value drivers

D0806519

value drivers

The Manager's Guide to Driving Corporate Value Creation

MARK C. SCOTT

JOHN WILEY & SONS, LTD

Chichester · New York · Weinheim · Brisbane · Singapore · Toronto

Copyright © 1998 by   John Wiley & Sons Ltd,
Baffins Lane, Chichester,
West Sussex PO19 1UD, England

National   01243 779777
International (+44) 1243 779777
e-mail (for orders and customer service enquiries):
cs-books@wiley.co.uk
Visit our Home Page on http://www.wiley.co.uk
or http://www.wiley.com

Mark C. Scott has asserted his right under the Copyright, Designs and Patents Act, 1988, to be identified as the author of this work.

Reprinted October 2000
Reprinted March 2002

All rights Reserved. No part of this book may be reproduced, stored in a retrieval system, or transmitted, in any form or by any means, electronic, mechanical, photocopying, recording or otherwise, except under the terms of the Copyright Designs and Patents Act 1988 or under the terms of a licence issued by the Copyright Licensing Agency, 90 Tottenham Court Road, London, UK W1P 9HE, without the permission in writing of John Wiley and Sons Ltd., Baffins Lane, Chichester, West Sussex, UK PO19 1UD.

Other Wiley Editorial Offices

John Wiley & Sons, Inc., 605 Third Avenue,
New York, NY 10158–0012, USA

WILEY-VCH Verlag GmbH, Pappelallee 3,
D-69469 Weinheim, Germany

Jacaranda Wiley Ltd, 33 Park Road, Milton,
Queensland 4064, Australia

John Wiley & Sons (Asia) Pte Ltd, 2 Clementi Loop #02–01,
Jin Xing Distripark, Singapore 129809

John Wiley & Sons (Canada) Ltd, 22 Worcester Road,
Rexdale, Ontario M9W 1L1, Canada

British Library Cataloguing in Publication Data

A catalogue record for this book is available from the British Library

ISBN 0-471-86121-9

Typeset in 11/13pt Palatino by Vision Typesetting, Manchester
Printed and bound in Great Britain by Creative Print and Design Wales, Ebbw Vale

Contents

About the Author

Mark Coleridge Scott is a director of Lake Capital Management, a principal investment group specialising in investing in professional service firms. He was formerly Executive Vice President and a founder at Lighthouse Global Network, a global marketing services group that was acquired by Cordiant Communications Group plc in August 2000. Before Lighthouse he served as Operations Director at WPP Group plc and prior to this worked for a number of years as a management consultant in Europe and the USA. He received his MBA from Harvard Business School and was educated at Oxford and Cambridge Universities. He is the author of *Reinspiring the Corporation: The Seven Seminal Paths to Corporate Greatness*, *The Professional Service Firm*, and *Heartland: How to build companies as strong as countries*, all published by John Wiley & Sons.

Introduction

"Value drivers versus cost drivers: the age old game"

Since time immemorial there have been two sorts of activities in companies; those that drive value creation and those that drive unproductive cost. The problem for senior managers has always been the same one that Lord Leverhulme apocryphally faced with his advertising budget: half is waste but which half, is a mystery.

This situation has persisted due to the veil of obfuscation which has hung over the internal workings of most companies. Historically, most larger firms have tended to be conglomerates of a heterogeneous blend of business units. Most managers have occupied functionally specific roles which they could master meticulously over the years even if they were counterproductive. Rigid departmental structures have limited the responsibility of anyone for the inefficiency of the overall production process. Rigid vertical hierarchies have ensured that orders and ideas have flowed one way only. The scope of most managers' responsibility has been finite, accountability for market outcomes fragmented, and the contribution of individual units to overall performance opaque. As long as the firm was big, everything was fine; more or less.

Then suddenly something changed around about the early '80s. The wave that had been building for decades began to bear down; the burdensome central overhead, slow cycle times, low rates of innovation, the lengthy internal transactions, failing peripheral businesses. Then – wham! The harsh reality of globalizing competition and capital markets hits home. The layers are stripped out. The overhead is slashed. The departmental structures are remodelled into cross-functional teams. Business units are given full economic accountability. Suddenly the Lever-hulme conundrum is solved. The dead wood is exposed to the light of day. The non-performing business units are sold off. The value driving activities are clearly identified and reinforced. Share prices soar.

Well that's what a lot of management books would have you believe. Not quite reality of course! There's no doubt that most companies have made enormous efficiency gains over the past two decades and stock prices have risen accordingly. But most companies still have a long way to go in identifying and honing their value drivers before they can claim to have reached world class levels of competitiveness. And the pressure is increasing, not relenting. Markets are continuing to globalize and an ever more international group of competitors is entering the fray. The average life cycle of most products is shortening. The speed of efficiency gains in production and the speed of market respon-siveness necessary to compete are increasing. Cost structures are shifting dramatically year by year as new producers come on line and new technologies propel shifts in business processes. Every-thing is moving faster and will continue to accelerate. Today's competitive "paradigms" will be tomorrow's old hat.

As a result, firms are having to reinvent themselves continual-ly. In the past a CEO might have had the luxury of ten years to show a steady increase in market penetration using an estab-lished manufacturing system to produce a well-tested product concept. Now the same CEO has only a couple of years to prove that he or she can create value for shareholders, otherwise they are out on their necks. To create value they have to understand precisely how the firm drives value and how that process can be accelerated. Nearly a quarter of the CEOs of *Business Week*'s top 1000 companies have turned over in the past two years, which suggests that many of them are not up to the job.

Of course, whilst all attention is focused on the CEO, it is the line managers who have to make it happen. The market changes under way pose tremendous challenges for the managers who are responsible for delivering the corporate strategy laid out by the CEO. It means they must be masters of rapid change. But more importantly it means they must understand clearly what actions do and do not drive corporate value creation and how they can influence them. Effective business management is founded on coordination of all the value driving activities of a company, not the perfection of one or two in isolation. Manufacturing strategy must *reinforce* the marketing strategy. The company's approach to motivating and retaining people must provide a backbone to its method of differentiating its products or services. A firm's approach to its balance sheet must be geared to maintaining the investment in R&D necessary to achieve product advantage.

Unfortunately, few managers are in the privileged position of being able to see a firm from a "strategic" perspective. Most companies are still structured departmentally and the managers running or working in these areas will tend to view the world from the perspective of their specialty. If you are in a marketing group you will be thinking about share of voice and price discounts. If you are in operations you will be thinking about scrap rates and inventories. If you are in human resources you will be thinking about relative pay scales. The ability of most managers to understand how their actions contribute to overall value creation is therefore limited. The result is that most firms still continue to bang into the same issue as Lord Leverhulme.

This book is intended for the manager or aspiring manager who is intent on understanding how they can contribute to value creation in their company. It follows a simple framework which should allow you to identify the key value drivers of a typical firm and to determine whether they are being effectively exploited in your own firm (see Figure I.1).The real winners inside corporations, those that rise to the top, will be increasingly those that understand how value is driven and how they can influence it. Managers who fail to understand the drivers of value in their company will continue to bear the brunt of the reduction of non-productive functions, whether termed "downsizing", "reengineering", "strategic refocusing" or some other epithet. They will be the victims of the Leverhulme conundrum.

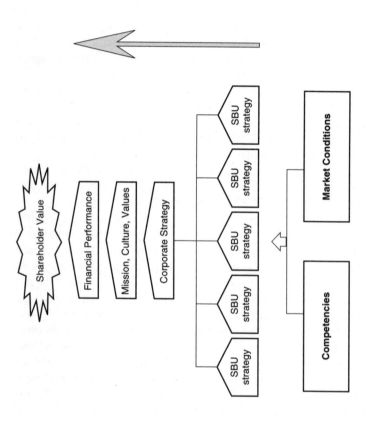

Figure I.1   *Value drivers roadmap*

1
Why are Firms in Business in the First Place?

"Motherhood and apple pie"

This question may sound facile, but it is not always an issue which is understood as crisply as it should be. The motives influencing management have undergone subtle changes over the last decade. It is these motives that are the prime driver of the way firms compete.

There can be no doubt that nowadays the principal goal of management is the enhancement of shareholder value. This means maximizing the returns generated to those people who have an ownership stake in the business. Shareholder value is another term for the total value of the equity of a firm or its "market capitalization". The market cap of a publicly traded firm is highly transparent. It is simply the number of shares listed on the market multiplied by the average price per share. For privately held firms it is a number which is not as easily measured but we will ignore this complication for a moment. As a shareholder, whether or not management is creating value is reflected in the movement of the stock as clear as day.

The capital markets have become highly sophisticated at identifying firms which are underperforming on the basis of the amount of value they are creating for shareholders. For all major quoted corporations there are brigades of analysts who spend their time determining how effectively the firm is delivering shareholder value. If the value of a firm's stock falls below what they deem to be an appropriate level, that firm will become the target for management change. If that change is slow in occurring the firm will probably become a target for takeover. This provides a clear incentive to management to ensure that, whatever else may occur, the stock price does not fall below levels deemed acceptable by the markets.

The value of the equity of a company is predominantly (but not exclusively) determined by the level of sustainable growth in its profitability and – the close relation of profit – the anticipated strength of the firm's cash flow (we will distinguish between these two measures presently since they differ in important respects). Therefore all eyes are on how well profits are moving in line with expectations. More specifically the markets will tend to look at growth in earnings per share or EPS.[1] The bulk of consulting activity going on in most firms, whether they are going through a restructuring to reduce costs or a rationalization process to strip away non-core assets, is to boost reported earnings per share. This impacts directly the market's valuation of the firm and hence the return enjoyed by shareholders of the company.

The markets are not the short-term speculators they are often accused of being. They will be concerned with the long-term prospects for profits growth rather than the absolute number in a single year. If, for example, a firm is investing in building, market share profits may be temporarily depressed. Strong revenue growth, however, may be an indicator of a windfall of future profits once the firm has established a dominant market position. If a firm cuts its investment in advertising to boost short-term profit, this may erode the long-term earnings power of its brands. The markets will usually build in these expectations by adjusting the value of the stock. As we will see there are many routes to maximizing long-term profits and there are many indicators of whether a firm is likely to get there or not. But, however a firm does it, it is long-term growth in earnings per share that the markets are concerned about.

So the purpose of a firm is to create value for its owners. Doesn't sound like rocket science! In the past, however, this has not always been so clear. Often the unspoken objective was to give the top managers a gentle and elegant ride, regardless of

---

[1] EPS is normally calculated by dividing the after-tax earnings of the company by the number of shares it has issued.

what this implied for the performance of the profit line. This might have meant corporate jets and antique collections at HQ. Many firms had an ethic of lifetime employment and the objective of the firm was to provide a guaranteed decent quality of livelihood for its employees. This was apotheosized in a large number of publicly owned companies. Even in the "commercial" oriented firms there were typically delicate tradeoffs between the brutal motive of maximizing annual profit and a broader range of goals, such as moral or intellectual leadership. Many managers still see size as the goal, usually measured in terms of total revenues rather than total capitalization. Size is often seen to confer prestige on a firm. Of course, high revenues do not necessarily correspond with high profits. Work can easily be won at a loss, eroding shareholder value.

These days are largely gone and virtually everyone, including state-owned enterprise, has woken up to this fact. Corporate raiders and turnaround managers have broken the backs of most of the old behemoths. The growth of investment funds have made blocks of shareholders, collectively larger than most of the firms in which they invest, and who are thus able to flex their muscles. Now everything is measured in terms of shareholder value. The firms that are not clear on this tend to be those that are in deep trouble. The only question we have to ask is whether the firm is doing the right things to maximize its return to shareholders by focusing on those activities which really drive value creation (see Figure 1.1).

MISSION AND CORPORATE STRATEGY: "SEEING THE WOOD FOR THE TREES"

Most modern firms are highly complex entities and are involved in managing a multitude of activities, products and services. Virtually every firm of any significance operates on an international footing. Because all firms have many faces it is usually hard to answer the question of how it intends to deliver maximum returns to shareholders. The trick of the excellent manager is to see the wood for the trees, to understand where the company is heading and how each particular piece contributes or doesn't contribute to overall value creation.

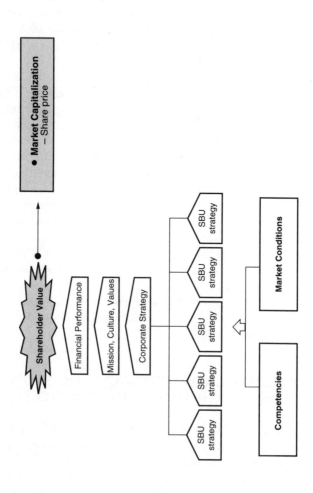

Figure 1.1   Value drivers roadmap

What is the firm's overall mission? What is its strategic goal? What chance has it got of getting there? As an issue of nomenclature, a mission is different from a corporate strategy. A mission is a conceptual intent to head in a certain direction; a strategy defines the way a firm intends to get there. Although you might think a firm's mission should be an easy thing to identify, it is in fact often one of the hardest things to pin down. You may refer to the mission statement issued by the Chairman which will appear in the Annual Report. Usually this sounds more like Keatsian poetry than a clear explanation of the purpose of the company. You may also read general statements about the firm in the press. But more often than not, it is an extremely frustrating process to get a clear sense of the overarching business rationale. This is why few firms meet international competitive standards.

So if the mission statement cannot tell you, who can? The reality is often surprisingly few people and they are individuals to whom you are not likely to get regular access and who might not be able to tell you clearly even if you could locate them. The missions of firms tend to evolve through layers of decision making over time. Often they are driven by something as illusive as a vision by the founding CEO. Occasionally the mission of a firm will be clearly stated and will appear to make some sense given the area of activity a firm is competing in. This will be your opportunity to see how well it meshes with corporate strategy.

Corporate strategy is the set of rules the firm follows to be able to deliver on its mission and should be geared to maximizing returns to shareholders. Most companies comprise a number of businesses which might be as diverse as specialty chemicals and ice cream or they could be as superficially similar as luxury eyeglasses and ski-goggles. These areas of activity are usually broken into Strategic Business Units (SBUs). An SBU can be defined as a business producing a product or service to meet distinct customer demands and requiring distinct competencies to satisfy those demands (we will get onto this presently). Corporate strategy is the business rationale that binds these SBUs into a cohesive whole which will deliver maximum shareholder value. Why does the particular firm you are looking at compete in both specialty chemicals *and* ice cream? What possible advantages can there be to competing in both areas? Why doesn't it sell its chemicals business and get into frozen chocolate bars instead?

The answer to these type of questions should lie in the corporate strategy of the firm.

In most sizable firms comprising a number of SBUs, each of these businesses will have its own strategy. Its managing director will hopefully spend a good deal of his/her time working out how to maximize value creation in his business area. Above him will be a board of directors who may potentially control a wide number of SBUs and who determine corporate strategy. Corporate strategy needs to account for a single issue; why is the firm competing in all the areas it is and how does it intend to create value through ownership of these separate businesses? It is impossible to know whether a corporate strategy makes sense without understanding the details of the SBU's that are being marshalled under that corporate strategy. There are some instances where the firm in question only competes in one narrow area which might qualify as an SBU. This will make your task simple. In the majority of instances, however, this will not be the case. In order to decide whether the firm has a viable corporate strategy you will need to understand the competitive nature of each SBU. In order to understand a firm it is therefore necessary to break it into intelligible parts. This process is called "business segmentation".

2
Segmentation

"Identifying an SBU can be like identifying a UFO"

Most larger firms compete in a wide range of discrete businesses. The easiest basis on which to isolate them initially are the Standard Industrial Classification Codes, an extract of which is listed in Figure 2.1. Sometimes a firm will span a wide number of activities and in other cases it will be more tightly clustered. Multiple businesses which fall within particular SIC codes will tend to be organized into divisions. However, you will see immediately the limitations of this set of classifications as a basis for defining the activities of a firm. Most firms compete in a set of apparently related businesses and therefore your list will be short. Of course, beneath the surface of the SIC codes lurk a very wide range of business areas. Our ice cream division, for example, may compete both in high end wrapped cones and also in ten gallon tubs for institutional use. Common sense would tell us that these are fundamentally different businesses.

The real problem with the SIC definitions is that they do not tell you what is necessary to achieve competitive advantage in these business areas. The requirements for competitive advantage in the ice cream cone business are very different from the requirements in the institutional market. This brings us to "segmentation". Segmentation means breaking up the whole on the basis of an underlying rationale. The trick is identifying that rationale. Segmentation of companies into SBUs is usually based on distinctions between how value is created in them. This can be broken down into two simple questions:

45.23   Construction of highways, roads, airfields and sport facilities

This class includes:
- construction of highways, streets, roads, other vehicular and pedestrian ways
- construction of railways
- construction of airfield runways
- construction work other than of buildings for stadiums, swimming pools, gymnasiums, tennis courts, golf courses and other sports installations
- painting of markings on road surfaces and parking lots

This class excludes:
- preliminary earth moving cf. 45.11

45.24   Construction of water projects

This class includes:
- construction of:
  - waterways, harbour and river works, pleasure ports (marinas), locks, etc.
  - dams and dykes
- dredging
- sub-surface work

92.6   Sporting activities

92.61   Operation of sports arenas and stadiums

This class includes:
- operation of the facilities for outdoor or indoor sports events:
  - football stadiums
  - swimming pools and stadiums
  - golf courses
  - boxing arenas
  - winter sport arenas and stadiums
  - field and track stadiums, etc.
  - private and local authority owned leisure centres

The facilities may be enclosed or covered and may have provision for spectator seating or viewing

This class excludes:
- rental of sporting equipment cf. 71.4011
- park and beach activities cf. 92.72

Figure 2.1   *Extract from the "Standard Industrial Classification" coding system*

1 What is the nature of customer demand?
2 What skills are necessary to satisfy that demand?

A SBU can be defined for our purposes as a business where the nature of customer demand and the skills or "competencies" necessary to satisfy that demand are distinct.

You will notice immediately that these criteria for segmentation are market driven. This is an important point. In the past a firm might have produced something and then gone looking for customers to whom to sell the product. This approach is rarely admissible today. Since it is customer sentiment which determines whether a firm succeeds or fails, it is always advisable to understand what a firm is delivering from the viewpoint of the customer. Most firms are facing ever-increasing competition in their markets and are having to become ever more focused in how they serve their customers. This means that they are continually having to refine their own definition of what business they are in.

If, for example, the company sells swimming pools, you might think that "swimming pools" would be a clear enough description of a SBU. However, within the swimming pool industry it turns out there are several distinct markets. There are the luxury pools, manufactured out of freestanding plastic, for middle class families in the suburbs. Then, at the opposite extreme, there are municipal pools constructed out of concrete foundations commissioned by city councils. The demands these two groups of customers place on a supplier of pools will be radically different. Whilst the institutional buyer will probably focus exclusively on the price of the building contract, the homeowner with cash to burn will be concerned about after-sales service. The skills the firm needs to compete in each segment will therefore be very different. One will require competencies in component manufacture and servicing networks, the other in civil engineering, project management and low costs.

CUSTOMER-BASED SEGMENTATION

The problem with customer-based segmentation is that the customer is usually a slippery customer. Defining one group versus another is often not as straightforward as the swimming pool example. There is a fairly standard list of first-screen criteria for separating out target customer segments. The first distinction firms usually make is between retail (consumer) markets and industrial (business to business) markets. In the case of retail markets firms will typically cluster consumers demographically on the basis of social groupings,[1] average household income,

---

[1] The standard basis of social grouping is ABC1, C2, D & E.

educational level, age or life-stages.[2] They may also be able to define customers by "user event". Private individuals who buy guns for hunting have a different "user event" in mind than a military customer who has a war to run. It may also be possible to distinguish between users according to the distribution source from which they purchase. The private individual, for example, will tend to buy his weapon through a retail outlet whereas the military customer will place a bulk order direct to the factory. Finally, it is common to group customers geographically, reflecting the challenge of distributing product to end markets.

Whatever the basis of customer segmentation, the firm will implicitly be attributing certain behaviours to the groups they are aiming to serve. Basic demographic segments, however, often do not give a real clue about the motivation or interests of real people buying things. One ABC1 householder might purchase soap-powder purely on the basis of price whilst another will pay anything to stick with her favourite brand. Two apparently similar firms purchasing machine tools might have quite different manufacturing strategies which create different priorities in terms of the performance of their milling machines. One may simply want a "low spec, low tech" version whilst the other requires variable speed and sizing capability with a zero error rate. Conversely, the same "purchase criteria" may be shared by individuals or firms which fall into quite distinct groupings based on first-screen criteria. This means it usually makes more sense for a firm to group its potential customers based on their purchase criteria which more accurately describe what motivates them to buy. Unless a firm understands these motivations it will not be able to sell what it makes effectively (see Figure 2.2).

In most cases, customers will have a standard list of purchase criteria which tend to include:

- price
- quality
- performance characteristics of the product or service
- speed of delivery
- after-sales support
- brand appeal/endorsement.

[2] "Life-stages" typically divides households into pre-family, family, empty nesters and post family.

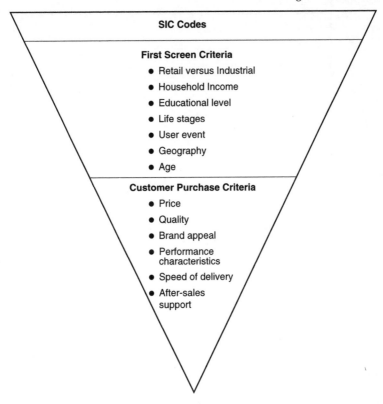

Figure 2.2 *Illustrative process for customer-based business segmentation*

In addition, there will be a number of criteria which are unique to the industry you are examining. You can identify these simply enough by asking customers about them. Having got the list together the next stage is to rank the criteria in terms of their importance to the customer. (If done properly, this requires interviewing a statistically significant sample of customers – quite a demanding task). Once you have a ranking this should expose quite clearly the difference in nature of what a customer expects from one product or service versus another. These differences will exist because the customers are either fundamentally different or because they are buying for quite distinct reasons. For example, the purchaser of the upmarket, private pool will

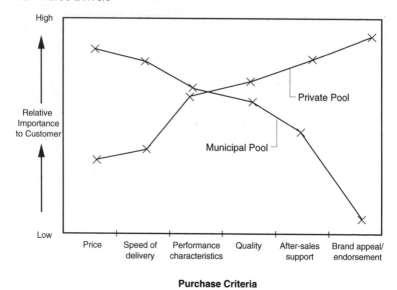

Figure 2.3   *Illustrative purchase criteria for different swimming pool segments*

probably place price lower on the list than will the institutional purchaser of a municipal pool. They may also conduct the purchase process in a quite different manner. Therefore, what appeared to be a single business in fact has all the characteristics of two quite different businesses (see Figure 2.3).

SKILLS-BASED SEGMENTATION

Once you have a grasp of the customer-based segmentation then you should consider the skills-based segmentation. Whereas the former is external facing, the latter is internally facing. It simply poses the question, do these segments place the same internal demands on the organization in terms of servicing customer needs? If we go back to our swimming pool example, servicing the private luxury pool market will require the firm to have an excellent capability at customer service. Servicing the institutional market, by contrast, will require it to have an excellent cost base. To be able to provide good customer service will require heavy investment in repair and service teams. To keep costs low will require a highly efficient installation process and low cost suppliers. These are quite different sets of capabilities.

In the case of the swimming pools, the criteria for segmenting the market in terms of customer needs bears a direct relationship to a segmentation based on the competencies necessary to meet those needs. This should come as no great surprise. Different consumer needs will put different demands on a firm trying to satisfy those needs, leading it to evolve a distinct set of capabilities. Things can, of course, also work the other way around. A firm can generate a new set of skills which will allow it to cultivate a new set of consumer expectations and needs. Before Sony came up with the Walkman, the commercial "need" for it did not exist.

The real challenge in performing an analysis of competencies is in making precise distinctions between the different skills necessary to fulfil customer needs. For example, a steel firm producing tubular steel for drains and steel rods for construction will need to compete on price to succeed in both segments. But the competencies necessary to deliver low costs in the two segments will differ radically. In the case of the tubular steel they will need to be expert at welding and shaping. In the case of the construction rods they will probably need to be running a mini-mill type plant. This brings us to the concept of the "value chain".

To segment a firm based on competencies it is necessary to understand the value chain of the company. The value chain is a description of the tasks necessary to deliver a product or service to market. A generic value chain is included in Figure 2.4 and we will explore this in more detail in a later section. For the purposes of segmentation, the main question you should ask is, in which areas of the value chain does the firm have to be outstanding to succeed in each customer segment? What skills or competencies are necessary to deliver an outstanding result in those areas of the value chain? Are they the same for each segment or do they differ radically? In our swimming pool example, a quick purview of the value chain shows clearly that the competencies to compete in the retail versus the institutional segments differ radically (see Figure 2.5). This almost certainly means that the two markets should be serviced by separate SBUs.

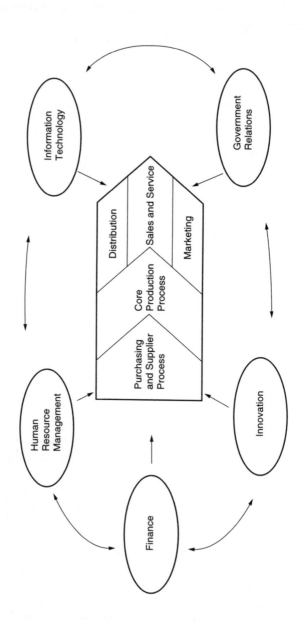

Figure 2.4 *The generic value chain*

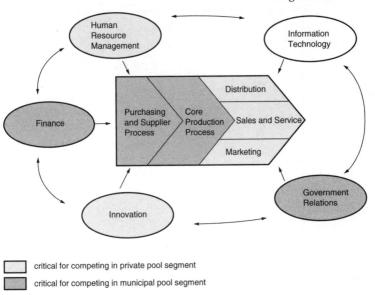

critical for competing in private pool segment

critical for competing in municipal pool segment

Figure 2.5 *Illustrative hierarchy of competencies necessary to compete in different swimming pool segments*

PULLING IT ALL TOGETHER

The synthesis of your segmentation analysis based on both customer needs and competencies should give you a clear sense of the discrete business areas in which a firm competes. If the competencies necessary to meet different customer demands appear similar then the segments can probably be grouped into a single SBU. Even though a child may be looking for different things when it buys a chocolate cone and a vanilla whirl, the same skills are necessary to satisfy that demand both in terms of manufacture and marketing.

Once you have a sense of the nature of customer demands and the competencies necessary to meet them in the major areas of the firm's activity, you should check how closely these businesses are clustered (Figure 2.6). It may be the case that your segmentation analysis results in one definition of SBUs whilst the firm organizes them quite differently. Assuming your evaluation is

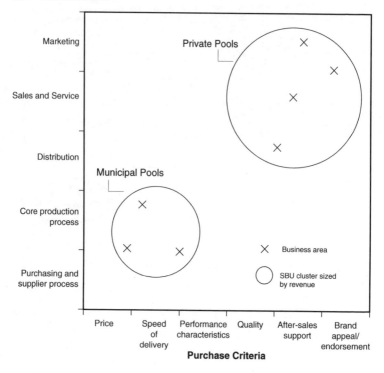

Figure 2.6   *Illustrative clustering of a firm's business activities into SBUs*

sound, it may be that the firm does not understand the markets in which it is competing. This will probably mean that it has failed to develop the competencies necessary to meet customer needs better than the competition. If a firm has failed to organize its business units to service distinct segments, you will almost certainly uncover performance problems as we advance through our analysis. The segmentation analysis will give you the foundation from which to understand the basis of value creation in each segment. This will allow you to decide whether you believe the firm is well positioned to meet the competitive demands of the market (see Figure 2.7).

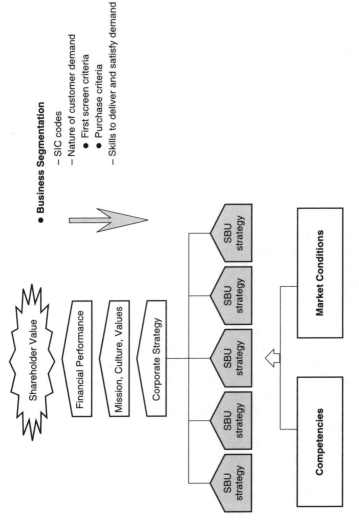

- **Business Segmentation**
  - SIC codes
  - Nature of customer demand
    - First screen criteria
    - Purchase criteria
  - Skills to deliver and satisfy demand

Figure 2.7 *Value drivers roadmap*

3
Ranking SBUs

"It's not just what you do, it's how you do it"

Often, people have odd conceptions about what a particular company does. Perhaps some part of it will be better known than others even though it contributes only a small amount to the overall business. Often firms will have an "image leader" in their portfolio. Most people, for example, would associate General Electric in the US with domestic appliances and not with finance, although the latter now increasingly contributes the bulk of its profits. Goldman Sachs would probably be best know for its M&A work whereas the bulk of its profits are made in trading. You should not fall into this trap. Once you have formed an opinion about the type of segments a firm competes in you should check how important these segments are to sustaining it. This will allow you to begin to understand the options the CEO has about how he or she might manage that group of SBUs to optimize returns to shareholders.

The first step is to attribute sales to each segment you have identified. This will be the clearest indicator of the relative size of the SBUs. Grouping these segments by SIC cluster will give you an impression of their overall weight in the company's portfolio. Next, assign operating profit numbers to each segment since it is profits, not sales, that are the prime factor in driving share value. Defining profits as an accounting term, and ensuring the numbers are comparable across segments, is not a straightforward process and we will come onto this later. But usually a basic number will be available which will equate either to operating or after-tax profits.

The relationship between the sales achieved by a firm in particular segments and the profits they yield is highly instructive. Clearly, if a segment generates large sales but does not contribute much to the corporate profit pile then the analysts will pounce. Alternatively, a firm may be dependent for the bulk of its profits from one or two segments, with the rest achieving decent sales but which are not converting it into profit. If these other segments lie outside the core clusters then the red flags should go up. Figure 3.1 illustrates the segments of our fictional swimming pool assembler on a contribution to profit/sales matrix. As you can see, it is having a nightmare with municipal pool projects, probably because they lie outside its areas of core competence which are in specialist garden pools. Is it a good use of shareholders money for the firm to pour investment into this

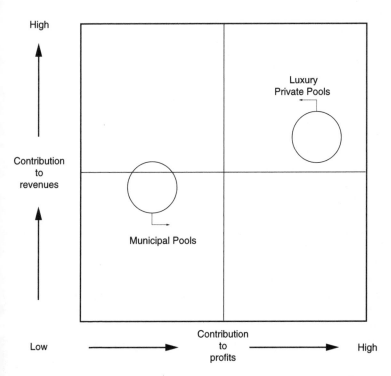

Figure 3.1 Illustrative SBU contribution matrix in the case of a fictional swimming pool producer/designer

area? Why is the CEO doing it? Is there something we do not know?

The performance of segments for a firm will not be static but will change over time, sometimes quite dramatically. The degree to which they are changing is just as important as their absolute size. The usual way of measuring change is to look at their average annual growth rate. It is always instructive to compare growth in sales with growth in profits. This can expose complex dynamics. For example, the segment that is yielding lots of profit currently may be experiencing zero revenue growth. Clearly this will pose dangers for the future profitability of the company. Alternatively, if a firm is experiencing low profitability but high growth in a number of segments this may augur strong future cash flows once these segments mature into large businesses.

Analysts typically will look at a number of key charts when creating comparisons between a firm's segments:

- size of segments versus their profit margin for the firm;
- percentage of total company sales versus percentage of total profits from segment;
- growth rate of the segment versus share of company sales;
- growth rate of sales versus contribution to profits.

These charts should give you an indication of both the performance and the role of the segments in the business portfolio. At this stage you should simply raise flags which you can examine in more detail further on. For instance, a segment which is small but with high growth may well be a high investment area which will yield rewards in the future. A segment which is large, low growth but highly profitable is likely to be the core of the business which provides the bulk of the cash flow. It may be unexciting but essential (Figure 3.2).[1] Some segments are likely to be showing much larger growth rates than others in both revenues and profits because they are at very different stages of development in their "life cycles". Different segments are therefore likely to pose quite distinct management challenges and present different value creation opportunities. This brings us back to corporate

---

[1] The seminal growth/share matrix is the Boston Consulting Group's matrix which is now a foundation stone of portfolio strategy.

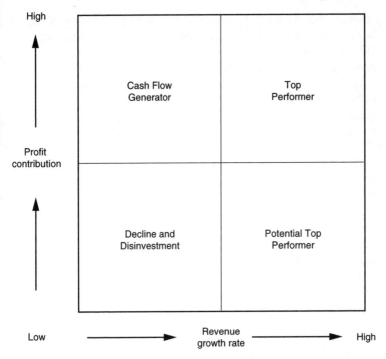

Figure 3.2 *Illustrative SBU contribution matrix for a given firm*

strategy and the logic binding the pieces together. We will return to this shortly.

THE GEOGRAPHICAL DIMENSION

"It's not just what you sell; it's where you sell it"

Since most firms of any reasonable size operate internationally, it is essential to understand in which markets they are strong and where they make money. The differential growth prospects of different markets make the geographical distribution of business units a major determinant of overall performance.

For each segment, try and break out the revenues and profits by geographical region. The key regions are Europe, North

America, South East Asia and Latin America, which between them comprise the bulk of the world's Gross National Product.[2] Although each accounts for a great diversity of countries, the economic characteristics of the countries within them will tend to be similar and they are increasingly operating as internal trading blocs. Breaking down the segments geographically will enable you to determine the dependence of the firm on different markets in its key segments. If you combine this information with some basic economic numbers on these markets such as GNP, GNP per capita and growth rates, you will be able to draw some powerful conclusions. If the firm makes all its money in markets which are extremely slow growth then you know that those SBUs will have a tough challenge in terms of sustaining earnings growth. If, on the other hand, the firm is well positioned in markets which are growing fast then you know it is taking effective advantage of the international business opportunity and earnings growth will be achieved more readily.

An analyst will typically look at a number of variables including:

- share of company segment sales versus market growth;
- share of company profits versus market growth.

From such information it should be possible to gauge how well the company is positioned relative to the market potential. If, for example, a diversified chemicals business generates 60% of company sales from low margin bulk chemicals in the low growth UK sector and has only a minor penetration in specialty chemicals in the high growth Far East sector, this should raise a red flag in the manager's mind. Unless a firm has a foothold in a high growth sector in a mature economy or, if they are in a mature sector and don't have a foothold in a high growth market, they will have problems producing growth in earnings up to par with the best competitors (see Figure 3.3).

---

[2] Gross National Product (GNP) is the measure of the overall output of an economy, equivalent to revenue in a company. For reasons of accuracy, it is in fact calculated on the basis of national consumption. Its primary constituents are public spending, private consumption, investment and savings, the net balance of trade and net property income from abroad. GDP is the measure used in countries such as the UK and differs from GNP in that it excludes net property income from abroad.

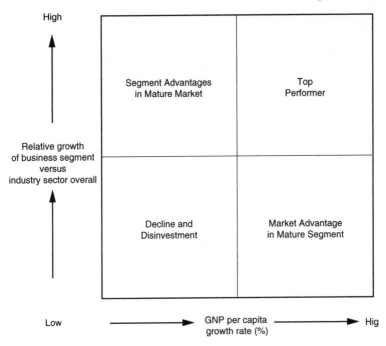

High

Segment Advantages
in Mature Market

Top
Performer

Relative growth
of business segment
versus
industry sector overall

Decline and
Disinvestment

Market Advantage
in Mature Segment

Low

GNP per capita
growth rate (%)

Hig

Figure 3.3 *Illustrative matrix of market exposure of SBUs for a given firm*

PULLING IT ALL TOGETHER

To complete your snapshot of the firm's structure you should cluster SBUs or segments which have similar customer and competence profiles and summarize the position of each cluster in terms of contribution to company sales, contribution to profits, segment growth potential and geographical market exposure indexed on the basis of percentage of sales achieved in high growth markets (see Figure 3.4). This will form the basis of your evaluation of how they contribute to overall value creation. Before we go further into our analysis of SBUs, however, let's step back to the issue of corporate strategy for a moment (see Figure 3.5).

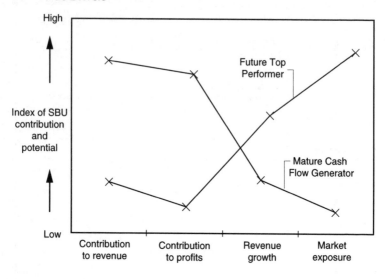

Figure 3.4 *Illustrative summary of SBU value contribution and potential for a generic firm*

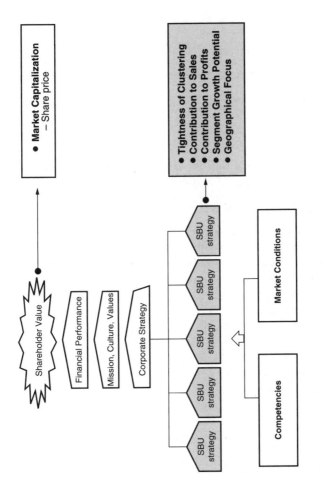

Figure 3.5   Value drivers roadmap

4
Corporate Strategy Revisited

"It's not how much you do, it's how well you do it"

It may be the case that the SBUs you have identified are quite similar in a number of respects and it is only when you get to the precise customer and competency details that the differences emerge. Alternatively, it may be the case that the SBUs identified differ radically. As we already discussed, corporate strategy should provide some compelling logic for these SBUs to be held by one particular firm. Otherwise they would be better off in the hands of other owners or as separate companies.

The tighter the clustering of segments into groups with similar customer requirements and competencies, the more likely it is that a firm will be able to manage its assets optimally to achieve competitive advantage. However, there are a number of strategies which can facilitate the extraction of value from apparently heterogeneous SBUs. In this chapter we will cover briefly four of the most prevalent:

- portfolio strategy
- vertical integration
- horizontal integration
- financial holding strategy.

PORTFOLIO STRATEGY

If the firm you are analysing competes in a tight cluster of business segments then your analysis will have shown that they are unified by a common thread, either of client needs and/or common competencies necessary to meet these needs. However, as your analysis may have shown, many firms manage a portfolio of businesses which would, on a segmentation basis, appear quite different. As in any portfolio, different pieces can play different roles. The key issue is whether the SBUs held by a company are indeed playing complementary roles. If they are not then the warning bells should sound.

The most common justification for a portfolio is management of a flow of funding between SBUs. Some segments may be highly profitable and contribute the bulk of a company's current earnings. They may also be at the top of their business cycle and entering long-term decline and therefore the focus of the firm will hopefully be shifting away from them. Other segments may be small on a revenue basis, currently losing money but growing at tremendous rates and will represent the future of the business. A portfolio approach would allow a flow of investment funding to pass between the cash-rich mature segment and the segment which is hungry for investment, in effect turning the corporation into an internal bank. Figure 4.1 illustrates the case of a bicycle manufacturer. Bikes made out of advanced materials are high growth but currently contribute little to revenues. They probably represent a future investment by the firm. Traditional road bikes are low growth but contribute the bulk of the revenues, providing the staple cash flow which is being invested in the new, high growth advanced materials area. Clearly, if an area is a high growth one and is already relatively large, as is the case with the mountain bike business in this example, then the earlier internal reinvestment strategy of the firm may have already paid off.

The key point is that different parts of the portfolio have different roles to play which reinforce each other. If a firm is pursuing a portfolio strategy then it will probably be using its traditional, profitable core to invest in higher growth opportunities for the future. A word or two of warning. What can appear to be a portfolio strategy can often be a failure of strategy. For example, a CEO who feels quite secure with the cash flows from his core business might consider this boring and start investing lots of cash in areas which are more exciting and attractive, and apparently high growth. If these segments have nothing in common with the core SBUs in terms of your segmentation analysis,

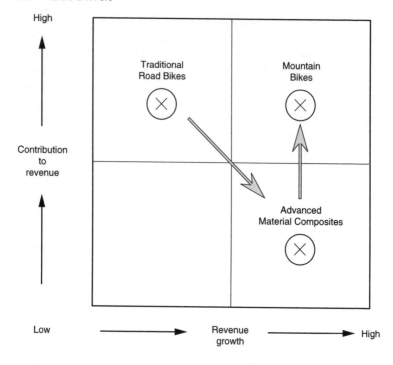

High

Contribution
to
revenue

Low

Revenue
growth

High

Figure 4.1   *Illustrative portfolio strategy of a fictional bike manufacturer*

then beware. How can the firm compete in this new area in which it has no expertise? Why should it be better than established competitors who really understand the business? Will it ever make real money in this area or is it a mad whimsy?

There has always been a tendency for companies to be tempted to diversify into high growth areas. In the early 80s, for example, certain property companies started getting into areas as far removed from their core business as film making. The problem is not simply that a firm may not possess the skills to enter a completely new industry (try and find a synergy between mortar and movies!), but also that the process can make the CEO take his eye off the ball in his core business. His construction business is pumping out cash and he simply starts bleeding it to fund other ventures. What could be more exciting for shareholders than to get into film? Gradually the level of investment in greenfield site development to sustain good productivity falls away, competitiveness is eroded and the good managers start joining competitors. Before the CEO knows it, he has to issue a profits warning and the firm is in jeopardy. So what if the movies are great!

Portfolios of assets should be subjected to the same segmentation analysis as any other business. Unless the SBUs in a portfolio have some operating commonality then a portfolio strategy should be treated with suspicion.

Risk Management

Portfolio management based on a flow of funding between SBUs is not the only justification for running a portfolio. A related reason is risk management. All business segments have different risk profiles associated with them. This will relate to the volatility of earnings in the markets in which they compete. Put simply, this means that the drivers of change, the level of change and the timing of change between profitable and unprofitable periods will differ. (We will come onto what drives the differing profit characteristics of different business segments shortly.)

The most common risk reduction rationale for a portfolio is to hedge out the different business cycles of the segments in it. The CEO may anticipate that his swimming pool business will boom for two years because of hot summers, increased economic activity and because the competition have been slow to get their act together. After two years are up he anticipates that business will take a dive because all these factors will shift. However, he believes with equal venom that the market for UV sunbeds will show precisely the inverse cycle, maxing out in about three years in a counter-cyclical pattern. He may, therefore, choose to hedge out the risk of a downturn in pools by developing a position in sunbeds. This will, theoretically at least, limit his exposure to cyclical market changes (see Figure 4.2).

Another type of risk is purely a function of the nature of the business rather than of shifts in the business cycle. For example, investing in biotech may offer the possibility of extremely high rewards for a company if it delivers a successful product. There is, however, an extremely high risk of it not doing so. The risk is

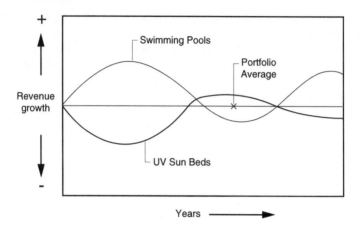

Figure 4.2   *Illustrative business cycle profile of different SBUs*

not that the market will move: if you can come up with a cure for cancer it will sell. The risk is that the compound will not work or meet statutory approval. The reason the CEO runs this risk is because the payout will be concomitantly large should he pull it off. This is the immutable law relating risk and return. The CEO may, however, wish to mitigate the risk associated with this bet by also investing in an area where the odds of success are much higher. Producing an enzyme which will increase the speed of fermentation of beer, he believes, is a fairly sure outcome. By combining the risk profiles of those two very different businesses he will hope to lock in what he considers a reasonable level of risk and, therefore, return for the company overall. This is called the "Expected Monetary Value" of the portfolio (see Figure 4.3).

Again, however, portfolios of SBUs with very different risk profiles should be subjected to segmentation analysis. If the nature of client demands and the nature of the skills required to meet them are very different, what powerful argument can be put forward to support the view that this company can effectively manage very different sets of assets better than competitors focused on tight clusters of segments? It is because portfolios can be used to paper over cracks and blur the underlying performance of segments that they are now out of favour with the capital markets. As we will see, "core competence" is king of contemporary management thinking.

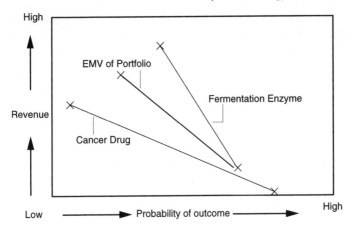

Figure 4.3 *Illustrative intrinsic risk profile of different SBUs*

VERTICAL INTEGRATION

The other common rationale for tying together SBUs which are not tightly clustered is vertical integration. All firms are composed of a value chain of those sets of activities necessary to deliver a service or product. In reality, however, most industrial activities and some service activities are composed of several value chains strung together. For example, the production of a car will start with the manufacture of steel and glass. This will then be integrated with basic metal components to form substructures such as wing mirrors. In parallel, companies will be producing electrical, glass, rubber and mechanical components. These will then be assembled into that familiar shape we all know and love, finished, distributed and sold. Certain companies may choose to integrate these separate value chains into a single value chain which they can then control. In the case of the automotive manufacturer, this would mean owning component manufacturers at the back end and distributors at the front end.

Why would they do this? The usual thinking behind vertical integration is that it will lock in a competitive advantage that would not be available to the firm were it to turn to independent suppliers. For example, an auto manufacturer may believe that by owning its own supplier of glass, it can achieve shorter delivery times and hold less inventory by owning that supplier. Or it might be that the supplier has a proprietary technology that confers a decisive product benefit which the auto manufacturer does not want shared amongst competitors. It may also believe that there are large margins to be won in these supply businesses which it does not want to surrender to independent owners.

Whatever the rationale for vertical integration, the recent trend has been the breaking down of integrated structures. Since, in line with our segmentation analysis, many of these different parts of the total industry value chain have very different requirements for success, firms are often better off focusing their resources on a single piece of the value chain where they can gain decisive advantage. For example, certain parts of the automotive value chain may require large scale operations in order to achieve competitive unit costs, such as the manufacture of glass for windscreens. A captive supplier may not be able to achieve the minimum competitive scale and therefore that part of the business will achieve a low return on capital. Others parts of the value chain, such as managing dealerships, may offer high returns on capital given the positioning and competencies of the firm. Concentrating resources here instead of dispersing them across the external value chain may offer a much higher overall return for shareholders.

Many of the advantages of integration can be achieved through developing strong relationships with suppliers, distributors or marketers. This has been a major feature of the strategy of many Japanese firms in the 80s. If the firm in question occupies the core, high value added section of the industry value chain it can exercise tremendous pressure over both upstream and downstream suppliers. For example, manufacturers of automotives control the key part of that business and are relatively few in number. By contrast, suppliers of electrical components will occupy a far less strategic part of the value chain, be far greater in number and therefore have a relatively weak negotiating position. In this situation the auto manufacturer can effectively exert the same pressure on these independent suppliers as if they owned them outright. If the firm is sensible about it this will not simply take the form of lower prices but rather of a genuine partnership to deliver greater customer value. For example, they can insist on certain quality standards, they can impose certain delivery schedules so as to minimize their own inventory, they can collaborate to ensure that innovative product features are rapidly introduced. And they can do all this without tying any capital up in that lower margin part of the business chain.

The other benefit to partnership versus possession is that it reduces the fixed cost component of the business. As we will explore in a later section, all costs in a business can be divided between fixed and variable costs. Fixed costs are usually items such as plant and machinery or office space and, in some markets where there are restrictive labour practices such as Germany, employees. The problem with fixed costs is that they do not go away when revenues suffer a downturn. Whilst a firm can cut back on raw materials and electricity it cannot so easily close plants without incurring a large cost. If the sales blip only lasts a year, it would seriously damage the firm's future if it had to fire half its employees, for example. If a firm partners up with suppliers instead of owning them, the loss of flexibility associated with fixed costs is reduced. In essence these fixed costs are turned into variable ones and can be adjusted to suit market conditions, increasing the firm's agility.

The reciprocal side of good value chain partnerships is that the smaller firms in the relationship can also benefit. For the producer of electrical components for the automotive sector, an alliance with a major buyer will allow it to invest in production technology with a fairly certain return on investment. It will also allow it to achieve highly competitive quality standards and a decent cost structure. Armed with these advantages, it will be able to compete aggressively for independent contracts against suppliers who have not enjoyed such a relationship. They can, of course, also wind up with an unhealthy dependence which will leave them exposed when there is an economic downturn in their partner's business.

Virtual Corporations

Over the coming years it is likely that partnerships will be carried to a new level of sophistication with the formation of "virtual corporations". Virtual alliances are formed when a group of firms come together temporarily to deliver a specific service or product which alone they would be unable to produce viably. Typically each partner will bring a particular skill to the party and together they will represent a set of complementary competencies that cannot be achieved alone. Often when the project has been completed these alliances will fall apart once more. The number of instances of virtual companies being formed to meet temporary market demand is growing fast, from telecomms through to financial services. At heart they are an acknowledgment by the firms participating that they cannot do everything themselves and should focus on perfecting the areas they are good at.

In the past, the widespread vertical integration of business has probably had as much to do with the desire for perceived dominance by the CEO as with achieving high returns for shareholders. Size can be sexy. This has now been almost universally replaced by an imperative to achieve the highest return possible on capital employed in the business. In this light, most companies have been forced to conduct the type of analysis we have gone through to compare the contribution of their SBUs to the bottom line. In many cases this has resulted in the breaking up of integrated value chains and the emergence of specialist firms in each area. Of course, the process of disintegration and reintegration is highly cyclical one. As soon as a firm perceives an advantage to integration it will take it. This decision will, however, almost certainly now be based on a calculation of value creation for shareholders.

HORIZONTAL INTEGRATION

The logic for horizontal integration is quite different from the logic governing vertical integration. Horizontal integration is an alliance of two SBUs which share a common value chain or a point on that value chain. This might take the form of common marketing or distribution channels or common suppliers or a common production process, for example. The integration of the two SBUs may confer various types of competitive advantage based on that point of synergy. For example, a CEO who runs a lawnmower business and decides to buy a power-tool business may be able to manufacture the electric motors for both sets of products on the same production line. This will help him maximize the utilization of his productive assets, lowering unit costs significantly below those of non-integrated competitors. Alternatively, a CEO who has businesses that manufacture both bicycles and bike helmets may be able to leverage his relationships with key distributors to effectively double sales achieved through those channels. Likewise, a firm which produces both T-shirts and shoes which carry the same brand name can achieve scale economies in its advertising which is then depreciated over a larger set of inventory.

Horizontal integration clearly matches more closely with the guidelines we have laid out pertaining to segmentation. Two segments which are related in key aspects of their value chains are more likely to have a compelling businesses "synergy" and to be clustered in terms of customer characteristics and the skills necessary to compete. If you look at the patterns of acquisitions among firms over the past two years you will see that most of them obey the logic of horizontal integration. This tends to make shareholders much more comfortable than do diversified acquisitions because they know with some certainty that the management team have experience in extracting value from this type of business. For example, the Saatchi & Saatchi's rumoured bid for Midland Bank, a major retail bank in the UK, when their core competence was in advertising, led to a collapse in share price of their company. In contrast Asea and Brown Boveri, who share many operating synergies in power and plant construction, have been handsomely rewarded by the markets for their decision to merge to form ABB.

FINANCIAL HOLDING STRATEGY

All the advantages we have discussed so far that might be extracted by a firm from its multiple holdings are operating advantages. That is say, there is something about the relationships between its SBUs which helps the firm deliver a product or service more efficiently than the competition. However, even if there are no apparent advantages from an operating standpoint from multiple holdings, a firm may persuade shareholders that it can extract incremental value from disparate assets through efficient financial management. The "financial holding" strategy simply involves acquiring an ever-growing portfolio of companies to fitten, fatten up and then sell on or merge.

Financial holdings have a single core competence: they know how to raise money from the capital markets and how to deploy it against productive assets with great efficiency. For example, a small manufacturer of automotive components may historically have been family owned. The family may have been extremely wary of having too much debt on the balance sheet, fearing that this would endanger the business should there be a market downturn. A financial holding may realize that this business is easily capable of coping with twice this level of debt and still meet interest payments comfortably. Indeed, it may believe that the discipline of meeting these interest payments will force it to introduce cost-cutting measures which are long overdue and have been masked. By buying up such family firms, the holding can immediately achieve a high return on the equity of shareholders by leveraging up the capital structure through a leverage buy-out or LBO. (We will discuss the mechanics of this in more detail in a later section.)

In addition to the value driving effect of leverage, a holding which has a large amount of debt in its capital structure will probably be much more sophisticated in its dealings with the capital markets. A small firm reliant on debt from its local bank may have been paying a standard rate of retail interest. By contrast, in spite of the increased risk associated with the business because of higher debt on the balance sheet, the holding may be able to issue debt to the markets at a much lower coupon rate. This will enable it to return money to shareholders more efficiently. Typically, it will also be very competent in a number of other financial areas. Firstly it is likely to optimize the tax structure of the overall portfolio with great efficiency. The family-held manufacturer of automotive components, for example, may have had all its manufacturing based in the UK and be subject to a tax rate of 36%. The holding, by consolidating its earnings internationally, may be able to write off losses incurred in other parts of the business against this stream of earnings and lower overall taxes. In a similar fashion, it may be able to secure corporate debt against different sets of assets in its portfolio and thereby lower the risk for lenders and the level of interest it has to pay on it. All these feats of financial engineering will increase returns to shareholders.

Although the primary competence of most holdings is managing the balance sheet, the majority will also possess skills in how to boost profits rapidly. This will mean that they are familiar with managing down working capital, reducing headcount, and introducing rigid financial management systems. Typically they will acquire a firm and then insert their own management to instil these disciplines. These sorts of groupings tend to consist of companies which will be responsive to a formulaic approach. The reasons for this are obvious; that once you learn how to turn around one firm the same skills are easily transferable to companies in a similar situation. The important point for our analysis is that such holdings are not attempting to leverage operating synergies between the companies they own; they are simply trying to leverage their own skills as financial managers.

Pure financial holdings, and particularly the LBO funds, tend to aim for rapid rises in the value of the assets they manage. In order to deliver ongoing growth in earnings per share they usually rely on continued acquisition of new firms and divestiture of firms they have already squeezed dry. The result is a churn of companies in the portfolio rather than long-term growth of a set number of "members". This trick is harder to pull off as the number of basket cases going cheap on the market begins to dry up, as is the current situation. It should not be surprising therefore that many holdings are changing their role to become proper operating firms. What started as purely financial plays are evolving into more focused, horizontally integrated groups of companies claiming operating synergies.

PULLING IT ALL TOGETHER

So is There a Corporate Strategy?

"Integration" is a word often bandied about by firms to justify their ownership of a wide set of businesses. However, unless there is a compelling commonality or clustering of SBUs, the claim should be treated with appropriate caution. Your segmentation analysis will have given you pointers as to whether a firm appears to be positioned in businesses where it can achieve advantage through operating synergy. If the operating synergies appear weak, you should test for portfolio and integration advantages. Is there any compelling advantage the company can bring by holding these SBUs under its umbrella? Do they share common pieces of the value chain? Are they selling to similar customer groups? How much transfer selling is there between the SBUs as a percentage of the firm's overall turnover? If none of these is the case there is probably a failure to optimize shareholder value (see Figure 4.4).

Roughly speaking, there has been a 40-year cycle of management thinking regarding the logic governing corporate strategy. In the 60s and 70s it was fashionable for firms to assemble large collections of highly diverse businesses. This period saw the appearance of the diversified conglomerates such as ITT in the US and Hanson in the UK. By the mid-80s these large behemoths were felt to have lost focus and to have drifted. This mood has propelled a movement towards focusing on "core competencies". Firms have shed non-core activities and focused resources on those areas where they have a unique skill or knowledge. Typically this has meant that there is a tighter clustering between the various business segments or SBUs of such firms. This phase has been contemporaneous with the ascendancy of the concept of shareholder value and the increasing sophistication of capital markets. It has also gone hand in hand with the opening up of markets to global competition and the loss of local monopolies. It is therefore tempting to declare that core competence is king. However, it is clear that there are a number of routes to optimizing shareholder value. The issue is whether that route is being pursued coherently and effectively.

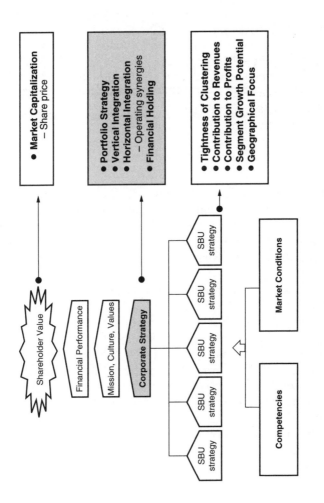

Figure 4.4 *Value drivers roadmap*

5
How Well is the Firm Doing?

"The bottom line is the bottom line – or is it?"

At this stage you should have a sense of how the pieces of the firm are arranged and how they hold together. Before moving into more detail, now is the time to ask yourself how the firm is doing overall and how this relates to the clustering of SBUs. This will lay the groundwork for more incisive inquiry about SBU strategy.

There are a large number of indicators of overall company performance which you can turn to. Indeed, the range of numbers offered in the annual report will be utterly overwhelming for the average manager. If the firm is publicly quoted, the best way to get a general snapshot is obviously the share price. Charting the movement of the price against the market or industry sector index over the last five years on a quarterly basis will give you a good idea of what the market thinks of the relative performance of the firm. Another good measure of the anticipated relative performance of the firm, used by all analysts, is the Price/Earnings ratio or PE. This is simply the total value of the stock of the company divided by the annual after-tax earnings of the company. It can also be calculated by dividing the share price by the earnings per share. If the PE ratio of the firm is higher than the average for all stocks in the sector then the market will be saying that it thinks performance has been and will remain good and therefore justifies a premium over other firms. The PE ratio will, by its very nature, respond closely to anticipated movements in the earnings per share.

If the firm is not quoted, the ratio most analysts will quote is overall growth in annual pre-tax profits. If earnings growth has been good then this is a reasonable sign that the business has been doing well. This will be particularly so if the operating margins[1] achieved by the business have been increasing over time: this will suggest that it has been able to charge more for its products or services, either because they are better or because the firm is focusing on areas where it has a competitive advantage. One word of warning: profits numbers have to be treated with some caution as they can be influenced by a number of factors which are independent of underlying performance. These can include the profit boosting impact of acquisitions, the treatment of balance sheet items such as depreciation and also by decisions regarding the timing of write-offs. We will come to these in more detail presently.

RETURN ON EQUITY

The real guts of your evaluation of overall company performance, however, should focus on an analysis of the firm's "Return on Equity". ROE is a basic measure of how efficiently money is being earned for shareholders on the cash they have invested. This ratio directly drives the share price of the company. Quite simply it is calculated by dividing the after-tax profit achieved by the firm by the book value of the equity on the balance sheet. This ratio can be compared between companies (bearing in mind the reservations already raised) and will give a sense of relative performance from a shareholder perspective.

However, much more interesting than the absolute ratio is an understanding of how it has been achieved. Return on equity is driven by a wide number of features of the business strategy. Firstly, it is influenced by the efficiency with which assets are being deployed to generate sales. This is often referred to as asset turns and is simply calculated by dividing total revenue by the total book value of assets on the balance sheet. Secondly, ROE reflects the efficiency with which sales are being converted

[1] A firm's operating margin is its pre-tax income as a percentage of revenues before interest and other non-operating charges.

into profits, or the profit margin, as we have already discussed. Thirdly, the ROE of a firm is driven by the amount of leverage in the balance sheet or the amount of debt relative to book equity. As this ratio increases, so will the volume of earnings, after the payment of interest on the debt, that can be returned to shareholders. Therefore, debt will boost the earnings of shareholders. Obviously this only works as long as the business can comfortably pay its interest; otherwise it goes bust. Most debt arrangements with banks come with covenants specifying a number of financial ratios they must achieve for the bank to maintain a credit line with that company. The most important of these is interest coverage. This is simply how many times a firm's earnings, before interest charges and before tax, are able to cover the interest payments on the company's debt. Usually a coverage ratio of four to five times is adequate but once it starts falling further you know warning lights will be flashing with the bank manager. It may be this unhealthy level of debt which is allowing the firm to achieve an unusually high return on equity. But clearly this will not be sustainable if it goes bankrupt! Leverage is commonly measured by dividing the book value of equity in the business into the total assets on the balance sheet. The higher the ratio, the greater the leverage of the balance sheet.

If these three ratios are multiplied together they will give the return on equity of the business (Figure 5.1).[2] This will enable you to see not only how good the return on equity is in absolute terms but how it is being achieved. For example, the consumer goods manufacturer may be sustaining good returns simply by pumping up the level of debt on the balance sheet. Its competitor, by comparison, may be sustaining very high margin levels because it is offering outstanding customer satisfaction with its high quality merchandise. It is likely that this is going to be a much more sustainable source of advantage since any firm can leverage up its balance sheet but not every firm can satisfy customer needs such that customers will pay a premium for the product or service. Again, a third firm may be achieving a good return because it is achieving good utilization of its assets by outsourcing manufacturing successfully. In general this is likely to be a less unique source of advantage than a strong customer

[2] This formula is commonly known as the Du Pont formula.

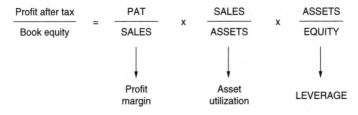

Figure 5.1 *Standard return on equity formula ("Du Pont" formula)*

franchise but it is more sustainable than leverage. By exploring these three ratios you can begin to corroborate your suspicions about the quality of the firm's results and consequently how sustainable those results are in going forward.

CASH FLOW

The other key measure of overall company performance you should focus on is cash flow. Cash flow is the lifeblood of a company. If it runs out, the firm dies just like a human being. Cash is different from profit. Profit is merely an accounting item, not bank notes in the company's account which can be used to pay interest and cover working capital needs. The two are, however, related. All firms keep a float in their bank account but they are also receiving and spending money in an ongoing cycle. The object is to end up with more cash than they spend. The net result of these flows through the year is "cash flow". "Profit", by comparison, does not take account of the fact that cash may not have been physically paid or received. It also does not account for capital expenditure in a cash sense. Shareholders cannot eat "profit" but only cash.

In order to convert the profit number to cash flow it is necessary to do a number of things. Firstly, you must subtract the net working capital at the beginning of the year from the position at the end. Working capital is cash tied up in items such as inventory and bills which have not been collected. It is also bills the firm itself has not paid, which effectively lend it cash to play with. "Net working capital" is the difference between what the firm owes to suppliers and how much cash it has tied up in inventory and in unpaid customer bills. If net working capital has grown during the year it will have eaten up cash. Secondly, you must add back depreciation. Depreciation is simply a notional charge relating to the annual "consumption" or usage of assets which have been purchased. Depreciation can be written off against tax over a certain period as a charge against profits and it can generate a cash benefit equivalent to the tax rate times the depreciation number. However, it is not an actual cash outgoing. Thirdly, you must subtract any capital investment in such things as machinery. This will have been paid for in cash unless it is being leased in which case you can ignore it. Having done all this, the final number you end up with is the firm's cash flow during the year (see Figure 5.2).

What can cash flow tell us? As we will discuss in a later section, the value of a firm's stock is ultimately determined by the cumulative value of the anticipated cash flows of a business into the future. This is literally how much dosh would hit the pockets of owners (unless the firm decided to use it to fund acquisitions or new investments). As your calculation of cash flow will have shown, a firm's cash generating ability is determined by its profitability, how much capital it ties up in working capital such as stock and receivables, the rate at which it depreciates its fixed assets and its level of capital investment. All of these numbers are excellent indicators of a firm's underlying performance.

You should also compare the cash flow of the firm to its profit. If the ratio of cash flow to profit is very much lower than that of a comparable competitor you should be on your guard. There could be a large number of reasons for this (as we will come onto) but it may corroborate your observations about the company's strategy. For example, a firm with a low ratio may be engaging in a period of heavy capital investment which will give it a competitive advantage in the future, or it may simply be carrying a lot of redundant, slow moving stock. Conversely, a firm with a high cash flow ratio may simply be harvesting a mature SBU without investing adequately in its future. Or, by contrast, it may be managing its working capital needs excellently. This ratio will allow you to begin to pose these questions although you will not yet be able to answer them. We will deal with how to examine these in more detail in our finance section in Chapter 7.

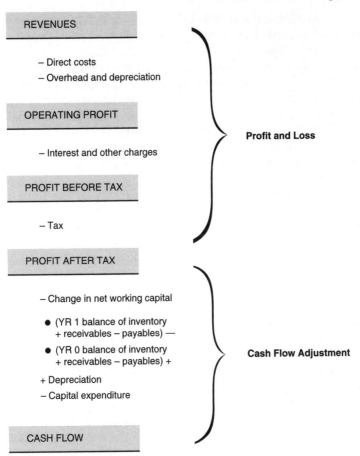

Figure 5.2 *Illustrative simplified calculation of cash flow from a P & L statement*

PRODUCTIVITY

Another good indicator of a firm's overall competitiveness is its productivity. Productivity is a measure of how efficiently sales are being generated from assets. The assets we have considered so far in our analysis of ROE are the capital assets of plant and machinery which are included on the balance sheet. But there are also those assets which do not appear on the balance sheet:

people. People are important. More and more businesses are recognizing their dependence on the quality of their people to sustain the competitive advantage enjoyed by their firm. This is not only true of service businesses which now constitute the bulk of the Gross National Product (GNP) of most western economies but also of industry, which is having to become increasingly good at anticipating and responding to consumer needs. In many manufacturing organizations it is the quality of the workforce that is the critical determinant of quality and unit costs. Unfortunately it is not always an asset base which comes up on the radar. That is a big mistake.

The easiest way to gauge the productivity of the "human asset" base is the change in the ratio of revenues per employee over time. This is simply an indicator of the level of output they are able to deliver. This number can, of course, be driven by a large number of factors. Most significantly over the last five years it is likely to have been boosted simply by a reduction in the company's headcount. In most cases this will have been a one-off benefit that cannot be repeated annually. Also, history has shown that after major head cuts there tends to follow a creeping re-employment drive to support revenue growth. Somebody, after all, has to do the work! The more meaningful productivity numbers will be gained by normalizing for the years where there has been headcount reduction. In this context, productivity improvements are more likely to be the product of better deployment of resources against SBUs. It will also reflect the calibre of employees, their level of motivation and the impact of training. All these things are more likely to be sustainable sources of productivity gains than one-off headcount reductions.

The second key productivity measure is the change in value added per employee. Value added is the difference between the sales price of the finished item or service and the value of the material, time and finance inputs that go into making it. Quite simply it is the value the company adds to its inputs. Whilst there are a number of complex routes to defining value added, for the purposes of our analysis, the simplest way to measure it is the change in pre-tax profits per employee. A large number of variables influence the profit number which may distort it as a measure of value added. However, it will give you a pointer towards the change in the ability of the workforce to command a premium for its activity in the marketplace. Again, a change in value added could be attributable to a number of things. A service business enjoying an increase in value added may be shifting into more profitable market segments or it may be achieving an improving reputation which enables it to increase its prices faster than competition. It may also be slashing headcount. The relationship between value added and revenue per employee is instructive. A movement apart may be an indication that a firm is moving into more or less profitable segments of activity (see Figure 5.3). Alternatively it may signal a loss of ability to charge a premium because workers are left unmotivated after a downsizing spree and cannot bother to iron out product errors.

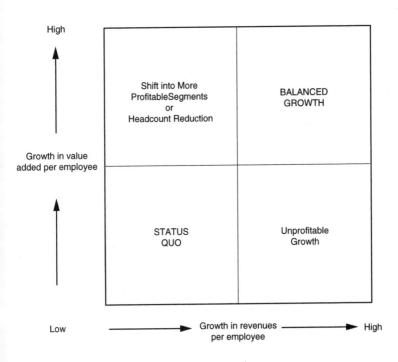

Figure 5.3 *Illustrative productivity trade-offs in a generic firm*

PULLING IT ALL TOGETHER

Before we move on to deepening our understanding of how value is driven in individual SBUs, you should balance your assessment of the company's overall performance with your evaluation of the mix of SBUs under its charge. Do you believe there is a strategy unifying them which is driving value creation? Or is value being created in spite of this corporate logic? A summary of the issues you will need to examine is shown in the "Value Drivers Roadmap", Figure 5.4.

After examining the primary drivers of value creation in SBUs we will return to the issue of corporate strategy and overall performance.

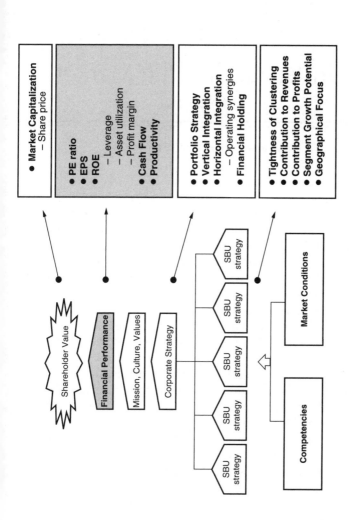

Figure 5.4 *Value drivers roadmap*

6
Understanding the Market Context

"SBUs don't compete with themselves"

SBUs do not operate in isolation. Their ability to create value is driven largely by the markets in which they compete. To understand the challenges facing a SBU you have to get a clear understanding of the nature of the marketplace around it. For example, a margin of 10% might be healthy in the consumer electronics business but lousy in the software business. Furthermore, it might be a viable strategy to compete on the basis of premium quality in software but in the electronics business this would be a disaster. These critical distinctions are driven by the nature of the marketplace.

Because of the apparently overwhelming complexity of most markets there is a dangerous tendency to generalize; for example, the manufacture of low grade paper might be dismissed as a nightmare of price-based competition – an area to be avoided. However, it is almost certainly the case that a well positioned firm will be able to achieve good margins in it. It will do so by understanding the key drivers of that market and configuring itself to meet those challenges optimally. Having said this, it is certainly the case that some markets are more attractive than others. An evaluation of the relative attractiveness of market segments should govern a firm's choice of which SBUs it chooses to invest in and the skills it develops to ensure a competitive position in that particular market.

Before embarking on an analysis of the market, it should be

pointed out that the relevant unit of analysis is the SBU, not the corporation. As your segmentation analysis will have shown, the nature of client demands will differ radically by SBU and this is one of the key drivers of market conditions. Also the relevant market will tend to be the local national market for the SBU's goods or services. The nature of competitive conditions tends to differ on a national basis and will almost certainly differ radically on a regional basis. This is true even for the most globalized markets such as the manufacture of aeroframes or cola distribution. In order to render the process of analysis manageable it is wise to focus on the limited number of markets which contribute the bulk of sales in the key clusters of SBUs for the company you are examining.

So what shapes the nature of a market? Simple. *Competition*. The level and nature of competition will be the prime driver of the attractiveness of a market and will determine how a firm has to position itself to create value. The key job for the manager is to understand the relative level of competition, what drives that competition and how the firm must position itself to compete successfully given these dynamics. This can be done with the aid of the market model depicted in Figure 6.1 which summarizes the major drivers of competition in a market.[1] The drivers themselves are pure common sense. The art comes in weighing them into an overall evaluation of the market and then deciding how an SBU should be positioned in it to optimize returns and whether the SBU in question is able to achieve such a position.

COMPETITION: DIFFERENTIATION VERSUS LOW COSTS

There's competition and there's competition. Broadly speaking, competition can be divided into two generic types; competition based on price and competition based on differentiation. In order to compete in situations where price is the dominant customer purchase criteria it is necessary to be a low cost producer. In order to compete where the major driver is differentiation, the

---

[1] A number of similar models have appeared over the years. The archetypal and most well known market model is Michael Porter's "Five Forces" (see Bibliography).

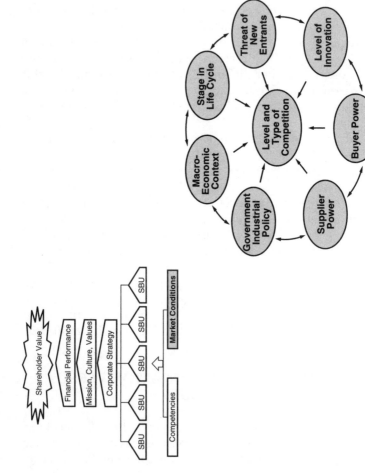

Figure 6.1   *The market model*

key is a unique product or service attribute. Clearly these are fundamentally different propositions. In industries where competition is based on differentiation, costs may be high but higher prices can be achieved to produce a favourable overall margin. In industries based on cost competition, equally healthy margins can be achieved but only by cutting costs down to the bone (see Figure 6.2). Firms can build successful businesses pursuing strategies on either basis as long as that strategy is well suited to the market. For example, trying to differentiate light bulbs and hoping that customers will pay more is probably doomed. Similarly, competing on price in the perfumes segments on the basis of low cost packaging will probably not fly, faced with competition from the Italian fashion houses. By contrast, aiming for rock bottom unit costs in the light bulb market, say 20% below that of competitors, will probably confer decisive advantage. Similarly, investing 10% of revenue in advertising for a perfume brand might also enable a firm to capture decisive levels of market share.

Probably your first instinct will be to say that most markets value both low unit costs and high levels of product performance and brand attributes. In fact, it is usually very difficult for a firm to be both low cost *and* differentiated. In order to differentiate a product or service, a firm will have to invest in building a loyal

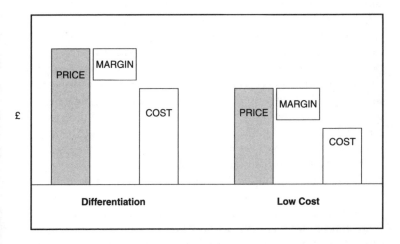

Figure 6.2   *Generic basis of competition: low cost versus differentiation*

customer franchise. It will probably also have to invest in keeping its model's leading edge. This will almost certainly prohibit it from competing on the basis of low costs. It is, fortunately, usually the case that customers of these type of businesses will not be particularly price sensitive. Therefore introducing low cost products will simply be a self-damaging exercise since they will be perceived to be "downmarket" by image-conscious consumers, as well as reducing profits. Conversely, firms which are competing on the basis of low price are likely to have to invest in outstanding production technology to lower their operating costs. They will have to focus on keeping their price points competitive. This will prohibit them from investing in differentiation efforts without destroying their margins in the process. Besides, this will probably be a futile exercise since what the customer will value is competitive pricing, not lots of bells and whistles. Attempts to combine both strategies can result in a firm being uncompetitive on both axes (see Figure 6.3).

There are, of course, apparent exceptions to this rule. Japanese car manufacturers, for example, would appear to achieve low unit costs and to successfully differentiate their vehicles from competitors by incorporating the design integrity of more classy vehicles in their mass production models. The key in these cases is to consider what constitutes differentiation. The trick employed by low cost manufacturers can be to introduce features which would appear to be differentiating when in fact they are simply exploiting methods of lowering costs. A redesign of a door panel section may be aesthetically pleasing but it might also permit easier manufacturability. In addition, the goalposts for a differentiated product are always moving. What is an innovation one day will be regarded as standard the next. Increasingly an innovation will probably not be a point of differentiation for long before it falls into the low cost domain. This can give the impression that the two axes are collapsible but, in fact, they rarely are.

Firms pursuing differentiation strategies will tend also to be pursuing "niche strategies". This should be no surprise. In order to differentiate a product a firm typically has to focus on those consumers for whom those bells and whistles *are* relevant. Armani clothes, for example, will not be to everyone's taste or, more importantly, to everyone's wallets. Niches do not necessarily have to be small but they will certainly be a subsection of the

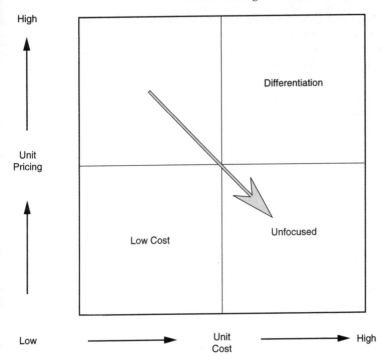

Figure 6.3 *Generic competitive strategies: low cost versus differentiation*

general market for a particular product. The important thing for a firm pursuing a niche strategy is that the niche is defensible. Competitors competing on price will typically not be targeted enough to operate in niches because they will rely on high volume to maintain decent profit margins. But the sands are ever shifting. A large, price-based competitor may decide to launch an upmarket product specifically to attack a niche. Yamaha has chipped away at Harley Davidson's market for roadsters, for example. Niches tend to draw a lot of attention; this is why firms competing in them are usually able to charge premium prices. It also means that they have to keep a weather eye on large, price-based competitors who might be lured in.

Before beginning your analysis of the market you should make sure you are clear what is the basis of competition in the industry you are examining. The primary hallmarks of a market which is based on differentiation will probably be high levels of marketing spend and relatively low unit volumes. The reverse is likely to be true for an industry based on low unit costs. Industries which are "stuck in the middle" and demonstrate both sets of characteristics typically will be markets in flux and suffering low margins. A firm can achieve high margins and a good return on investor's money through either competitive route. Different routes will suit different markets. The critical question to remind yourself to ask is whether the firm you are evaluating is able to meet the competitive requirements of the market.

DOWN TO DRIVERS

So, what are the competitors up to in the industry you are looking at? The best place to start is with shifts in market share and price. Market share does not necessarily correlate with profit but it can provide useful pointers. This means looking at the degree of consolidation versus fragmentation of the market and how it is evolving over time. If the market is carved up amongst a handful of large players and there have not been major changes in the distribution of market shares for some years it is likely that it is an orderly market. In this scenario it is probable that all players concerned are achieving good levels of return on equity or else they would have engaged in aggressive plays for market share. It will probably be the case that prices have increased steadily with inflation. Obviously the most extreme form of a cozy relationship is an established oligopoly or, in the exceptional case, a monopoly. If, by contrast, the market is fragmented and shares are low, with two or more dominant players battling for share, this will probably be a market which is highly competitive and where margins are low. Prices may have declined in real terms. This, of course, does not mean that it may not convert into a highly profitable situation once market shares have been consolidated or balanced.

The basic measure of market consolidation is a concentration ratio. A C4 ratio, for example, would correspond to the total market share represented by the top four competitors. If you compare changes in this ratio to the average annual change in unit prices and you know the average profitability of SBUs in that market, you will be able to draw some conclusions about how the level of competition may be driving profitability. What should be apparent, however, is that this gives you little understanding of the basis of competition and therefore what skills are necessary to create shareholder value.

THE MARKET MODEL

The market model depicts the seven primary factors that drive both the type and the level of competition in a marketplace:

1 Stage in the product or service life cycle
2 Threat of new entrants and ownership changes
3 Level of innovation occurring
4 Buyer power
5 Supplier power
6 Impact of government industrial policy
7 Macroeconomic context.

Weighing the impact of these drivers will allow you to understand why a market is as competitive as it is. This should enable you to answer the question of whether a firm is capable or incapable of sustaining competitive advantage in that environment (see Figure 6.4).

Stage in the Product or Service Life Cycle

A product or service, just like a human being, has a finite life. This is usually characterized by an early period of high growth, a period of development, followed by a plateau of middle age, then the harvesting period of retirement where bank accounts are emptied and enjoyed, followed by death when cash is redistributed to fuel new lives. All markets pass through cycles which may vary in shape but will usually obey the same pattern, although over different time periods. At each point in the life cycle the market is likely to witness different dynamics and place different demands on the firms competing in it. For example, in the evolution of the PC industry, the early stages

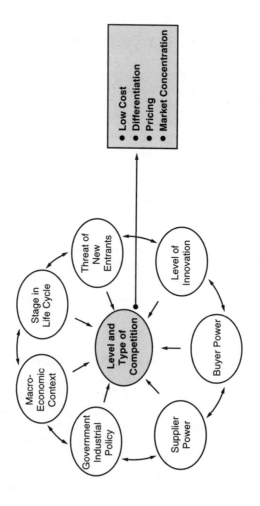

Figure 6.4   *The market model*

were characterized by a scrabble for market acceptance by a number of small players; profits were non-existent and cash flows were negative as they invested madly to achieve a consumer standard. Then one or two standards became dominant and market share was consolidated in a handful of large players. They achieved healthy returns as their early investments matured. Then, following expiration of key patents, a whole range of new competitors entered and started manufacturing at extremely low cost without any of the product development overheads of the early players. As a result the average margins achieved by the original firms began to fall and they were compelled to revise their product strategies and introduce a new round of innovation to position themselves at the head of a new life cycle. The same pattern is true for most industries, from pharmaceuticals to trainers. The difference is how long it takes each cycle to work itself through.

The primary descriptor of the shape of a life cycle is the industry growth rate. High growth will typically mark the early and development phases and tail off as the industry matures. In the early stages of the life cycle, there will be room for new entrants as growth comes from increasing volume rather than stealing share. It is also usually possible to charge full prices when demand is soaring. This means there is lots of cash to be made by all to fuel capital investment. As growth slows, the industry is likely to consolidate and competitors will battle with each other for share. The only means to grow is to take business away from one another. The growth rate, therefore, is a fundamental driver of both the level and the nature of competition, starting with innovation and a bid to set standards and ending with a shift to cost-based rivalry.

The life cycle for most product and service categories has shortened considerably over recent years and the market dynamics associated with the average life cycle have become exaggerated as a result. The standard industry life cycle nowadays is, in fact, the product of many life cycles; one life cycle begins and another begins to die each time a new round of product or service innovation occurs. If a firm cannot keep the ball in the air by innovating then it will gradually decline along with the old curve (see Figure 6.5).

The first thing you should identify is where on the life cycle

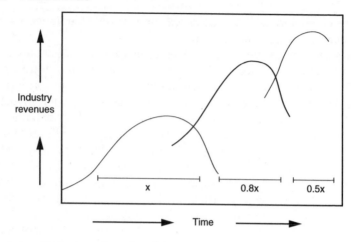

Figure 6.5 *Illustrative generic cumulative industry life cycle*

curve the products or services which account for the bulk of the industry's activities fall. Secondly, you should estimate the likely length of the upcoming curve. This will allow you to make a prediction about the demands placed on the firm as it moves along the curve. This analysis requires you to draw your own best version of the life cycle of the industry which is not easy. Tracking the industry growth rates over the previous five years and plotting it against known innovative product launches will give you a sense of what the curve looks like. If the curve is marked by low growth, ownership is split between a couple of large players and prices are stable, then they will probably be harvesting it for profit. If, on the other hand, it is mature, low growth and market share is changing hands that may be a sign it is a dying elephant's blood bath. Prices are likely to be falling fast. If you feel that the curve is coming to an end that may be a sign that a major substitution of underlying technology is about to occur. If, on the other hand, growth has been flat for 20 years without a major decline, then it may be a great cash spinner for incumbents. This would probably be the case in industries where the technology is stable and which are dominated by brands, as is the case with certain basic consumer goods categories such as cereal.

Threat of New Entrants and Ownership Changes

More competitors means trouble. If a significant firm is in the process of gaining a foothold in the market this is a sure signal that there will be an increase in competitiveness and pressure on profits. New entrants might seek either to gain this foothold through acquisition or through investing in start-up operations. The trouble with new people is that they always want to change the rules. A change in ownership of a company will usually disrupt the cosy, unspoken competitive agreements that have existed in the past. Typically, the new player will want to demonstrate to shareholders that it can extract value from the deal and will aim for rapid market share gains. Equally, if a firm is investing in a greenfield operation it will typically behave very aggressively to ensure that it can reach critical levels of utilization to deliver a return on that investment. Unless the market is growing fast enough to accommodate the entrant without detracting from the sales of incumbents, blood will be shed. The incumbents typically will respond to the appearance of a new competitor by lowering their prices to reduce the latter's viability and bring it under pressure from its own shareholders.

The counterpart to entry is exit. The regular exiting of firms from a sector may signal growing concerns over the viability of profits. Of course, the disappearance of a losing firm may also signal a return to healthy profits for the remaining competitors since a dying dog will tend to drag prices down in its bid for survival. More disturbing is a situation where a number of firms are suffering low margins but are unable, for whatever reason, to exit the sector. This will keep margins low for the foreseeable future.

The key drivers of the level of migration are the barriers to entry and exit. These drive both the incidence of new competitors and the ability of old competitors to get out and hence impact the margins of other players in that industry. In some segments the investment costs necessary to enter a business can be tremendous; there may be proprietary technologies which are not accessible except through high levels of investment in R&D. It may require huge investments in production facilities to achieve requisite economies of scale. It may be extremely difficult to win the set of client relationships necessary to build a business base (this would be the case in many professional service areas for example.) All these factors will pose formidable barriers to new entrants and hence limit any increase in the level of competition experienced by the sector. In general, the more consolidated a sector is, the more difficult it will be for a new player to establish itself unless there is a major change in the underlying technology or they do so through a major acquisition. For example, Direct Line Insurance in the UK has crept successfully under the door of the insurance giants because information technology has enabled it to price itself lower than firms carrying a large traditional distribution overhead.

Conversely, it may be very difficult for flagging players to leave the sector. This may be for emotional reasons such as the perceived need by the company's CEO to keep a foothold in that industry in order to retain credibility. Or it might be because of the costs of laying off workers due to regulation in the local market: these may outweigh the benefits of any exit. Or it might be because management cannot see any other area of business activity to which they could viably migrate. It is hard to teach an old dog to dance to a new tune. If a player who is doing poorly cannot get out it is likely that the level of competition will remain high and the profits of all the players will remain depressed.

The challenge is to evaluate the level of entry and exit that has recently occurred and to make some predictions about how this will alter in the future. To do this you will need to list and then rank the barriers both to entry and exit in the segment you are scrutinizing. Figure 6.6 lays out a simple illustrative example of this in the pharmaceutical industry versus the advertising industry where entry and exit barriers are fundamentally different.

Level of Innovation Occurring

Closely related to the issue of entry and exit is the process of innovation. The rate of product and service innovation has increased dramatically in recent years. The average life cycle for a new car has dropped from six years in 1980 to under two years in 1995 and is continuing to fall. The average life cycle for a PC has fallen to between six and nine months. This means that a firm may happily be producing a product with reasonable levels of

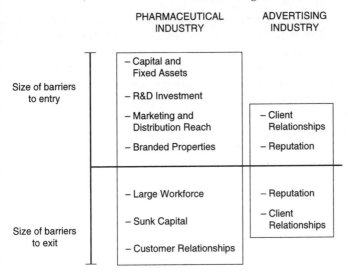

Figure 6.6 *Illustrative drivers of entry and exit barriers in two distinct industries*

profit when a substitute is launched and pulls the rug out from under it entirely. This is not an uncommon occurrence! The emergence of in-line skates, for example, caught manufacturers of roller skates napping. And does anyone use a typewriter any more?

Typically in situations where total substitution has occurred a technology will have been quite old, investments will have been depreciated and consequently profits will be high. Management may be operating under the assumption that this will go on for ever or, if they are aware it will be swept away, they will take it for all the cash they can while the sun is still shining. This is appropriately called "harvesting". The only problem with harvesting is that something has to be done with the cash released from the business. Returning all of it to shareholders in the form of a dividend or share buy-back can be perceived as an admission by management that it cannot put the cash to use. In the long term this will erode the market value of the firm and shareholders will lose out. Therefore, excess profits from a highly mature segment where there may even be the whisper of a substituting technology on the horizon should be treated with appropriate caution. Unless the firm has an ability to counter or ride the wave of an impending substitute technology then it will be seriously damaged.

More common, however, than the outright substitution of a technology is the relentless upgrading of an existing technology. The improvement of car models, the upgrading of specifications on software packages, the changes in food flavourings are often incremental upgrades rather the erasing of an old concept by a new one. Of course, the impact of those incremental changes may be an effective substitution over a longer time frame. In markets where substitutive upgrading is occurring rapidly you would anticipate the level of competition to be high. The levels of investment necessary to upgrade annually will erode earnings per share and there is likely to be aggressive pricing in order to win rapid customer acceptance. There will be a regular to-ing and fro-ing every few years as players jostle for position. The firms that thrive will typically be nimble and aggressive.

Innovation does not only occur in industrial settings with traditional R&D departments. It is also an increasingly prevalent feature of service businesses. Ten years ago investment banks drew very little of their income from trading derivatives whereas today such instruments are their life-blood. Ten years ago no consulting firm had even heard the term re-engineering and now it is the staple of their business offer. A logistics company delivering parcels across Europe will use fundamentally different systems than it did ten years ago. Those firms that failed to upgrade are probably no longer in competition with the likes of UPS or DHL. What usually makes innovation in service businesses different from innovation in an industrial setting is that the R&D process is far shorter and less capital intensive. The innovation is often simply an ingenious concept which a smart person has concocted. The time and effort comes in perfecting the delivery of it in the marketplace through a process of refinement. Because of the fewer R&D requirements, the entry barriers into many service areas are far lower than the entry barriers into industry. Any business school professor can set up a consulting firm. Many major service providers, from contract cleaning to distribution, have simply sprung up out of family concerns. As a result, service industries will, on the whole, be far less consolidated than their industrial counterparts. This usually means that long-term earnings prospects will be more volatile and have more risk attached to them for shareholders.

Technology is not the only source of product substitution. Substitution can also occur due to nothing more than evolving consumer taste. Fashion moves swiftly and somewhat unpredictably, driven by a wide range of cultural factors such as the latest pop bands and clothing fads. Doc Marten's shoes might surf the wave for five years then fall off the other end. The main weapon in the corporate armoury to harness the power of consumer tastes is brands. Like any product, brands continually have to reposition themselves to avoid obsolescence. Brands, however, tend to be more enduring than technology-based products. The big ones such as Coke and Levi's may have been around for over a century and their positions are virtually unassailable because of their extraordinary hold on consumer emotions. The entry barriers for new brands are usually higher than those for a technology-based product. The cumulative spends on advertising and communications by mature brands constitute a huge hurdle for new entrants. As a result, the mortality rate of new brands is around the 80% mark in the mature western economies. In segments where brands, rather than the underlying product technology, are the differentiating features you will probably find a lower rate of innovation and new entrants.

The best way to predict how innovation will drive the level of substitution is to look at the historic intervals between effective substitutions or step changes in technologies. In general, it is reasonable to assume that the speed of substitution will show an ongoing acceleration over historical trends due to changes in underlying technology. Usually, before an impending substitution, sales will begin to stall as customers anticipate new models with higher performance characteristics. This pattern is very typical in fast-moving areas such as software and computer games. If industry sales growth has slowed over a relatively short period, it will probably be a signal that new technologies are anticipated by the market. You should check the press for reports on changes or innovations in the pipeline. The imminent expiry of key patents will probably augur a round of substitutive upgrading. If the level of research activity in the industry, measured in terms of patents per thousand employees, is heating up that may also point in the direction of substitution.

Of course, it is equally possible that the industry you are looking at has shown no major innovation for 50 years. This might be the case in the basic bakeries market, for example, where a handful of brands have an established place in the consumer's mind. Unless there is the possibility of consumer taste shifting dramatically, it is unlikely that such brands will be displaced.

One stumbling block is that innovation does not necessarily have to manifest itself in the product; it could also be in the process that creates it. In the case of bread baking, for example, oven technology has changed very rapidly over the past 20 years and has radically altered competitive dynamics. The family-run bakery on the corner of the street is a dying phenomenon. Changes in production technology can pose just as large a substitutive threat as changes in basic product technology. They are also probably more pervasive, driven by the quest for increased productivity. In terms of determining the rate of process change the best indicator is the rate of change in unit output per dollar of capital employed. We will come onto the issue of process technology in a later section.

Buyer Power

Love 'em or hate 'em you can't do without 'em. As you might expect, the nature of customers has a tremendous influence on the level of competition in a market. If there is a change in buyer needs, perceptions or, indeed, whims, someone will be there to satisfy it, potentially to the cost of the other firms in the industry. There is a circular debate about whether innovation amongst producers fosters changes in consumption patterns or if evolving consumer demands create a need which firms are forced to learn to satisfy. We won't get into that here. Let's just say that if we regard the customer as king we won't go far wrong. Whilst this sounds like a banality it is a rule that the majority of firms fail to respect. Even if firms take the rule seriously, it is equally likely that they fail to convert it into meaningful action. How many times have you received great service from your local telephone or gas company? The great thing about being a customer is that you usually have a choice.

"Choice" is an expression of a customer's ability to exert influence over a market. For analytical purposes the idea of "choice" can be broken down into two concepts:

- a purchaser's negotiating power versus a supplier;
- the cost for a purchaser to switch between suppliers.

Clearly the two ideas are related; if switching costs are low the level of negotiating power a customer holds will increase. However, the two forces can also exist independently. A company buying computer networks for their offices may be an important client and therefore their negotiating power is high. But they may also be unable to switch suppliers without replacing some of their existing LANS which will weaken their negotiating position.

The most basic driver of negotiating power is the relative size of buyers versus suppliers. If the principal group of buyers is much larger than the average size of suppliers it is likely that the buyers will use their strength to reduce prices. Equally, if the buyers are highly consolidated and the supply industry in question is less consolidated then it is likely that the buyers will hold the balance of power in negotiations. The effect of this balance of purchasing power is graphically illustrated in the retail sector where concentration has allowed retailers to stock increasing volumes of own label brands whilst continuing to distribute what in essence are competitive brands.

The second key driver of negotiating power is the degree of dependency in the supplier-buyer relationship. In many industries this relationship will be very close. The logistics system of the buyer may be intimately tied into the logistics system of the supplier. This would be the case if the buyer was operating a just-in-time (JIT) inventory system for example. Alternatively the supplier may have worked closely with the buyer to hit certain quality control standards such as ISO 9000, 9001 or 9002[2], which the buyer would have to forfeit if he moved to another supplier. In some cases the buyer may actually have a financial stake in the supplier to ensure that standards are maintained and delivery is efficient. Clearly the more central the supplied component is to the product or service of the buyer the less likely it is that the

---

[2] The ISO standards are one form of a number of major quality control standards used by companies specifying certain quality performance levels through parts of their entire value chain.

buyer will choose to exert excessive negotiating pressure, whatever their relative size.

Having negotiating power and using negotiating power, however, are two distinct things. The common reason for a buyer not to
flex their muscle is that playing that card carries a cost. Someone
buying a high blood pressure medication is likely to be loyal to
brand even if the price gets out of kilter. Similarly, a CEO who has
used a firm of management consultants for the past ten years, and
has come to depend on the judgment of the senior partner, will
probably be loath to change firms. The reason they choose not to
exercise their bargaining power is because of switching costs.
Switching costs are the price it will cost a buyer to change
suppliers. These costs might be literally financial or they might be
emotional. The person who adores Heinz baked beans will probably enjoy a financial benefit by switching to own label. They may,
however, suffer a terrible emotional trauma if, for instance, their
neighbours or friends see a cheap bottle of wine on the table when
they come round for dinner. It may also strain one of the tenderest
human emotions upon which companies prey: loyalty. For other
types of buyers the cost of switching may be very low. The
supermarkets, for example, have all developed their own label
products, therefore they are in a good position to negotiate tough
terms with branded suppliers since they can always dump them if
a lesson needs to be taught. In general, switching costs will fall
away dramatically as the degree of interdependence of the value
chains of the supplier and buyer diminishes.

The size of switching costs will be reflected directly in the level
of rivalry in a market and hence on the margins achieved by
protagonists. As a result, firms invest heavily in preserving
whatever switching costs they can. There is no rational reason
why, for example, Kellogg's has sustained tremendous market
share for a great many years despite a yawning price point
premium. It has done so by investing heavily in advertising and
brand promotions to bolster the feeling amongst consumers that
the emotional cost of switching would outweigh the cost advantages. Similarly, McKinsey extracts the highest fees in the management consulting industry when CEOs could readily turn to a
number of cheaper suppliers. However, McKinsey has invested
in building an alumni network which is unrivalled. Hence emotional switching costs are high and this enables fat margins to be

maintained. Emotional relationships, whether nurtured through brands or personal trust, are the most effective means of mitigating buyer power.

The key question to ask yourself is whether there is a gap between apparent switching costs or the negotiating power of buyers and the margins the firm is achieving. If there is a gap, then you have to ask yourself whether you believe this position is sustainable. It may be the case that the level of investment necessary to sustain the gap is not tenable. It may be that a rival firm is intent on winning the clients away using tactics that will make it clear to them that switching costs are in fact much lower than they thought. Always assume that the situation is dynamic and that a compelling rationale will be necessary to maintain a gap between buyer power and margins. In general, the greater the level of buyer power the more the industry will be subject to swings in pricing. In downturns it will probably be squeezed hard. Firms which have failed to invest in establishing a modicum of customer loyalty will be the first to suffer.

Supplier Power

The importance of the supply side is often overlooked by analysts. It is, however, a significant driver of profitability. The issues at play are the mirror image of those that drive the power of buyers; negotiating power and switching costs. If the supply industries are much larger than the firms in the industry you are looking at, and if that supply market is highly consolidated, it is likely that they will impose harsher terms and supply costs will be higher. The market for diamonds, for example, is dominated by De Beers who can to some degree dictate the market price – as a small retailer on Fifth Avenue you are in no position to negotiate terms, and you certainly have virtually no ability to switch. Consolidation need not occur simply at the original supplier stage. It often also occurs at the distribution stage. If, for example, you are a builders' merchant, there may be dozens of manufacturers of electrical cable from whom you can purchase, in theory, but in practice this will not do you much good if there are only two major distributors.

In some supply areas there is a genuine market for inputs

which no single supplier or buyer can influence singlehandedly. Many raw materials, from corn to aluminium, are traded on exchanges and prices are determined by overall movements in the markets rather than by a relationship between a single buyer and a supplier. The price will follow movements in the balance between general market supply and demand rather than to the peculiarities of a particular business arrangement. For many other supply areas, however, the nature of the relationship will determine the outcome.

Related to scale are, of course, switching costs. If a business can only get hold of an input from a single source, or if even the most temporary disruption to the supply of that input will cause chaos in the manufacturing chain, then it is likely the buyer will stick to a tried and trusted supplier. McKinsey, for example, will pay highly to recruit Harvard graduates because if it fails to do so competitors will quickly get an upper hand in claiming the top intellectual calibre available in the market. This means that even if the head of McKinsey does not personally get on with the Dean he will not risk switching out of Harvard. Similarly, a whisky distillery that is dependent on a certain type of peat to add flavour to its grain, will probably not negotiate peat diggers out of business even if they are a low-skilled labour group.

It is high switching costs, and the perceived risk associated with dependence on limited sources of supply, that have driven many firms to vertical integration. The question to ask is whether the reduction in risk to supply afforded by integration outweighs the possibility that the new owner will not know how to run that firm to maximum effectiveness and erode its competitiveness by giving it a captive internal market. As with buyers, the greater the power of suppliers the more easily they will be able to pass on costs to customers. Unless the buyer can do likewise with his customers, he is likely to suffer periodic margin squeezes. If the industry you are examining is outgunned both upstream and down then it will have serious problems in market downturns.

Impact of Government Industrial Policy

Government plays a crucial role in determining the level of competition in certain markets. Within a single national market, a western-style government's main concern will be to maintain an even playing field. This means maintaining a free, un-manipulated balance between supply and demand which permits the setting of prices through market forces.

In all markets there is a relationship between supply and demand which establishes the prices achieved called the "demand and supply curves". The curves will shift as the relationship between demand and supply alters, resulting in new price outcomes (see Figure 6.7). Pricing curves can suffer peculiar distortions which alter the pricing equilibrium that would exist under normal competitive conditions. The most obvious example is when a single firm captures a disproportionately high percentage of market share such that it exerts inordinate power over both suppliers and buyers. This will distort the pricing structure, almost certainly to the cost of the consumer. At this point the government will usually step in and issue an antitrust suit, limiting the firm's ability to distort prices. BA in the UK and Microsoft in the US have, for example, both been subject to government intervention. The widespread phenomenon of privatization which has swept the globe for the past ten years, has often involved the breaking up of just such monopolies. For the firms concerned this is usually a profoundly uncomfortable experience since they become subject to the power of the market to

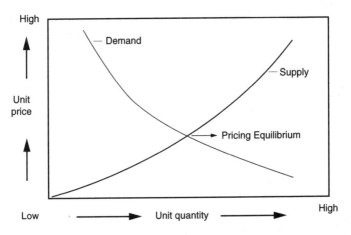

Figure 6.7 *Illustrative demand and supply curves in stable market conditions for a generic industry*

set prices. For the consumer it is usually a delightful experience since it means more cash in their pocket.

Since most businesses now operate on an international footing, the role of government extends far beyond the price setting process. Public policy can directly confer competitive advantage on firms versus their international competitors. A plant exporting cars from Wales, for example, may benefit from a subsidy it received to establish its manufacturing site there. This will enable it to price lower than a German firm importing cars into the UK which have been manufactured in Bavaria. It is almost always the case that firms competing in international markets which have their origins in different countries will enjoy differential government treatment. One government may impose regulations relating to the ability of firms to fire employees. If a firm enjoys free labour practices in one country whilst another with its manufacturing base in a different country doesn't, the latter will face distinct challenges. Similarly, a government may introduce regulations in a market governing the infringement of patent rights which enable a local firm to exploit an idea belonging to a foreign competitor without paying for its development. This will place the foreign competitor at a distinct cost disadvantage in that and other markets.

The interesting thing about favourable government regulation is that it does not necessarily result in a long-term advantage for the beneficiary. Spain's high import tariffs under Franco, for example, simply fostered a set of industries which were so pampered that they have been blown away now those tariffs have disappeared. On the other hand, there can be little doubt that the low costs of capital enjoyed by Japanese firms as a result of tacit government support helped many Japanese industries get a strong, low cost base position from which to penetrate foreign markets.

The depth and complexity of government regulation is overwhelming and can easily leave the manager with a bad headache. The only question that you really need ask yourself is whether one firm appears to be enjoying advantages as a result of government policy which another firm is denied. Usually this will be because they have their HQ or manufacturing base in different markets. If this is the case, clearly it can be beneficial but only as long as it is sustainable and it is not disguising fundamental weaknesses in the operation. If, once you have analysed a firm's competencies, you find that it is weak in key parts of the value chain, no amount of favourable government treatment will paper over those cracks for ever. At best they will provide a breathing space.

Macroeconomic Context

All industries are subject to the vagaries of the general economic environment in which they compete. Interest rates go up and down, exchange rates shift, domestic and international demand fluctuates through macroeconomic cycles. No firm is free from these contextual constraints. As these macro variables shift, so too does the level of competition experienced by players in any particular market. It doesn't take much of a slowdown in growth in GNP for weaker firms to begin to feel the pressure on shareholder returns. The size of the market for which they are competing will contract and unless they are able to maintain customer loyalty, the basis of purchase criteria will revert to price. Nor does it take much of an upward shift in interest rates to badly affect a firm with too much leverage in its balance sheet. Equally, a firm with an export dependency on key markets with depreciating currencies will immediately feel pressure in terms of the prices it is able to sustain.

Different industries will be affected quite differently by similar changes in the economic context. An industry which is immature, high growth and dominated by a small number of innovative firms may be able to sustain prices far more effectively than a mature, declining industry in a period of economic downturn. Conversely, a mature industry of staple products with a high degree of consolidation, competing on low margins, may not be affected as dramatically by a slowdown in general consumer spending as will an industry charging high premiums for non-essential purchases. Industries which operate globally and where competitors are not dependent on single markets are also likely to experience lower levels of increased rivalry than firms which are competing for a share of a contracting domestic market blighted by recession.

Not only do different industries behave differently as the

economic climate changes; distinct segments of an industry will be affected differently. A niche focused on wealthy clients, competing on the basis of strong brand values may be able to weather slow growth much better than a broad segment competing on the basis of value for a more price discerning customer. A segment built on the basis of close client relationships and high levels of customization may be able to pass on rising costs more effectively in an inflationary period than a mass market segment sold on the basis of price. As we have already discussed, it is because different business segments may behave quite differently with changes in the macroeconomic context that many companies maintain portfolios of fairly diverse SBUs.

Major Determinants of Macroeconomic Context

The macroeconomic context of an industry is driven by far too complex a set of factors for us to cover in this brief evaluation. Also, developments in each national economy are influenced by changes in the global economy which further confounds any simple platitudes. However, to simplify somewhat, the three most prevalent determinants of the market context under normal conditions are:

1 GNP growth
2 inflation and interest rates
3 exchange rates.

All three factors are closely interrelated. They also tend to move in a cyclical fashion, although determining the intervals and size of movements is an art few governments have mastered completely. Clearly, GNP growth will affect the size of the market available for firms in an industry to chase after. If a market shrinks, competition will typically increase as firms compete to maintain revenues. Inflation and interest rates will affect the cost of capital for firms in an industry, lower market values and put pressure on them to pass on costs to customers in the form of higher prices. The ability of different industries to do this differs dramatically and hence the level of rivalry that upward shifts in these variables will produce also differs. Changes in exchange rates will clearly affect the competitiveness of exporting firms. In industries which are highly traded, adverse exchange rates will again quickly tighten the ferocity of competition whilst domestic industry may feel the effects to a lesser degree in their imported inputs.

As a manager it is important to understand the sensitivity of an industry and its distinct business segments to shifts in these variables. Changes in macroeconomic variables are beyond the control of any firm and no firm in a local market can escape them other than by shifting the basis of their activity into another market. They would not appear, therefore, to be factors which differentiate one firm from the next. However, the ability of firms to manage through changes in the macroeconomic context varies dramatically and is a major driver of competitiveness. If one firm is better at holding prices with loyal customers because of past investment in strengthening its brand, it will suffer less than a firm competing on price with a transient customer base in a period of economic slowdown. If a firm is able to diversify its customer base abroad, it will do better than a firm focused on the domestic market during periods of relative currency decline due to high inflation.

In terms of gauging the future level of competition in an industry, you will simply be concerned with how sensitive current profits are to shifts in the key economic variables. This is typically called "sensitivity analysis". If GNP growth slows what will happen to pricing? Are there weaker firms who will be forced to enter a pricing spiral? If inflation and interest rates rise, are there a significant number of players whose profits will decline and who will aggressively compete to grow their market share to compensate? If there is a steep appreciation of national currency, will this reduce the ability of players to export and will they therefore turn on each other in their domestic market? The precise reactions any change in the macroeconomic context will produce is clearly dependent on the nature of the companies who dominate the sector and their ability to maintain profits without aggressive pricing. Going beyond sensitivity analysis, and trying to predict how economic variables will shift, is an art beyond the scope of our market modelling.

PULLING IT ALL TOGETHER

So, having worked through an analysis of the market in which an SBU competes, what do you do with it? The first thing to do is to assign a score to the key drivers and aggregate these into an overall weighting reflecting the level of competitiveness. If you do this for each of the markets in which the SBUs compete, you can then chart these scores against what you know to be the operating margins they have achieved. Ideally you would also chart these scores against the margins achieved by competitors. Figure 6.8 illustrates this type of analysis for our hypothetical swimming pool segments.

	Stage in Life Cycle	Threat of New Entrants	Level of Innovation	Buyer Power	Supplier Power	Government Industrial Policy	Macroeconomic Context	Overall Level of Competitiveness*
SBU 1	3	3	4	3	4	4	4	4
SBU 2	2	2	3	3	3	3	4	3
SBU 3	1	1	2	1	2	2	3	2

* Unweighted
1 = Low attractiveness   5 = High attractiveness

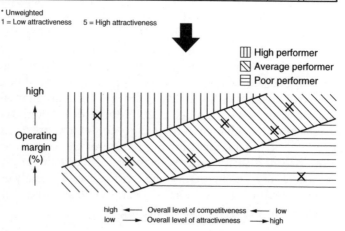

Ⅲ High performer
Ⓝ Average performer
⊟ Poor performer

high

↑

Operating margin (%)

↑

high ◀—— Overall level of competitveness ◀—— low
low ——▶ Overall level of attractiveness ——▶ high

Figure 6.8 *Illustrative market attractiveness evaluation for generic segments*

This process will throw up lots of red flags. If one of the SBUs, for example, competes in an industry which seems, on the basis of your analysis, to be fairly uncompetitive, but the firm is achieving low margins, then you will know it has a problem. If the situation is the reverse, then you know it is doing something right. At this point you will not be able to say precisely what is making the SBU behave as it is. You will, however, know whether the SBU is competing in an attractive market, broadly what skills are necessary to compete in it and whether it is excelling or not.

Armed with this information, you should quickly turn back to the issue of corporate strategy. Is the firm in question focusing its resources in those segments where profit will be most readily won? If you plot the attractiveness of the segments you have analysed against the relative weight of these segments in the firm's sales portfolio, this will immediately raise the issue of whether it is banking its future on areas which you believe will yield good profits. Performing the same analysis against share of profits will give you a further pointer. A firm which is generating 50% of its profits from a segment which you believe is going to suffer margin erosion due to substitute technology and new entrants will clearly be facing a bleak future. Conversely, a firm which has only a small and declining amount of revenues from this source will probably have read the tea leaves in the same way as you. A firm which has focused its activities in sectors of low anticipated rivalry will probably be able to sustain premium profits with comparative ease (see Figure 6.9).

At this point you will still not know precisely why a firm is performing as it is in a particular segment and whether it could indeed do better, although you may now have some pretty good ideas. A marketplace may be tremendously tough but a superb player will be able to achieve high returns and vice versa. Very profitable businesses have often been built in areas which other firms have abandoned as unprofitable. The rules of the market are there to be broken by the innovative competitor!

Your segmentation analysis will have told you something about the nature of the customer and nature of the competencies that characterize each segment and therefore what skills you believe are necessary to extract good profits from it. Your market analysis will have told you something about the nature of com-

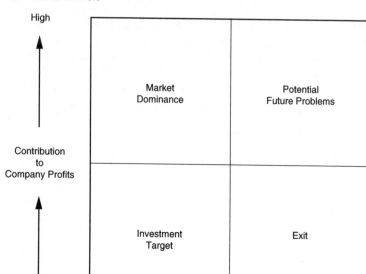

Figure 6.9   Illustrative SBU market prioritization matrix

petition, the type of demands it places on firms competing in it and the key drivers of value creation (see Figure 6.10). The next question to ask is whether the SBUs you are looking at are capable or incapable of meeting those demands or even reshaping them altogether. This requires understanding the firm's value chain or the internal drivers of value creation (see Figure 6.11).

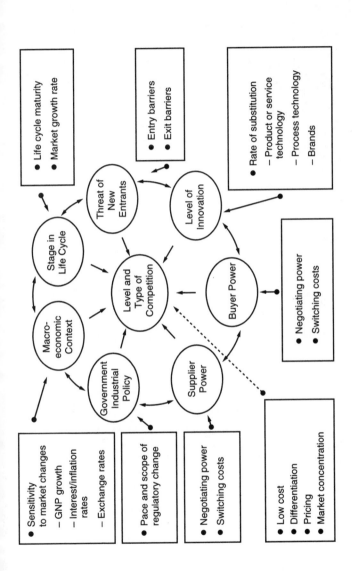

Figure 6.10   *Market model summary*

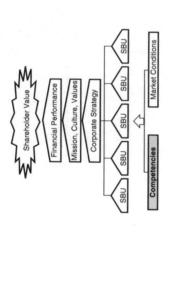

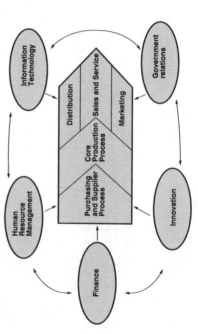

Figure 6.11   Value drivers roadmap

7
Core Competencies

"Can we hack it?"

Different market conditions will obviously place different demands on firms competing in them. If a market is characterized by intense competition based on price and customer loyalty is low then tight costs will be vital. More specifically, it may be necessary to have large-scale manufacturing which will lower unit costs. If however, a key area of competition is speed of delivery then outbound logistics will need to be superb. In most companies there will not be a single factor which enables the firm to compete effectively or the absence of which will destroy it. Rather there will be a hierarchy of requirements, some of which need only be done to minimum necessary standards and others which must be perfected or else. This is called the "skills hierarchy". For example, a manufacturer of plastic waste bins may have to meet certain basic specifications in terms of product quality such as not having gaping holes. However, if unit prices exceed a certain amount then the local council will not continue to purchase from that supplier, holes or no holes. In designer watches, by contrast, a distributor may feel happy introducing a price increase every six months. But if the speed of new model introductions stretches out to a whole year then he will look elsewhere.

You should be able to complete a first cut skills hierarchy on the basis of your segmentation and market analysis. Figure 7.1 illustrates the skills necessary to compete in the business traveller end of the commercial airlines industry. These skills are split

Figure 7.1   *Illustrative skills hierarchy for competing in the business traveller end of the airline industry*

between those that are a necessary minimum requirement to compete in the market, called "threshold skills", and those that would differentiate the service from the pack and confer significant competitive advantage. Of course, this is all very well in theory, but how does a firm deliver these skills in practice? It delivers by excelling in those pieces of the value chain which house these skills. An airline competing in the high end, transatlantic market, for example, may decide to differentiate itself on the basis of in-flight customer service. This will place great pressure on its HR function in terms of training staff, and probably on its inbound logistics in terms of sourcing outstanding fresh food, as Figure 7.2 illustrates. The tighter the fit between the skills hierarchy and the value chain, the more competitive the firm will be.

Of course, to be really powerful, it is necessary to take this analysis a step further and hypothesize what would have to be done right in those crucial steps of the value chain to excel. For example, saying that an electric fan manufacturer needs to achieve very low manufacturing costs to satisfy price sensitive

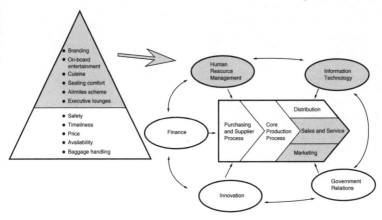

Figure 7.2 *Illustrative skills hierarchy and impact on the value chain of a firm competing in the business traveller end of the airline industry*

customers is not entirely helpful. Should this be done by introducing robotic automation or should it be done by sourcing cheaper components? This brings us to an evaluation of competencies.

VALUE CHAIN STRATEGY

All firms, whether industrial or services, have a value chain. In the case of a service firm the configuration of the core elements may look different. Figure 7.3 compares the value chain of a generic manufacturer of electronic consumer goods with that of an advertising agency. Each part of the value chain requires a strategy to ensure that it drives value creation for the firm overall. For a piece of the value chain to have a strategy means that the individual managing it is clear about what capabilities the firm requires to deliver effective market impact. Usually they have many choices. For example, the head of marketing in an fmcg[1] company, faced with a situation of declining share in her

---

[1] fmcg = fast moving consumer goods such as foods, detergents, personal care products etc.

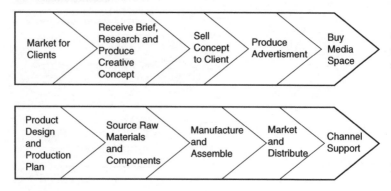

Figure 7.3   *Illustrative simplified value chain of a generic manufacturer versus a generic advertising firm*

core cereal brands, may choose to invest heavily in promotions and to cut the unit price to force a comeback. This may simply precipitate a price war which she has not got the cost structure to support because of a comparatively weak manufacturing base. Had she invested in a more intelligent use of advertising spend she may have been able to gain such a huge share of voice that she would have gained a decisive advantage. The difference between having a strategy and not having a strategy is important here. Each area of the value chain will have a manager who has to cope with the day-to-day exigencies of running a business. These can be overwhelming. If she has formulated a strategy, she will focus her attention on those areas which will produce most impact in delivering a result. If not, it is likely that this area will be run sub-optimally and that weakness may impact the firm's ability to compete.

The core elements of the value chain can be grouped into seven areas:

1 operations strategy
2 marketing, sales & service strategy
3 innovation strategy
4 financial strategy
5 human resource strategy
6 information technology strategy
7 lobbying position with government.

Whilst we will discuss the individual pieces of the value chain as if they are discrete this is absolutely not the case in practice. Firms succeed by ensuring that the entire process necessary to deliver a good or service is attuned to achieving the single goal of competitive positioning in the market. This requires coordination across the entire value chain, even if certain pieces of it are more critical than others. Historically, most firms have divided the overall process functionally into its separate parts. The reason for this is simple. Marketing requires marketing skills whilst manufacturing requires engineers. The pieces of the value chain were specialized because they required specialist skills, producing the departmental phenomena which still drives most of the business structures in firms today. There is now an increasing shift away from this departmental view of competencies, to managing the value chain holistically. The SBUs that do well in a particular segment will not simply be excellent in one part of the value chain. They will ensure that the entire value chain works to support their differentiating attributes. As we will come onto, it is the ability of a firm to integrate all its departmental skills behind a single goal that gives it decisive advantage over the competition. This process of integration is the role of senior SBU management.

It is also important to be clear on the relationship between a company's value chain and its SBUs. Certain parts of the value chain are likely to be common to all its SBUs. For instance, a firm may have a centrally organized HR function which manages the payroll or recruitment for all the individual firms in the company. The IT strategy for the group may also be administered through a central resources unit with a single budget. By contrast, each SBU will probably have its own marketing group and control its own operational flows. It may, however, operate through a shared sales force. Large elements of the finance function such as treasury are likely to be performed centrally. The rationale for centralization is almost always cost reduction. A finance group of 50 people servicing 20 SBUs is more cost effective than 20 SBUs each with ten people. The degree to which functions are performed on a group-wide basis or left to the discretion of individual SBUs will vary depending on the firm's overall structure and strategy. The more closely SBUs are clustered, the easier it will be to centralize non-client-facing functions, leaving the SBUs to concentrate on what they are good at, adding client value. If, however, functions are centralized in an environment where the needs of SBUs are very different, cost savings can be outweighed by operational disruption. In performing your evaluation of the value chain you should, therefore, work out at what level functions are managed and whether this means they deliver optimal value to the SBUs.

Pulling it All Together

In terms of focusing your energies you should concentrate on those pieces of the value chain which come out top of your skills hierarchy and which are the principle drivers of value creation. The objective is to see how well the key pieces of the firm's value chain are positioned to contribute to meeting the competitive demands of the market place.

OPERATIONS STRATEGY: "THE GUTS"

The operations of a company are the basic processes that drive the delivery of a product or service. In a manufacturing context the usual perception is that the operation is confined to what happens on the factory floor. But the production line extends beyond the factory. It starts with how the inputs are sourced and ends with how the goods or services are delivered to the customer. Operations strategy is the process of ensuring that these core processes are functioning efficiently to deliver a satisfactory customer result. For purposes of analysis, the core operations of a company can be broken into three pieces:

- the purchasing and supplier process
- the core production process
- the distribution process.

The Purchasing and Supplier Process

So far we have only considered the negotiating power of buyers versus suppliers in determining pricing. However, supplier relationships are more subtle affairs than this. The quality of the relationship is often the key to the ability of the purchasing firm to compete. This is not just an issue of price. The speed and accuracy, for example, with which suppliers deliver product can make all the difference to the efficiency of a production process and to the quality of product or service that it pumps out. Even though an electrical component may constitute only one thousandth of a percent of the total value of a Boeing plane, if it fails the plane goes down. Whilst recognition of the importance of managing inputs and supplier relationships is nothing new, the received means of dealing with it has changed significantly in recent years.

As we have already discussed, the dominant historical paradigm was for backward integration to ensure complete or significant control of the supply side. A key development has been the shift away from outright ownership to maintaining flexible ties between suppliers and buyers through partnership. This uncoupling has occurred in many industries for good reasons. Experience has shown that specialization yields decisive benefits in achieving world class specialized competencies. Long, integrated chains, by contrast, tend to lose that focus. Captive suppliers also tend to become complacent because they have a guaranteed internal customer. With the increase in international competition, firms have been forced to concentrate their energies in their heartland areas of competence. These developments have made the partnership paradigm a more compelling one.

Effective partnership has also been greatly facilitated by developments in IT. Creating strong informational links between a supplier and customer permit more efficient transfer of goods and services. A traditional factory will typically hold a large amount of inventory to ensure that its production lines are not idled by supply shortages. Carrying this inventory incurs a cost by tying up cash. They will also typically carry out laborious quality inspections of that inventory to ensure that component faults don't result in poor product. Both these procedures are based implicitly on the idea that the supplier is not to be fully trusted. The mentality is territorial. IT has begun to change this. A firm can cut inventory down to a minimum by ensuring that it informs its supplier precisely of the sequence, volume and timing of its production flow in advance. In the most extreme cases, the timing of their production cycles can be linked. This is appropriately referred to as Just-In-Time or JIT and reduces the need for a buffer of inventory to be maintained. Even if a firm cannot pull this off, it should be able to ensure adjusted volume forecasts are sent to suppliers in real time so that they can gear up production speedily.

In terms of quality inspection, it is increasingly the case that suppliers and customers will negotiate to meet compatible quality standards such as ISO 9000. They may impose the same quality control system and follow the same statistical process management techniques. As with the JIT inventory management process, these approaches to quality control are based on a high degree of trust and an extensive sharing of ideas and information. Some manufacturers may even make a capital investment in a supplier in order to bring them up to speed on these approaches.

Of course there are a large number of instances where the need for such a close relationship between supplier and customer does not exist. This might be the case where an input is a traded commodity and can be bought on a commodity exchange, as with many metals, minerals and basic food materials such as grain. In this case a firm can usually lock in a price for delivery of that commodity at a fixed date in the future. There is no need even to know the names of the raw material producers.

It is tempting to think of many service businesses in the same light as a firm sourcing from a commodity exchange; the main input is people and people are a commodity. There are over three billion of them, after all. Of course that is not the case. Successful service companies tend to maintain strong ties with the best universities and to cultivate an image with potential recruits much as they would with customers. The sophistication of their recruiting techniques is likely to impact directly on their level of competitiveness. McKinsey's ability to attract the best students, for example, has enabled it to corner the market in terms of raw intelligence for which it can consequently charge its clients a premium.

Down to Drivers

In evaluating the efficiency of the supply chain there are a number of key indicators to look for. You will already have a sense of the relative size of suppliers and of the switching costs for the firm in question and therefore its relative negotiating power. You should also ask whether it has developed good relationships with the right suppliers, given the nature of its core production process.

The first key indicator to look at is how significant a cost is inventory. The sign of a good supplier relationship is that a firm does not carry excessive inventory. From the balance sheet it is impossible to separate out finished goods inventory from inbound raw materials inventory and you will, therefore, rely on obtaining numbers from the company itself. If this number is very large relative to the cost of goods sold then it may have a problem in the way it handles supply. Low inventory turns[2] suggest that it is having to pile up a buffer. If the firm has an arms' distance relationship with its suppliers you will probably be able to guess why this is occurring.

The second key indicator is the unit cost of inputs. You should benchmark the unit cost the firm pays compared to the prices quoted by other suppliers. If the supplier is captive or has a long established, cosy relationship with the firm this may be permitting it to pass on uncompetitive costs. High prices may also be a function of the strong bargaining position of the supplier.

The third key indicator is quality. How important is the quality of material inputs to the quality of the product or service produced? If the only quality targets that need to be met are basic specifications, then the need for a close supplier relationship will be lessened. If, however, the components are complex and the quality requirements stringent and highly specialized, then the value of a close relationship will increase. What evidence is there of a quality problem which may be attributable to suppliers? What is the company's scrap rate[3] compared to major competitors? Do suppliers have a quality accreditation such as ISO 9000? For a service company the same criteria apply. What is the average calibre of recruits versus the competition? Does the firm have a good reputation on the major university campuses? We will explore this issue more closely in the human resource section presently.

[2] Inventory turns = Cost of goods sold divided by inventory, or the number of times inventory is restocked in a year.

[3] A firm's scrap rate is the percentage of finished or semi-finished goods which are discarded because of product faults.

As with all relationships, supplier relationships are subtle and shifting. They are very much contingent on a company's individual approach. Unless the relationship is a good one, both cost and quality are likely to suffer regardless of the rigour of delivery specifications and penalties for non-compliance.

The Core Production Process

The core production process will convert a raw or semi-processed input into a customer deliverable. In the case of a paper manufacturer, for example, it will incorporate the sieving of wood pulp, the laying and pressing of fibre, the drying of fibre and the cutting and rolling of lengths of paper. In a service industry, such as insurance, it will be constituted of document receipt, sorting, data input, form processing and preparation of customer communication.

What should be immediately clear is that each of these processes can be divided up into discrete pieces. This is exactly how traditionally production processes have been organized. In the manufacture of barrels for whisky distillation, for example, the hooper would make the iron rings, these would then be passed to a person binding the wooden slats together who, in turn, would pass it to someone sealing the gaps with tar and finally to a person who would plunge it into water to make the wood swell etc. Each step is specialized and performed by a separate group of skilled workers. Between each person there will typically be a pile of work in progress or "WIP" waiting for the next person to pick up and work on. Because different parts of the process take longer than others, WIP will tend to accumulate in some areas much more than others, requiring the addition of more workers or machines at those crucial bottlenecks.

Whilst this "batch" type system is still common in many manufacturing and service settings, it is being superseded by other approaches. In the manufacture of products which are standardized and high volume there was an evolution to continuous, production-line technology in the 70s. This means that instead of there being handovers between stages, WIP proceeds automatically from one stage to the next. This is typical of many of the basic manufacturing processes that produce all our familiar objects, from tins to tyres. The advantages of it are that it reduces WIP, eliminates the need for labour and also shortens the "throughput time". Throughput time is the time it takes a single piece of product to travel the length of the production line. Clearly, the longer it is on the line the more capital is tied up in WIP, even if it is moving rather than static. More important still, continuous production reduces the "cycle time" of a process. Cycle time is the time between two pieces of finished goods falling off the end of the production line ready for sale. Cycle time determines the overall capacity of the production process or how many finished products it can pump out per day[4]. The faster it can pump stuff out, the more utilization it will get out of its capital assets and the lower will be its unit costs. An automated process is likely to increase the utilization of a plant and thereby reduce unit costs.

Continuous flow manufacture is not suited to all products. In instances where one part of the process is much slower than another it may be best to stick to a batch system and build up a buffer of inventory to keep the other pieces utilized. In general the speed of the entire process will be determined by the slowest part of the process. If the slowest part involves a massive machine, or is a piece which cannot be changed easily, then the speed of the entire system will be dictated by it. This means that the cycle time of that particular machine will be the same as the cycle time of the entire system. When the difference in cycle times of different parts of the process are very pronounced the system is probably "out of balance". Conversely, in a system that is balanced, the cycle times of each part of the process will be similar. In other words, a plastic component coming out of one machine can reasonably be expected to be sucked immediately into another because it will have just finished its last piece. If a system is out of balance WIP will rapidly accumulate between the production stages. WIP is the calling card of a bad production process.

Automation was in essence a balancing and speeding up of a batch system. Processes have undergone more radical shifts over the past ten years. This brings us to that feared word "reengineering". In the core production areas various attempts have

---

[4] The capacity of a production process can be calculated by dividing the number of hours the line is operating by its average cycle time.

been made to entirely rethink the way the process is organized. One form this has taken in some industrial settings is a shift away from a batch process of steps performed by separate operators to an integrated process performed by a single operator. In the case of a component manufacturer, for example, this means that a single person sits at a position surrounded by all the machine tools necessary to hone the piece. The benefit is that the cycle time is reduced because there is no longer the delay of handovers between operators. Also the task is less boring for the operator and therefore quality is likely to improve. The same philosophy has been followed in some service industries such as insurance. Instead of a claims form, for example, being handed from one person to the next and often getting lost in the process, it might be handled by a single individual who processes all the transactions on their PC. The result is less errors and faster processing, hence lowering costs.

In service businesses the usual form that reengineering has taken has been to collapse traditional department structures into cross-functional teams. In the case of the advertising industry, for example, the client brief was turned into a piece of advertising through a laborious and lengthy procedure of handoffs between departments, from account management to creative to media people, ad infinitum. By breaking these structures down and grouping a cross section of functional specialists into client-facing teams the length of that process has been cut dramatically. Figure 7.4 illustrates the transition from a traditional to a more innovative process structure in an advertising setting.

Down to Drivers

Timeliness

Whatever the manufacturing process chosen by a company, the first thing that matters is that it is able to meet market demand in a timely fashion. Most companies face a clear choice between trying to chase demand and holding stock in anticipation of demand. In so doing they are always juggling the costs associated with carrying inventory versus the damage to customers of stock-outs. Chasing demand requires flexibility and responsiveness and, if got right, means low inventory costs. Not getting it right can risk stock-outs. The stock approach simply requires

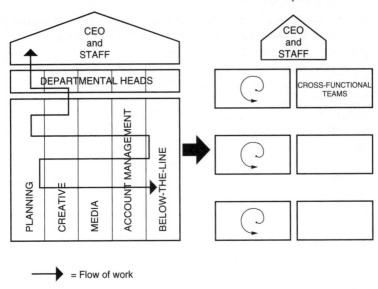

→ = Flow of work

Figure 7.4 *Illustrative restructuring of departmental structures in an advertising agency*

the setting of a steady rate of production but does risk the cost of excess inventory in slack months and possible stock-outs at peak demand. The growth in availability of sophisticated optimization planning systems based on linear programming is making the process of capacity management a more scientific one.

Quality

The other basic requisite is that the manufacturing system is able to meet acceptable quality standards. There are many techniques available to help managers maintain quality performance levels, the most common of which are statistical process control charts. Each vital section of the process will have tolerances within which it has to operate. In the case of a machine stamping out a plastic component, these tolerances may be expressed in terms of certain surface attributes such as the distance between screw holes. An operator sampling every twentieth piece or, better still, making use of an infrared sensor, can make a note of the measurements on his computer. At the end of an hour he will be able to see what proportion of components are being produced outside the acceptable tolerances for that piece. Typically this information is represented in terms of standard deviations from the mean. If too many pieces are falling several standard deviations out, there will be a problem and the machinery can be adjusted.

But clever use of numbers can only get you so far. Equally important to quality as statistical control is the well-being of the workforce. If staff are demotivated and bored, quality is likely to suffer immediately. This is why measures such as the introduction of teams, where efforts have to be collaborative, or the move to single operators, where the employee "owns" the entire process, can result in great leaps in quality.

Total Quality Management, Quality Circles and a wide range of other initiatives have been explored over the years. Whilst there is no point in us getting into these here, they are all recognition of the fact that quality is something that has to be managed into a manufacturing system through ongoing attention to laborious detail. It cannot be ordered in: it can only be learned over time. This brings us to the concept of the "learning curve". As a firm and its employees gain experience with a manufacturing or service process over time, the unit costs of whatever it is producing will usually fall as a result of the cumulative ongoing tweaking of the process. There is always an initial period during which a new process has to settle down and operators make blunders. If you are looking at a process which has been established for several years you can reasonably expect them to have traveled down the learning curve and the rate of improvement to have slowed (see Figure 7.5). If the process has been long established and the blunders are still going on, this means trouble.

The classic hallmarks of a production system which is unable to support quality standards is the quantity of scrap and rework that it generates. Scrap is finished or semi-finished product which has to be binned because of an irreversible flaw. Rework is product which has to be sent back through the system to correct a fault which occurred earlier in the production process. Scrap and rework absorb both raw materials and production capacity and are therefore costly. Moreover, typically only a percentage of errors will be caught by the quality inspection process and hence some faulty goods will arrive in the hands of customers. If the scrap rate is high it is likely that customers are being bombarded with substandard product. This costs any firm dearly in terms of reputation and customer loyalty. Regaining ground lost through

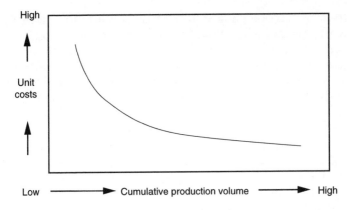

Figure 7.5   *Illustrative learning curve for a generic manufacturing firm*

poor quality requires a firm to boost its marketing expenditure, hence the costs of poor quality extend well beyond the cost of raw materials and production time.

Unit costs
The third key in the manufacturing process is utilization. Manufacturing usually represents the major capital item for a firm. If it is an insurance firm this may take the form of IT systems and the space they occupy. For a manufacturer of cars it will be the hardware of the production line. These items will almost always be fixed costs which can not easily be shrunk back or expanded overnight. The key for all firms is to ensure that these assets are highly utilized. Since every unit produced will have to share the costs of the equipment on which it is produced, it is in the interests of the firm to ensure that as many units as possible are produced on it. This will drive down unit costs and increase the firm's cost competitiveness. One of the main goals of any production process is, therefore, to ensure that its capacity utilization is high. For many firms this can be a major battle, particularly as the amount of output the market can bear will alter year by year and the volume of capacity in the market will also vary.

Even if a firm manages to utilize its productive assets to a very high degree this may not be sufficient to give it competitive unit costs. If one manufacturer of cars produces one thousand roadsters a year whilst its nearest rival produces three thousand, even if the former is operating at 100% capacity utilization it is likely to have higher unit costs. Why? Because there are "scale economies" associated with the production process. Scale economies mean that the larger the production process, the lower will be the costs of each unit it produces. Most industries have a minimum level of scale beneath which firms will be rendered non-competitive. This is why the large-scale Japanese plants pumping out cheap motor-bikes were able to decimate their more specialized counterparts in Europe and the USA operating from smaller plants. Scale economies arise because the incremental cost of adding capacity tends to be lower than the cost of the nuts and bolts basic model. For example, doubling the capacity of a small paper mill may not require twice the land, the new machine will probably not cost twice the price of the smaller model and the cost of utilities will not rise in a straight line (see Figure 7.6). If an industry does have scale economies, then ensuring that a firm is operating at competitive scale will be vital in enabling it to attain competitive unit costs.

Pulling it All Together

So, as a manager short of time, patience and without an engineering degree, how do you evaluate a production process? The first thing to do is to map out the process you are evaluating. Every service and industrial process will have its own peculiar charac-

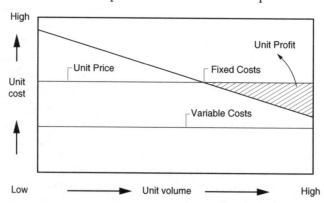

Figure 7.6   *Illustrative scale economies for a generic manufacturing firm (excluding the effects of cumulative volume on variable and fixed costs as a result of the learning curve)*

teristics. Figure 7.7 illustrates the relatively simple "process map" of an advertising business. Ideally you should understand which are the most important stages by assigning a dollar value to the material and human assets tied up in each stage and by determining which are the most time consuming steps. If you have the cycle time of each step in the process, you will be able to estimate its capacity and its current capacity utilization (see Figure 7.8).[5] This will enable you to make a judgment about where the system may need to increase capacity to increase the speed of delivery of product by removing "bottlenecks". In the case of the service business you might also distinguish between aspects of the process which are client facing, adding visible client value, and those that are behind the scenes (see Figure 7.9). This will enable you to determine whether energies are focused where most market value can be added.

Assuming you have a reasonable picture in your mind of the process, the first question to ask is whether the process is "capable" of meeting customer demands. You should have a robust list of these demands from your segmentation analysis and industry analysis. If, for example, cost is the primary purchase criteria then the system has to be able to deliver low unit costs. This may mean it has to operate at a minimum critical size to achieve basic scale economies which would be the case in most heavy industry, for example. If, by contrast, frequent new product features are vital to consumers, then the system has to be flexible enough to run multiple product lines without destroying costs. It will probably also have to be able to operate viably on short production runs. If we are talking about the manufacture of pacemakers then clearly the system will have to be able to guarantee 100% quality as its primary objective.

Most production systems will have to meet one or more of four distinct requirements:

1 timeliness
2 quality
3 low cost
4 flexibility.

---

[5] Capacity is calculated by dividing the operating hours of a system by the cycle time of the system and utilization is calculated by dividing the number of pieces actually produced by the absolute capacity of the system.

Account Management	Planning and Research	Creative	TV Production	Media Planning and Buying
Receive client brief				
Crack client brief				
Present to client				
	Creative brainstorm			
		Create storyboard		
Rehearse presentation				
Present to client				
Choose director		Finalize mechanicals		
	Produce media plan			Produce media plan
Brief director			Brief director	
Internal approval			Internal approval	
Present to client				
Preproduction meeting			Preproduction meeting	Present plan to client
Sign and send to finance				Media plan approved
Preproduction meeting with client				
			Shoot	
Send copy to client				Book media space
				Invoice client
Send film to station				
Close job and invoice				

Figure 7.7 *Illustrative simplified process map for a generic advertising agency*

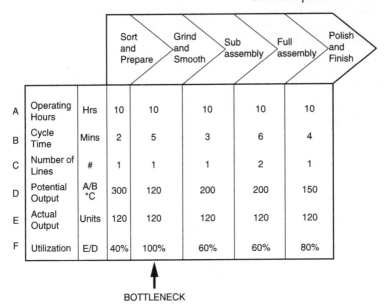

			Sort and Prepare	Grind and Smooth	Sub assembly	Full assembly	Polish and Finish
A	Operating Hours	Hrs	10	10	10	10	10
B	Cycle Time	Mins	2	5	3	6	4
C	Number of Lines	#	1	1	1	2	1
D	Potential Output	A/B *C	300	120	200	200	150
E	Actual Output	Units	120	120	120	120	120
F	Utilization	E/D	40%	100%	60%	60%	80%

BOTTLENECK

Figure 7.8 *Illustrative evaluation of a simplified process map of a generic manufacturing firm*

Each of the above imposes different demands on the system and every competitive situation will require differing levels of performance against these criteria. There are sometimes trade-offs to be made between them. Flexibility, for example, can have a high cost associated with it. On the other hand, getting one right can also have a beneficial effect on others. High quality might lower costs by reducing scrap and rework. Most production systems have to focus on a couple of key dimensions in order to be "capable" of meeting market requirements to competitive standards (see Figure 7.10).

Having decided whether the system is capable you need to find out how well it is performing. There are a number of key indicators to look at, depending what the capability requirements are. If quality is the key issue, then you can use the defect rate, the scrap rate or volume of rework that is generated. These statistics will usually be quoted as a ratio of a thousand finished items. If the issue is unit costs, then you will need to find out the fully loaded cost of a finished unit. This will include direct

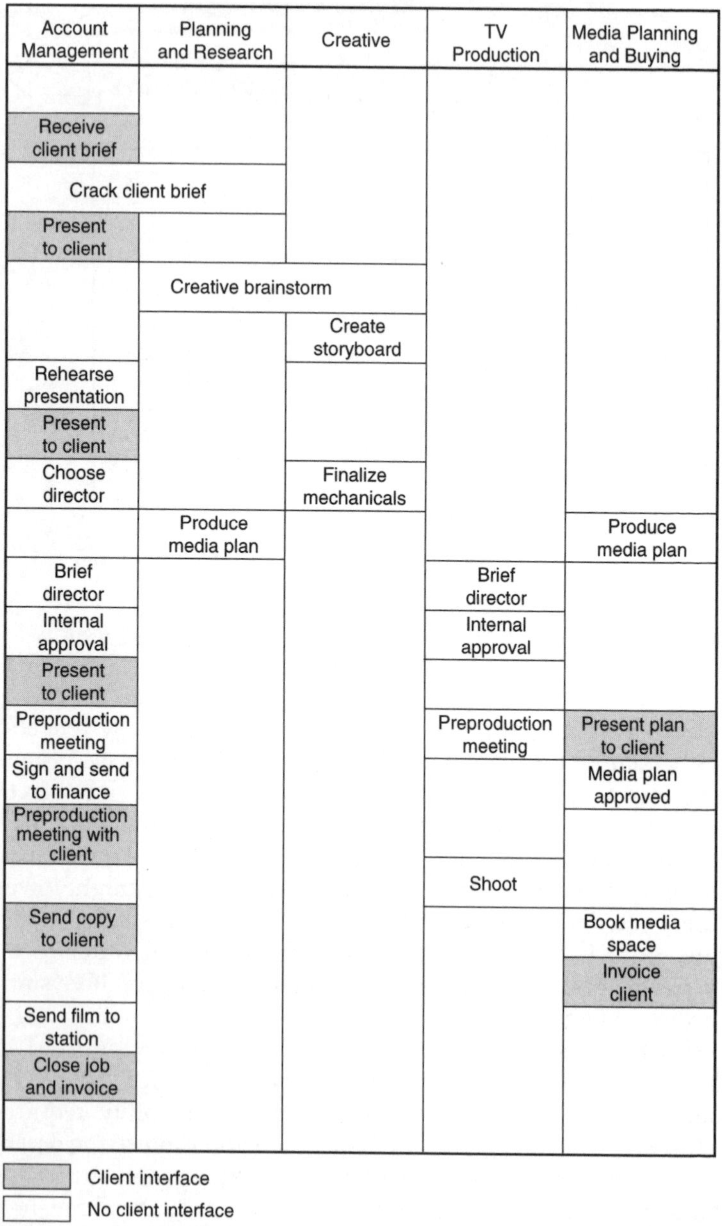

Account Management	Planning and Research	Creative	TV Production	Media Planning and Buying
Receive client brief				
Crack client brief				
Present to client				
	Creative brainstorm			
		Create storyboard		
Rehearse presentation				
Present to client				
Choose director		Finalize mechanicals		
	Produce media plan			Produce media plan
Brief director			Brief director	
Internal approval			Internal approval	
Present to client				
Preproduction meeting			Preproduction meeting	Present plan to client
Sign and send to finance				Media plan approved
Preproduction meeting with client				
			Shoot	
Send copy to client				Book media space
				Invoice client
Send film to station				
Close job and invoice				

■ Client interface

□ No client interface

Figure 7.9 *Illustrative simplified process map for a generic advertising agency showing areas of client interaction*

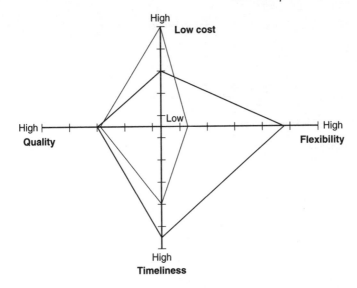

Figure 7.10 *Illustrative generic trade-offs in selecting a manufacturing strategy*

material costs, direct labour, overhead and scrap. We will cover this in detail shortly. You will also want to check the firm's capacity utilization versus industry standards as well as its levels of inventory and WIP. If the issue is flexibility, then you will want to find out the average changeover time between setups which will govern how fast and at what cost a firm can switch product lines. If the issue is timeliness, you will want to determine the average cycle time and throughput time of the process and therefore how rapidly the firm can get an order through the system (see Figure 7.11).

The Distribution Process

In our definition of it, the distribution process covers that group of activities between the product leaving the factory or office door and the customer receiving it. This stretches from stock-keeping, order fulfilment, distribution to wholesalers or dealers and then, finally, the push through retail onto customers. Usually much of the outbound value chain is independent of the manufacturer because it requires local market presence. How-

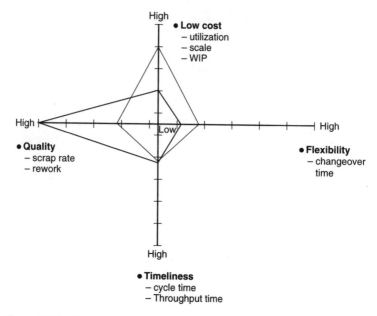

Figure 7.11 *Illustrative generic indicators in the inter-related dimensions of manufacturing strategy*

ever, many firms combine their own wholly-owned distribution and sales force with the use of independents. Even firms competing in the same segment may adopt quite distinct configurations in their outbound logistics chain. (Figure 7.12 illustrates the very different routes to market taken by two fictional toy manufacturers). Adopting the right route to market is a major determinant of the success of a firm because it influences the way the firm is perceived by its customers and how able it is to respond to their needs.

Down to Drivers

For the purposes of your analysis of operations, you need simply to ascertain its level of performance against three basic criteria:

- speed to market
- inventory levels
- unit cost.

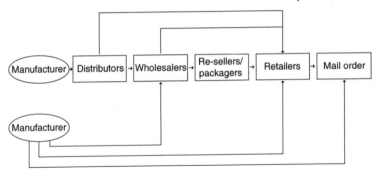

Figure 7.12 *Illustrative routes to market for two fictional toy manufacturers*

The time it takes a product to get from the manufacturing site to the place where it will be purchased by the end consumer is a key determinant of how responsive the firm can be to changes in demand. This may simply take the form of shifts in seasonal volume or it might take the form of more fundamental shifts in customer needs as one product is substituted by another. The speed with which a firm can respond to these changes will profoundly affect its level of competitiveness. If, for example, it takes two months for a new software game from the US to get onto the shelf of a Japanese store, that will be a major disadvantage if it takes a local manufacturer only two days. In a market where rapid product innovation is a major purchase criteria, speed to market will be particularly vital. For exporting firms, penetrating foreign distribution mazes can be a major factor impeding their timely market impact.

The issue of finished goods inventory is closely bound up with speed to market. It will cost a manufacturer dearly to hold a large volume of finished goods inventory which represents idle cash. If the distribution system is slow and unresponsive, a firm will be forced to accumulate inventory to handle surges in demand. A good distribution system will maintain a steady flow of product and allow the manufacturer to pass off the cost of inventory to the distributors responsible for pushing it to market. It will also provide timely information to the manufacturer about shifting patterns of consumer demand which will allow it to avoid accumulating superannuated stock. In an environment where unit costs are tight this will be a critical differentiator.

Overall unit distribution costs differ radically from product to product depending on their value added. The cost of distribution as a percentage of total unit value will determine the viable distance over which a product can be distributed. Transporting a ton of bottled water from China to the US will incur distribution costs which are disproportionately high compared to their market value. Importing Chinese software, by contrast, will incur a charge which is low compared to market value. The means of reducing distribution costs is to site manufacturing close to the end market. For most products there is usually a trade-off between distribution costs and the costs associated with siting manufacturing closer to end markets. Typically, the process of reducing the length of distribution lines adds manufacturing costs as scale advantages are lost in smaller manufacturing units supplying local markets. The trade-off between distribution and manufacturing cost advantages will tend to differ firm by firm. However, if the sum of manufacturing and distribution unit costs exceeds that of competitors then you know the firm is doing something wrong.

A firm's ability to compete on the dimensions of speed and costs in the outbound logistics area has been altered dramatically by IT. It is now possible for a firm to get sales data direct from the point of sale and aggregate this information on a daily basis to determine what to dispatch. They can also identify clearly where stock resides in the distribution chain. Concurrently, there has been an emergence of specialist logistics firms such as DHL and UPS able to deliver small consignments cost effectively to end customers. The costs of long distance distribution have fallen dramatically over the past 20 years with the growth in international trade. As a result many firms are able to achieve levels of responsiveness, inventory management and unit distribution costs which would have only been available to the most sophisticated companies in the past. This is one of the reasons why the value added of the outbound logistics chain is shifting relentlessly downstream to the pieces which most closely touch the customer. What matters is that the guy buying the Armani shirt gets good sales support and ego massaging. Speed to market and low inventory are becoming threshold values, a minimum competitive standard. Increasingly, managing the customer experience is where the value will lie.

Pulling it All Together

We have treated the three parts of the production chain in isolation and evaluated their performance relative to the goals set by the market. In reality, of course, they need to work effectively together to ensure that the system is balanced and able to meet customer demands. If the core need is flexibility it is no good having a flexible manufacturing system which can achieve rapid changeovers if suppliers are slow to respond and distribution will not accept a change of model without elaborate briefing. It is no good having an outstanding outbound logistics system which can deliver components to the shelves in a week if it takes a month to switch over manufacturing lines. Similarly, if unit costs are the main purchase criteria then achieving scale manufacturing will do no good if distribution remains highly fragmented and expensive. As a manager the key thing to understand is the degree of alignment of the three pieces of the production chain behind the task of meeting key customer purchase criteria. This will directly influence their ability to drive value.

Figure 7.13 summarizes the key value drivers in the operations area of a typical company's value chain.

MARKETING, SALES AND SERVICE STRATEGY: "THE SELL"

If manufacturing makes the stuff, it is sales and marketing that convinces the customer that the whole exercise has been worthwhile. As such, for most western companies it probably represents the stage of greatest value added in the value chain. This is not how it is usually perceived. During the 80s the Boards of many companies became dominated by finance professionals as firms were gripped by anxiety concerning takeover and also by a sense that acquisition was the surest and fastest way to achieve growth. Marketing professionals, by contrast, are rarely major participants at Board level outside the fmcg companies.

The cross marketing has to bear is that it is often perceived to be "soft". Large amounts are invested in it but it is usually hard to establish a quantifiable relationship between this investment

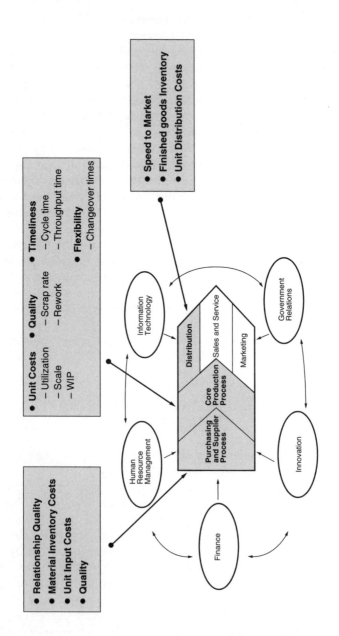

Figure 7.13 *Value drivers summary*

and the bottom line. Therefore calculating return on investment is a virtual impossibility in many marketing areas. The result is that the budgets associated with marketing tend to be highly cyclical, following underlying shifts in the economy rather than an intrinsic business logic of winning competitive advantage. At the risk of over-generalization, marketing strategy tends not be a strategy at all so much as a tactical response to short-term market conditions.

Marketing is also a hard beast to define. It spans a vast territory, from pricing decisions through to the development of advertising copy, from corporate identity to customer loyalty schemes. The thing that brings these strands together is that all of them directly influence how the customer feels about the good or service she or he is purchasing. Irrespective of the exact tools used, marketing strategy should integrate all the activities of the company into a single moment of truth with the customer. Figure 7.14 illustrates the various potential influences on customer opinion for an average fmcg brand. Many of these levers are under the control of the marketing group and it is the effective coordination of them that makes the difference. Clearly, depending on the brand and the target customer group, some levers will be

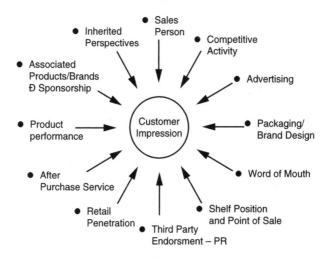

Figure 7.14 *Illustrative example of the diverse influences on customer opinion for a typical fmcg brand*

more important than others. This brings us back to understanding the customer which is where marketing begins.

Customer Segmentation

As we have already discussed, for every product or service a customer purchases there will be a hierarchy of customer needs. This hierarchy can be divided into *threshold values* and *differentiating values*. Threshold values are those necessary to get a product or service on the radar. In the case of airlines, basic guarantees of safety would be one of these. Differentiating values are those necessary to ensure that we purchase one product or service over another. In the case of airlines, a more generous air miles scheme is potentially a compelling differentiator.

The problem with customer needs is that they almost never hold true for all customers of a company's product or service. Whilst for the purposes of our segmentation of SBUs, we worked on the assumption that all customer needs would be the same, for a marketer this definition would be far too crude to be useful. Most products will service a wide range of customers, each of whom will have a subtly different hierarchy of purchase criteria. To be able to manage a marketing effort effectively a firm has to ensure that these different needs are understood and customers are clustered into similar "groups" which enables them to be targeted. Customer targeting is the very foundation stone of marketing strategy. Once customers are clearly understood, then the firm can put in motion a set of measures to ensure they market to them in a meaningful and fruitful way.

In evaluating the effectiveness of a firm's marketing efforts you can begin with two simple questions:

1 How well do you believe the firm in question understands its customer groups?
2 How well do you think its marketing activities are geared to winning the loyalty of those customer groups?

Typically, certain customer groups will be much more profitable to a company than others. Bad firms won't know which they are. The dangers of this are pretty obvious. Firstly, a firm can expend a tremendous amount of resource on non-targeted marketing activity which is highly unproductive because customers aren't interested. Secondly, it can carry on merrily without realizing or admitting its level of profit dependency on key customer groups; if these groups get lost in the scuffle then that firm could be in real trouble. This is, by the way, not an infrequent occurrence.

The Virtue of Loyalty

A key measure of the success of a marketing effort is its ability to win the loyalty of these key customer groups. Client loyalty is always closely related to profitability, both in services and industry. Acquisition of new clients is typically very expensive compared to servicing existing customers well and retaining them because a firm always has to invest significantly to hook new clients and reel them in. They may have to be winkled out from a competitor brand or they may have to be lured to bite when all their instincts tell them not to do so. The cost of acquiring them will be depreciated over the life of their relationship with the company. Therefore, the longer the life the less that initial amount will be as a percentage of revenues. In the case of an advertising agency, for example, which has just won a major account, they will have to staff up and learn about the client's business, all of which will probably mean it will lose money in year one. In year two it may break even and by year three should be on a nice earner.

The second thing about loyal clients is that they tend to be less price sensitive. Every time clients review contracts they will put them out to competitive tender or, in the case of a consumer who is fed up with a household product, they will weight up the attributes of an alternative product. This will usually result in highly competitive pricing. The result will be that, even should the company retain the business, it will probably do so on a less profitable basis. Finally, if a relationship has been long-standing, that revenue stream has less uncertainty surrounding it than a new revenue stream. This will make investors and creditors more comfortable with the "quality" of earnings; they will therefore charge less for the use of their capital because of lower risk, which will boost the value of the equity of the company.

The ongoing profit of a customer relationship is called the "lifetime value of a customer". For many industries such as air travel, credit cards and cars, where loyalty is strong, this value can be truly staggering. The unfortunate thing about loyalty is that from a marketer's standpoint it is not as exciting as customer acquisition. Typically, very large sums of money are spent trying to enlarge the customer base when it might be more productive to build the loyalty of the core customer group and win incremental revenues from that source. Customer acquisition means sexy TV campaigns and lots of press coverage. Relationship building, by contrast, puts an emphasis on direct mail, loyalty cards, frequent usage discounts and company magazines. Not surprisingly, spending on loyalty-building communications is growing at rapid rates whereas advertising has been flat for years in real terms and shrinking as a percentage of the overall marketing mix.

Of course, new customers are not quite the evil we are making out. In reality, growing the customer base is important as an investment in future profitability and for sustaining market share and competitive position. Therefore a firm will want to make sure that the rate of customer acquisition does not fall behind that of competitors. This should not, however, be at the expense of reducing customer churn and achieving loyalty which is intrinsically more profitable.

Sales Versus Marketing

So how do sales and marketing fit together? Whilst they are often mentioned in the same breath, in reality they usually operate under separate management. The sales force, control of wholesaler, distributor and retail relationships will typically be managed by the sales director whilst marketing will fall under the remit of the marketing director. Where, between the two stools many of the crucial decisions regarding competitive positioning, fall (such as product pricing and volume forecasting) differs company by company. In general, the marketing group will concern itself with communicating brand values whilst the sales group will concern itself with getting product into the hands of customers. In many companies the marketing groups have grown substantially over the past 20 years with the acknowledgment by management that the customer is king. More recently the role of marketing and the position of the marketing function in many companies has begun to change. The way marketing interfaces with sales is also shifting with it.

More sophisticated companies are waking up to the fact that it is not simply traditional communications such as TV advertising or direct mail that influence consumers' decision-making processes. They are also influenced by the reputation of the company, the quality of after-sales service they receive, the attractiveness of product presentation in the retail environment and a plethora of other stimuli. If marketing is defined as management and coordination of all the inputs into the "moment of truth" with the customer, then its scope is significantly broader than the more classical definition of what constitutes marketing. It also implies that a much wider set of people in the company needs to be involved in delivering the marketing strategy. As a result there is a developing trend to instil marketing competence throughout the company rather than to isolate it in the marketing department. In the case of an auto manufacturer, for example, this might mean that the R&D department works closely with marketers to understand evolving customer tastes. It might also mean that, at the sales end, the dealers are consulted regularly about their interpretation of effective communications. Most importantly, it will probably mean that a wider set of people from different functional areas of the company are brought together in teams to ensure that the company's efforts are focused on delivering what the market wants. Customer-focused teamwork is simply another word for marketing, of which the advertising communications activities and customer contact at the point of sale are a part.

In most service industries marketing and sales are effectively integrated. The person delivering the service is often the same person who communicates the brand in the most powerful way to the consumer or client. In a consulting firm it is usually the partner servicing an account who will persuade that client to recommend their services to fellow corporate CEOs. In a bank it is the personal account representative who will usually be seminal in encouraging a client to make use of a broader set of banking services. The fact that, in most service businesses, the "company" and the customer interact directly rather than through an intermediary means that face-to-face contact becomes by far the most powerful means of delivering the brand.

The integration of sales and marketing in most service businesses probably goes a long way to explaining why many service companies experience much higher rates of customer loyalty than do product or industrial companies. The emotional bond that can be built by the firm if it operates effectively is very strong. Nevertheless, it is increasingly common to find service businesses engaging in the same type of advertising and communications as their fmcg counterparts. Even professional service firms such as Arthur Andersen are now major spenders both on TV and in print. The reason is simple: they are under pressure to increase their revenue base which means they have to recruit new customers. As we have already discussed, this poses a new set of challenges in terms of profitability compared with the more traditional focus on customer loyalty and incremental sales.

Down to Drivers

Where, as a manager, do you begin to get a grip on this gelatinous octopus called marketing? The first thing is to form a basic outline of the firm's key customer groups. You will already have conducted a provisional customer segmentation on the basis of their purchase criteria. To understand whether the marketing effort is well focused it will probably be necessary to refine this. Marketers usually begin their customer segmentation by classifying consumers according to their volumes of demand or frequency of usage. They will then cross reference this with a number of other criteria. In the case of a packaged goods company, they might look at the social grouping of these clusters using basic demographic definitions such as social strata, age, gender or life stage. In the case of a business-to-business firm, such as a supplier of office furniture, they might segment customers on the basis of industry sectors and size of company. The heart of their segmentation, however, will tend to be more complex screens based on the emotional values surrounding the brand for these consumer groups. Figure 7.15 illustrates such a segmentation filter for consumers of a "sophisticated" alcoholic beverage such as sherry.

Why would a firm bother going through this laborious process and pay agencies large amounts of cash to do it for them? The answer in many cases is that they don't. They treat customers as a

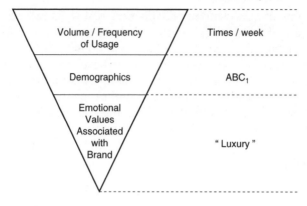

Figure 7.15   *Illustrative customer segmentation filter for a typical consumer brand*

homogeneous glob. The problem with the common denominator approach, as we already discussed, is that customers are not created equal.[6] Some will be much more profitable for a company and others of marginal benefit. Moreover, each cluster will respond fundamentally differently to messages put out by the company and will expect different things from it. Unless marketing communications is, at least, reasonably targeted against these needs then it may not only fall on deaf ears, it may also incur damage. As a loyal user of a heart drug it will not comfort you to receive direct mail telling you that new users can get first time annual discounts! It will also allow focused competitors under the door.

How can you tell whether a firm is targeting customers effectively? The key indicators are yield per customer or revenues per customer and the retention rate of customers over the course of the year or the annual rate of "churn". You would anticipate that as yield increases and churn decreases, all else being equal, profit growth would rise correspondingly. If churn and yield are moving in positive directions it is a reasonable bet that the firm in question is doing a good job of targeting existing customers. As already discussed, this does not mean that it can afford to ignore new customers. The trick for a firm is to ensure that the two groups are targeted differentially. You should compare the

[6] For more detail on this see Garth Halberg's "Not all Customer's Are Created Equal" in the Bibliography.

firm's rate of new customer acquisition against its rate of churn. If the rate of acquisition is high and churn low then you know it will be achieving a good job. If acquisition is high but churn is high you would expect its bottom line to be affected adversely. In a matrix of churn against client acquisition, a mature firm that has low churn and low acquisition will probably be performing much better than a firm which has high acquisition but high churn. The exception will be an industry which is in a high growth phase, as might be the case with a new software company for example (see Figure 7.16).

Assuming a firm has a decent understanding of its customer base, what levers does it have at its disposal to influence their behaviour? There are basically three key instruments on the control panel:

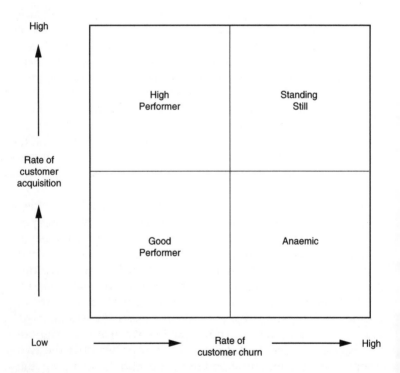

Figure 7.16 *Illustrative matrix of the relationship between customer acquisition and churn*

- brand positioning and communications strategy
- pricing and promotions strategy
- sales and service strategy.

At the risk of sounding like a broken needle, the question you have to keep in mind is: How well are these targeted at key customer groups and how well are they coordinated to win loyalty?

Brand Positioning and Communications Strategy

Marketing communications starts with the brand. But what is a brand and what is a product? This debate has now been raging for decades with no resolution. Its medieval counterpart was the dichotomy of the body and the soul. For our purpose, we can settle for a simple distinction. Whilst a product has a set of physical attributes, a brand has a set of emotional attributes which can condition our appreciation of the physical aspects of what we consume. More recently there have been attempts to place valuations on the brand as distinct from the product so that they can be put on the balance sheet as assets. There is no doubt that brands are assets. Harley Davidson would certainly lose share if it changed its name to Honda Civic. But putting a strict, separable value on it is pure inventiveness on the part of analysts who do so. Like the soul and body, a brand and the product that embodies it cannot be clinically separated.

Brands tend to last for a very long time. They usually outlive the products on which they are founded and get bounced from one product upgrade to the next. IBM, for example, was first used on a brand of weighing machines! Kellogg's was deployed on a health spar! The big brands have often been around for over a century whilst the markets, the process and product technology around them have all transformed out of recognition. If they last a long time, brands are equally hard to build up. The incidence of successful new brand launches is low unless they are tagged onto a fundamentally new product concept. As a result strong brands are tremendous assets to their owners and also constitute formidable entry barriers to players wishing to enter the market.

As we all know from experience, the strength of a brand helps determine what sort of price premium a product can win in the marketplace. We all pay more for Levi's jeans than for a generic. McKinsey can charge higher prices than Dr Spock Consulting. However, a brand does not simply condition the premium that consumers will pay; it also conditions preference. That is to say, if confronted with two identical chocolate bars comprising chocolate-coated fingers, it is far likelier that a consumer will buy a "Twix" made by Mars than they will a generic brand. There is, of course, a relationship between preference and price. As price rises above certain levels preference will fall away with it (see Figure 7.17).

So how are preference and premiums maintained? Put bluntly, brands are sustained through expenditure. Nowadays the number of potential avenues for this expenditure are vast as Figure 7.18 illustrates. In the past life was, by contrast, quite simple. Firms spent the bulk of their budget on advertising, first through print and latterly through TV. This has changed for a number of reasons. The first is the explosive growth in the number of channels which, with the birth of digital broadcast and cable, shows no signs of slowing. For advertisers this means fewer people watching each channel, and less ability to influence key consumer segments through simple media strategies. This

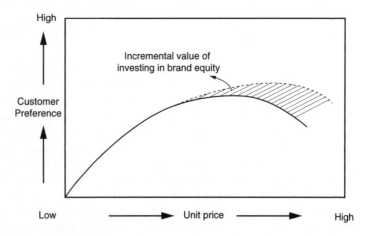

Figure 7.17   *Illustrative relationship between preference and price for a fictional brand*

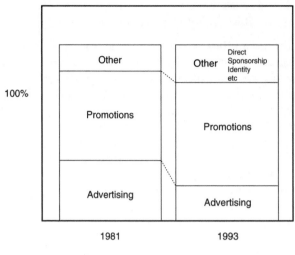

Source: Estimates

Figure 7.18 *Changes in the marketing spending mix in American consumer goods companies (1981–1993)*

has been combined with inflation in the prices charged by media owners as they have sought to fund the programming necessary to sustain a competitive share of audience. The result has been that the cost per gross rating point or GRP[7] has gone up considerably and therefore the levels of spend necessary to guarantee exposure to appropriate levels of consumers has been significantly raised. At the same time, there is increasingly widespread dissatisfaction with broad band media given the intrinsic inability to target customers: an 80 year old granny gets to see the same ads for the ski simulator as the 20 year old college student. This problem has been compounded by the increased clutter on major channels which has further eroded the effectiveness of advertising. Combine this with the intrinsic frustration of advertisers that a direct bottom line impact has always been hard to attribute directly to advertising investment and bingo. The result is a shift to "below-the-line", tactical activity such as promotions and direct mail which offer more focused targeting and an ability to calculate results more clearly.

[7] The number of GRPs is a way of expressing the total number of commercial impressions achieved by a piece of advertising.

Brand Equity Versus Short-term Profit

So, faced with all these challenges, how does a marketer choose her weapons? To start with, there is a fundamental distinction between advertising, direct advertising, sponsorship and the other large area of spend, promotions. Promotions offer a tangible benefit to the consumer on purchasing a product. This might take the form of a coupon which can be redeemed against future purchases or it might take the form of a temporary discount on face value. These measures are usually tactical in nature and geared to achieving rapid gains of market share versus the competition over discrete periods of time. In essence, they do not differ much from engaging in price point competition. Because of the imperative to maintain market share in highly aggressive recessionary markets, promotions have claimed a disproportionately large share of the total marketing budget over the past five years.

Advertising and sponsorship, by contrast, are designed to build brand equity. They are longer term and the results tend to be yielded over a number of years. Consequently, brands which have received a large amount of this type of investment over the years tend to have fairly stable market shares and to yield premium margins. The problem with this approach, as with all growth strategies, is that it requires patient investment. However, unlike investments in plant and machinery which can be depreciated over a number of years against tax, investment in advertising has to be expensed against revenues in the year it is spent. The net result is an immediate, non-deferrable cost and a deferred benefit. In an environment where CEOs are being held to annual EPS targets, advertising and sponsorship are therefore soft targets.

Direct marketing is something of a hybrid. Often it carries the same imagery as an advertising campaign but tends to be focused on responding to targeted customer group's needs. It can manifest itself in numerous ways, from "junk" mail to unsolicited telephone calls. Intrinsically it is likely to result in more immediate and direct sales because it is usually targeted at fertile prospects. It tends to be a tool that is associated with driving revenue from an existing customer base whereas much of advertising is aimed at recruitment of new customers. "Direct" can also be very effective as a recruitment tool, however; as an American householder it is now not uncommon to have your answering machine littered with orchestrated messages from companies. This is, of course, being increasingly upstaged by the new technologies of the Internet. Response rates can usually be calculated with reasonable accuracy and campaigns can be driven off a firm's customer database. Because it is more targeted and more accountable, direct marketing is thriving in today's environment.

The relative swing away from advertising will continue to be propelled in the medium term by the proliferation of new, more targeted media. Internet and PC-based on-line services are leading the way to a new set of broad band technologies which will include TV and video on demand. In essence all these media behave much more like direct marketing and much less like advertising. The consumer can make a choice when they are prepared to listen to a commercial message and the marketer is likely to get much more opportunity to understand their behaviour as individuals and communicate with them accordingly. This will tend to swing direct away from "junk" towards quality in the medium term which will improve its effectiveness to the detriment of advertising.

Most firms actively pursue both short- and longer term communication routes, balancing their spend between promotions and advertising in order to trade off short-term profit objectives and longer term efforts to build the brand equity. They are also becoming ever more acute at utilizing non-traditional media in their communications mix. Devices such as event marketing, arts sponsorship, co-branding and network marketing are all expanding at tremendous rates. The bottom line is targeting and therefore maximizing return on investment.

Down to Drivers

The best place to start your analysis of the effectiveness of brand communications is to map the position of the brand. "Brand mapping" involves identification of the basis of brand appeal for the consumer. This may have a number of axes. In the case of our sherry example, one basis of distinction may be whether it is perceived to be traditional or contemporary. Another might be whether it is perceived to be for use on special occasions or for everyday usage (see Figure 7.19). Whilst one sherry brand may be positioned in one sector of this matrix, another might be quite differently positioned. Each brand will use a different metaphor to act as a prompt to the consumer about its positioning. In the case of the special occasion, traditional sherry the bottle may be a deep, heavy green for example. By contrast, a firm wishing to increase volume through everyday usage may choose to make its bottle bright blue to suggest that it is contemporary and "alive". The advertising copy should, of course, reflect these same brand values and build on the brand metaphors. Over time these metaphors will become inseparable from the brand itself, as with the Andrex puppy or the Kellogg's cockerel.

The first question "brand mapping" will raise is whether the brand is in the right place. Does the target consumer group strike you as one whose consumption rate of this product is likely to increase? What level of competition from other con-

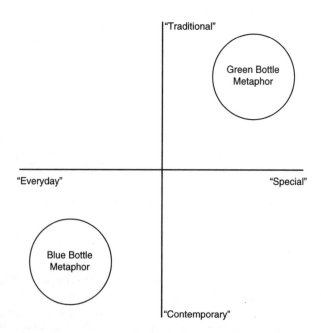

Figure 7.19   *Illustrative example of "brand mapping" in the sherry industry*

sumables is there for share of their pocket? In the case of sherry, for example, targeting the older drinker who use this product only on special occasions is probably not going to result in good EPS growth. If possible, you should calculate the growth rate of category consumption by target customer groups against their share of the firm's sales volume. This will give you an immediate sense of whether the brand is surfing on a growing or dying wave. As with all waves, consumer groups tend to ebb and flow over time. It is the primary job of the marketing director to ensure that the relevance of the brand is maintained despite shifts in consumer sentiment. This may mean subtly evolving the metaphor the brand uses or shifting the nature of the communications.

It may be that the product is targeted against a potentially lucrative set of consumers but the product or service just does not cut ice. Brand mapping should expose whether the metaphor used by the brand and the means by which it is communicated are doing an effective job against the target customer group. The most common way of determining whether the brand doesn't cut it are the prompted and unprompted recall numbers.[8] Recall numbers will tell you how many people from a statistically significant group of the population recognize the brand. This is a proxy measure because it does not tell you how many people actually intend to buy it. Some brands enjoy good recall but bad market share. If recall is much higher than market share then there are probably problems with the relevancy of the brand or it may simply be too highly priced for more than a niche set of consumers. This would be the case with Rolls Royce, for example. If awareness is low this is a good indication that something is wrong with the marketing effort (see Figure 7.20).

It may, of course, simply be that the firm is spending less on advertising. The standard measure of a firm's advertising activity is its "share of voice". Share of voice is the firm's contribution to total advertising spending in the category. The market share of the brand should, under normal circumstances, be reasonably close to its share of voice. If a firm's share of voice exceeds its share of market for a sustained period of time then you know that this spend is not proving the most effective use of resource. It

---

[8] Unprompted recall is the percentage of a sample of consumers whom would mention a brand when offered an indirect prompt that did not mention that brand by name.

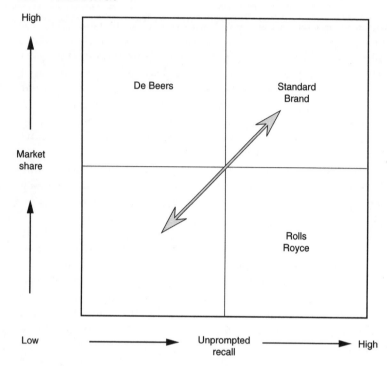

High

Market
share

Low   Unprompted   High
             recall

Figure 7.20 *Illustrative relationship between unprompted recall and market share for a typical branded good*

may be that campaigns have been poor or that market pricing is inappropriate. If the firm's market share is higher than its share of voice then it may be milking the benefits of previous year's investments. This will almost certainly not be a sustainable position (see Figure 7.21).

Both promotional spend and "direct" can be subjected to more scrutiny than advertising. Direct usually involves sending out mail to a set list of existing or potential customers. It is possible to track with reasonable accuracy the number of people responding to the mailing, and, in some cases, the volume of business resulting from it. This is continually being honed through improvements in the quality of underlying customer databases. Return on investment is therefore a number that can realistically be generated. This is roughly true of promotional activity where the

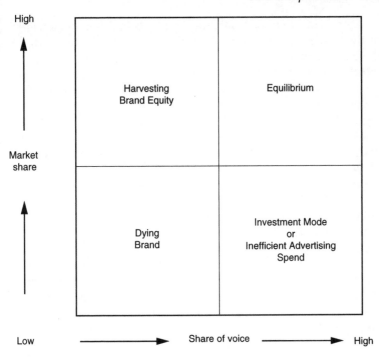

Figure 7.21 *Illustrative relationship between market share and share of voice for a typical branded good*

benefits accruing are usually immediately felt. If you take any increase in sales immediately after the promotion, assume a standard margin on these sales and divide this by the cost of the promotion you will get a reasonable sense of return on investment. One hidden cost related to promotions is that price discounting or couponing can damage the long-term equity of a brand. If, for example, a premium price is being commanded for a pair of Nike trainers, and Nike introduce regular couponing, a cycle of consumer expectations will be set in motion. Demand will tend to stall in expectation of future discounting, initiating a discounting cycle to maintain market share. In addition, Nike may no longer be seen as a quality leader since price is closely related to perceptions of quality. This medium-term risk will not be picked up in the calculation of ROI.

Many firms do not allocate their budgets to different elements of the marketing mix in a scientific fashion. Often this will be done on the basis of precedent and there may be corporate norms which brand managers have to follow. Often the balance of the mix will be dictated by short-term competitive pressures and shifts in the economy. If a competitor engages in price discounting and there is pressure to cut costs, the mix will tend to tip towards promotions and away from advertising. In periods of market growth the balance will tend to swing the other way as players attempt to maintain prices and build profit. The best overall guide as to whether a firm is investing or harvesting is to plot total marketing spend against market share. Obtaining overall numbers for marketing spend is not always easy because the individual budgets tend to be held by a wide number of people and many items could easily fall into general expense categories. If you can get the numbers and the firm in question appears to be wayward of the competitor balance of spend versus share, then the warning flags should go up. Comparing the spending mix will also be instructive. Is the balance between equity building and short-term volume driving activities in the long-term interest of the brand? In the case of the two brands in Figure 7.22, it is pretty clear that one is harvesting whilst the other is investing and a firm cannot harvest for too long without the soil drying up and blowing away!

In the aftermath of the global recession of the early 90s most firms have focused on cost reduction. With the ascendancy of cost control the marketing mix has shifted out of brand equity building into tactical sales generation. This period has also seen a shift of focus to core brands and the paring away of peripheral and non-core brands. The reasoning is simple: brands represent tremendous residual value but unlocking that value requires expenditure in marketing activity. By focusing that activity in core brands, firms are aiming to achieve a higher return on marketing investment. In order to further leverage those core brand equities there has been a growing trend towards brand extensions. The most prolific European example is probably the Virgin group whose single brand has been stretched from airways to vodka to pension plans. Most fmcg brands have also been repackaged in every conceivable form, shape and variant to extract maximum value from that intan-

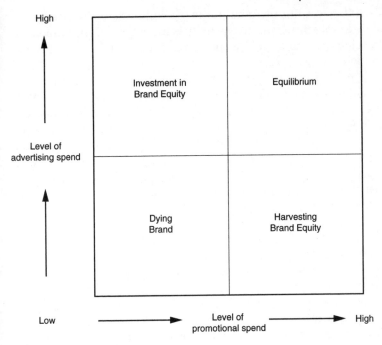

High

Level of
advertising spend

Low

Level of
promotional spend

High

Investment in
Brand Equity

Equilibrium

Dying
Brand

Harvesting
Brand Equity

Figure 7.22 *Illustrative relationship between long-term and short-term investment for a typical consumer brand*

gible asset. As a result, for many western firms their brands are
probably the most valuable assets they possess. The oddity is
that in most cases these assets are not included on their balance
sheets. Don't be fooled, however. The markets value them with
precision.

Pricing and Promotions Strategy

Everyone has their price and all products and services have their
price elasticities; that is the percentage of customers who are
likely to switch out of a product for each percentage rise in price
relative to the nearest rival. In categories where the elasticity is
low a producer may be able to sustain high prices for far longer

than they could in another industry without a major share erosion. In categories where elasticity is high, a small shift upwards in relative pricing will be enough to precipitate a market share landslide (Figure 7.23).

The shape of the price curve is dictated by the competitive dynamics of the market in which the firm finds itself in line with the market model we explored earlier. In classical economic terms, it is a function of the balance of supply and demand. However, a firm can influence its position on the curve through a wide range of actions. For example, a major investment in brand building will usually enable a firm to maintain a price differential which would not otherwise be sustainable. Similarly, the introduction of highly innovative product features or new brand extensions can increase the inelasticity of pricing. The more price sensitive a market is, the more a firm will have to invest to maintain a price differential over its competitors. If a market is very price sensitive most firms will simply opt to compete on low costs. Not surprisingly, therefore, the level of price elasticity of a market will usually equate closely to the pricing strategy pursued by a firm in it. It will probably also equate to the level of investment made in the brand since firms only bother to invest if they can extract a premium price to justify it.

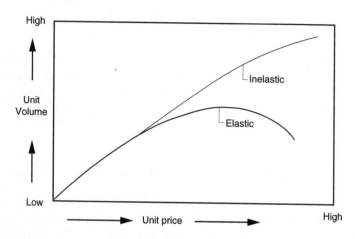

Figure 7.23 *Illustrative relationship between unit price and volume in two branded goods segment*

Pricing Strategies

In most markets there is always a delicate trade-off between price and volume. By raising price a firm can obviously drop margin straight to the bottom line. They will, however, almost certainly suffer an erosion of volume. Conversely, a firm can lower its price and enjoy an increase in volume sales. They will, however, damage their margin on those sales in the process. The trade-off for the company is how to maximize overall profit which is a multiple of unit sales and unit margin. In most industries there is a narrow range of pricing which will optimize the overall profit enjoyed by the company (Figure 7.24). The challenge for most firms is that this "sweet spot" is always moving with changes in the marketplace. Traditionally, therefore, firms have altered the price of their products and services with regularity to take advantage of opportunities on a tactical basis. A shoe manufacturer, for example, might drop prices in heavy shoes in the summer to boost volume in the slack months and pump up the price of flip-flops. He might also hold a "shock" discount which has not been anticipated by competitors to grab attention. Of course, most stores obey the laws of seasonality

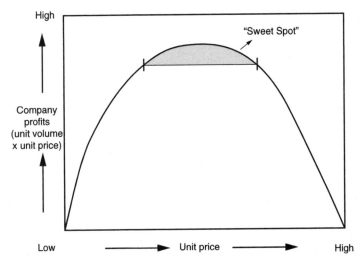

Figure 7.24   *Illustrative relationship between unit price and profit in a typical branded goods segment*

and hold discount sales along with all their competitors at certain times of year, most notably around Christmas. These are often timed with periods when stocks are changing and "dead" inventory has to be cleared, and have nothing to do with the prices that the manufacturers charge the retailers. The problem for branded goods companies in pursuing variable pricing strategies is that they are very laborious to administer and require close attention in order to avoid annoying retailers who may have differently priced stock at any one point in time. As a result some firms, such as Procter & Gamble, have moved to an "everyday low pricing" strategy which aims to maintain a consistently low price and obviate a need to continually change pricing structures.

Over the past few years most firms have been getting more sophisticated in their pricing strategies. In line with our customer segmentation, different customers have different levels of price sensitivity. This means they will have different senses of what constitutes value for money. By pricing goods differently for each group there may be opportunities to extract higher margins. Our shoe manufacturer, for example, might charge one price to price sensitive householders purchasing through catalogues and walk-in customers in a retail store a quite different price. Depending on the location and the target customer group, it is likely that the firm will face different types of competition. Differential pricing will allow it to match that competitive threat much more sensitively. The basis of the pricing strategy in this situation is called "value pricing". Value pricing means setting prices according to what value you believe a particular customer will place on a good or service. The opposite strategy is to price based on costs with a built-in margin. "Cost plus" pricing will tend to force pricing into a narrow range and suffers the limitation of being inward focusing. Value pricing is market facing and premised on the perspective of what constitutes value from a customer perspective. Not surprisingly, therefore, value pricing is the dominant mode in high value added service industries such as consulting and banking. Cost plus pricing tends to characterize industries where the dominant purchase criteria is price and margins have been whittled down to a whisper.

The most comfortable situation for any firm is to give the customer the impression that prices are low without actually surrendering margin. As a result many firms have refined to an art form the trick of shifting apparent price without lowering it. It is now common with large items to be offered with financing plans or deferred payment schedules. Furniture comes with a year's interest free loan, cars with monthly instalment plans. In nearly all cases, such schemes give the impression of lower costs, without the manufacturer in fact lowering prices. The most sophisticated pricing schemes often involve a single charge for unlimited usage. Open-ended railway passes are sold for a single, up-front payment; amusement park tickets cover unlimited rides. In most of these cases, the firm is making a bet that the customer will fail to use the service to the point at which they will break even on their purchase. Hence such strategies give the illusion of customer value whilst preserving the margin of the company.

Firms do not only price their products through the price points on the sticky label. They also have a variety of other means to effectively reduce the cost to the customer. The most common are multiple purchase discounts, either in the form of "buy-three-get-one-free" type promotions or in the shape of redeemable coupons. Although they have the appearance of encouraging loyalty and purchase volume, such tricks are effectively price discounts and have the same competitive effect. Because of the pressure on many branded goods companies over the past five years, the majority of firms have shifted marketing spend away from advertising and into price promotions. In many cases, this has simply sparked a vicious circle whereby competitors follow and initiate a downward price spiral. The beneficiaries have, of course, been you and me. Hurrah! About time!

The problem with price discounting is that its damage on profits is not temporary. For a start, it is very hard to raise prices again once price expectations have been lowered amongst consumers. Secondly, as with any drug, the substance leaves its mark on the character for a long while after the last dose has been taken. Price sends a clear signal about the brand. If a consumer finds it possible to buy an Armani suit for £50 she will probably begin to view it quite differently. She may begin to suspect that it is not as exclusive as she once thought; she might even suspect that the workmanship is not that great. Before long the collective consuming public will attribute a new set of values to the brand and its prestige will be unrecoverable without massive communications investment. For the company this might be a viable strategy since it will offset lowered unit margins with increased sales volume. But it does constitute an entirely different strategy which the company has to be able to support in terms of its cost position. There are usually no lack of competitors, all of whom will be all to willing to compete on price. The price fight is usually a very tough and damaging one. Amongst the most aggressive are the private label or store brands which require far less marketing support and can, therefore, compete effectively at a much lower price point than their manufacturer brand counterparts. With the growth in Asian and Latin American manufacturers, the price battle will be an ever harder one for most western firms to win.

Down to Drivers

The only issue with which you really need concern yourself is whether you believe the price point position of the firm you are examining is optimized and competitively sustainable. Do you believe it has hit the "sweet spot" on the pricing curve? Is it making use of opportunities to price differentially against different customer groups? Is it pricing on a value or a cost-plus basis? Has it made use of methods of lowering the apparent price point to customers without engaging in large amounts of promotional activity? Typically you would anticipate relatively high price points to correlate with either high share of voice or to an extremely targeted customer segment, as in the case of Rolls Royce for example. If neither of these characteristics are true then you need to ask yourself how wide the price gap can grow without a crash of share. Is a competitor firm engaging in an aggressive advertising campaign which will expose the brand as hollow? When will the firm need to restore the balance in terms of SOV? If the firm is pricing low, will it be sucked into a discounting war which will permanently damage the equity of the brand? If you anticipate a major pricing war which will drive down EPS, how well positioned is the firm to weather the storm? Can it really compete on the basis of low costs given its unit cost position?

Sales and Service Strategy

At the end of the day it is the sales force that delivers product. They are often somewhat unsung heroes. Historically the sales division has been viewed as a bunch of product-pushing road warriors. Nowadays, in better performing firms at least, they are understood to play a key role in sustaining the customer base and contributing to relationship marketing as part of the overall marketing mix. The motor dealer who ignores all the advertising that has stressed customer service and continues to treat customers like cattle is no longer the acceptable standard. The salesman delivers and embodies the marketing message. Sales is, therefore, a very high value added piece of the value chain for most companies.

Sales strategy touches a potentially large number of downstream pieces of the value chain, including distributors, wholesalers, retailers as well as end consumers. Typically most firms will manage their interface with the market through a mixture of channels. They may maintain a sales force to sell direct to certain types of end customers. They may sell to wholesalers as well as owning some of their own retail outlets. They may also run franchise operations in certain geographical markets. As a result, the chain of distribution between manufacturers and the end customer often will be complex. As we have already seen, it will also tend to differ firm by firm, even in the same industry.

The real complication comes with international sales and distribution. The structure and complexity of channels is likely to vary dramatically market by market in the industry you are analysing. A firm's ability to finance, structure and influence it will also vary. The level of sophistication with which a firm can snake its way into foreign distribution chains will have a major impact on its ability to export. And nowadays no firm can get very far unless foreign sales constitute a major portion of revenue. The reason? Simple. All the growth potential is in Asia and Latin America, precisely where distribution is the most fiendish Chinese puzzle known to man. Complexity means high cost and, potentially, slowness to market. Sales and distribution can therefore constitute one of the most effective barriers to entry for players trying to penetrate a foreign market, as American firms stepping into the Japanese arena have found.

One way round this that firms often employ is to site manufacturing close to the target market. This can have the effect of reducing the dependency on the local distribution chain and allowing the firm to develop far greater local market sensitivity. It can also have the benefit of making the firm itself appear "local" and better integrated into the idiosyncrasies of the key business circles. Of course, becoming local carries a price tag. If the firm requires a large manufacturing plant to achieve scale economies it might not be viable to site it in a one-country market. Instead it may be forced to operate across a region which will put the burden back on its management of the distribution chain. For large multinationals this poses a real challenge. In many areas of the value chain there are decisive scale economies, such as branding, manufacturing, sourcing and even management skills. Most multinationals are centralizing many of these activities to reap what cost advantages they can. Sales and distribution, however, remain staunchly local and fragmented. They require local knowledge and motivated local management. The result is a major tension in many of these firms between the forces of centralization and localization. There is no easy resolution to this tension and it is one of the major tasks of the senior management to harness it productively. We will return to this issue towards the end of this book.

Sales Versus Service

In many industries, making the sale alone is not enough. To ensure repeat custom, a sale has to be supported by high levels of customer service. With increasing market competition, standard approaches to customer service have improved dramatically in recent years. Most firms have a returns policy, provide customer information, maintain a complaints line and offer various types of quality guarantees. The higher the value added of the product, the more sophisticated the pre- and after-sales service tends to be. Contractors selling combat helicopters to the military, for example, will typically conduct lengthy trials with the buyer, hold sales meetings in exotic locations and guarantee progressive upgrades to armaments technology during the years after purchase. The concept of what constitutes customer service is also continually evolving. Whereas ten years ago it might have been a acceptable for an airline to guarantee a seat, now a competitive firm will have to support an airmiles scheme, guarantee legroom standards, provide an executive lounge and ensure performance against timely arrival standards. The explosion of new mediums for customer interaction such as the internet will help propel the thresholds for service to yet higher levels in coming years.

As a result of the focus on customer service, the service content of most products has increased. The cost of delivering a maintenance guarantee on a car, of managing an airmiles scheme, of administering a customer complaints service, all come at a price. As the sophistication of these service components increases so does their share of the unit cost bar (we will come to the cost bar in detail presently). Over time this can fundamentally alter the nature of the business in which a firm competes. British Airways, for example, looks less like a means of transport between two locations and more like an executive experience of luxury. Shopping at Harrods is less about buying merchandise than experiencing a sense of personal indulgence. This imposes potentially very different challenges on an organization. Is an airline which is staffed by logistics people and engineers able to focus its value added in service content? Is the retailer with an expertise in managing SKUs[9] and supplier costs able to sustain a compelling service environment? The transition of many industries from being product led to being service led will continue to cause a shake-out amongst firms unable to transform their skills set.

Service almost invariably has a cost associated with it which has to be recouped in higher prices. This means that the customer has to place a value on service and be prepared to pay for it. Service is not, however, always a customer purchase criteria. In industries where price is the dominant purchase criteria it is unlikely that a customer will be prepared to pay for bells and whistles. As the cost of the service levels necessary to support product differentiation rise, so firms face a stark choice in terms of strategy. They can either scrap service altogether and compete on cost, or they can aim for competitive service levels, differentiate themselves and recoup the costs through higher prices. As the minimum threshold of customer service increases, so the

[9] SKU = stock keeping unit.

difference between price competitors and differentiated players will tend to widen. This will make it very hard for firms to attempt to combine high service levels and low prices without getting shot on all fronts. The successful players in the airline industry, for example, tend to divide into premium service players such as BA and no frills low-cost players such as South West.

So whose responsibility is it to deliver customer service? In some businesses the sales force are the same people who deliver customer service. In most professional services, for example, the individual who gets the sale will only do so by ensuring complete customer satisfaction in the process. In an industrial setting, where a firm's customers are its retail buyers or wholesalers, the quality of support that the sales force gives them will constitute customer service. Often, however, the sales force of a firm will not have control over delivering service to end customers. A shoe manufacturer selling through independent retailers will not be able to control the courtesy of a salesperson. An insurance company selling through independent financial advisors will not be able to force them to smile every time they knock on a door. This "disintermediation" is potentially a major weakness, loosening control of the consumer. As a result, many firms invest heavily in tricks to re-establish direct contact with the customer. Complaint lines, web-sites, guarantees, couponing are all mechanisms to identify customers, log their personal details on a database and establish a direct line for ongoing communications and service delivery. Investment in brand communications serves a similar role in countering the process of disintermediation.

Down to Drivers

The key question to answer is whether the sales and service strategy of the firm supports the competitive requirements of the marketplace. A manufacturer of high quality shoes, such as Ferragamo for example, may require very careful management of the customer experience to achieve a sale. Therefore control of the retail environment is vital to sustain that brand equity. For a manufacturer of low grade running shoes this same necessity does not exist. Their aim is to get retail distribution as wide as possible without the overhead of their own distribution network.

For them good relationships with international wholesalers is the key.

To answer this question the first task is to understand the complexity of the distribution and sales chain. For example, in a consulting firm there is probably only one link between the consultants and the client. In the case of the manufacturer of electric cable there may be six or seven layers in addition to many alternative routes to the end user. Different elements of the distribution chain will represent different levels of value added. Also, as the number of layers increases, so the value added of the product or service will get distributed to a wider group of firms. The other effect of an increased number of layers is the degree to which the OEM[10] will understand the end customer. If all the knowledge of the end customer resides with independent parts of the sales and distribution chain then that firm will be rendered less sensitive in responding to changes in customer demand. The loyalty of customers will also be dependent on a set of circumstances largely out of their control.

The level of influence a firm can exert over the downstream value chain can be vital depending on the product or service. If Aston Martin, for example, are reliant on superb customer service to convey the performance characteristics of their car they will need to ensure that distributors are able to deliver it or the brand will be wrecked. This would imply the need for tight control. As we have already discussed, firms can exert control over distribution without necessarily owning it. To a large extent, this will be a function of how important their business is to the supply chain and how closely the relationship is developed. The insurance firm using independent financial advisors to distribute their products will nurture its relationships assiduously with them even though it has no direct control.

One gauge of the quality of this relationship is its level of exclusivity. If the Aston Martin dealer is also trading Mazda MX5s, it is probable that the relationship is not very good. Another indicator can be the size of margins awarded to distributors, retailers and sales channels by a manufacturer. The larger these margins the more value the company is having to surrender to distribute its product. Clearly, if the product is highly

---

[10] OEM = original equipment manufacturer.

competitive, a producer's negotiating position over margins will be strong and the value surrendered downstream will fall. A final indicator is to look at the quality of exposure the product receives in the sales environment. For packaged pasta in a super-market, for example, this would equate to the number of "facings"[11] it typically receives in the category. In the travel products industry it would equate to the position of the company's flight offers on the computer reservation systems used by travel brokers. As the quality of its relationship with the "trade" deteriorates, so will the competitive position of the firm.

If a firm has a good relationship with the "trade" or control of the sales and distribution chain, it is more likely that it will be able to deliver outstanding customer service. It is sometimes assumed that the success of a customer service process can be determined by the levels of customer complaints or returns. The problem here is that only a minority of dissatisfied customers tend to complain and the majority tolerate mediocrity in silence. One thing they will not do, however, is come back. The best measure of the success of a customer service process is whether the customer is sufficiently satisfied to come back. The only acid test, therefore, is the level of customer churn. If customers are loyal it is likely that a firm's service quality is targeted and high.

Once you have an understanding of the shape of the customer chain, the number of layers between the customer and the firm in question and the level of control it can exert, you should then ask how well this fits with the product or service being delivered. If, for example, you are analysing a luxury branded goods company your segmentation analysis will have shown that service standards are a paramount driver of perceptions of the brand. If your firm does not have any captive retail and relies on distribution through wholesalers it will be disadvantaged compared to a firm that has dedicated retail. For a manufacturer of computer chips, by contrast, all the customer cares about is reliable processing speed. Therefore ownership of wholesalers would simply distract the firm from focusing on achieving scale efficiencies in manufacturing. Nor will the firm care very much how many hands the product passes through before it comes to an end user

---

[11] A "facing" is a position at the front of a shelf where the packet is clearly visible.

since most of the value added occurs at the manufacturing stage of the value chain.

If a firm has an effective sales and service strategy then it should be well positioned competitively. That will mean that it is able to quickly gauge and respond to local market trends. A manufacturer of jeans in the UK, for example, might have been quick to see the growth of "grunge" and introduce looser fits. It will mean that it is quicker to market with stock, removing the need for heavy inventory costs. It will also mean that the firm's distribution costs as a percentage of sales value will be lower than the competition. All this should add up to either significant local market share or substantial price premiums, depending on which of the generic competitive strategies it is pursuing.

Pulling it All Together

Firms based in the mature western economies will depend increasingly on marketing to contribute the bulk of their value added. Basic manufacturing is shifting East and South to the low wage economies as the productivity advantage that fuels manufacturing-based competitive advantage is being fast eroded. This is happening even in places where product and process quality has formerly mitigated a labour cost disadvantage such as Germany. Product-based advantage is also becoming less sustainable as the rate of innovation increases and product life-cycles shorten. At the same time the sophistication of consumers, and the level of choice available to them, has increased dramatically. The result is that most western firms are pursuing strategies that involve getting as close to the customer as possible. This means that marketing is gradually moving from being a peripheral piece of the value chain to forming the very heart of it. Increasingly, manufacturing and R&D will see their orders delivered from marketing. Over time, many marketing intensive firms will probably shed manufacturing to specialist subcontractors and focus purely on managing customer attitudes and the customer experience. As a first step most multinationals are moving manufacturing to central regional locations, often in low wage environments, whilst boosting their marketing capability close to the consumer.

What does this mean for the brand? There have been periodic exhortations over the years that "the brand is dead". The most recent requiem was as retailer own-label brands began to bite into the territory of the traditional branded players. Own label has certainly taken a chunk of the market but its overall share has now begun to stabilize at around 15% in the US and most of Europe (although in the UK it is higher). The reason? Consumers want choice and they value brands. There has also been a requiem for brands in the wake of increased consumer scepticism. Where a vast gulf has continued to separate the price points of a branded products and their no-frills rivals, consumers have begun to ask, is that gulf worth filling with hard earned cash? The answer in many cases has been no. Many surveys have suggested that consumers have diminishing confidence in major brands. For these reasons the price premium enjoyed for many years by branded players has been brought in line with reality. However, this certainly does not mean the brand is dead. Quite the opposite will show itself to be true over the next decade. As western firms lose their manufacturing advantage to eastern and southern markets, their primary source of advantage will be their ability to understand and maintain a relationship with sophisticated consumers. The medium through which this trick is conjured is the brand. Asian firms without brands will be vying either to buy them or create them. The new consumers of the East and South will be vying to wear them and consume them. In short, the most valuable asset in the average company portfolio will be its brand, even if it is intangible. This will hold as true for service businesses as for industrial firms.

What does this mean for the marketing department? Will brand managers be promoted overnight to Board members? The answer is no. What will probably happen is that, as we have already discussed, the competencies of marketing will be invested in a broader set of people in the organization. The head of manufacturing will be more closely involved in interpreting evolving consumer tastes so that capital investment decisions can be made more effectively. The head of sales will work closely with the advertising managers to understand how prices can be sustained or raised through communications. Senior management will impose performance measures on the organization which directly reflect the level of satisfaction of the firm's customers. Instead of being a functional activity, marketing will become a corporation's way of doing business with all internal and external constituencies. The most successful firms will "live the brand".

All of this sounds great but where does it leave us as managers? We have discussed the three areas of brand communications – pricing, sales and service – as if they were separate activities. This is, of course, not how things work in reality. The key issue is how well the firm in question is coordinating the three levers of the marketing process to ensure that it meets or exceeds customer expectations. If, for example, a manufacturer of utility trucks is trying to raise prices, backed by heavy advertising spend, but distributors are failing to convey the right message to consumers at the point of sale, the strategy will nosedive. Equally, if a retailer is trying to convince customers that a piece of software is cutting edge but the manufacturer keeps cutting marketing support, lowering prices and discussing its upcoming new versions in the trade press, the retailer will probably dump it. Even if the firm excels in one or more of the key levers, unless all of them are well coordinated it will not matter. As with all areas of the value chain, focus and coordination win the day.

Figure 7.25 summarizes the key value drivers in the marketing, sales and service area of a typical firm's value chain.

INNOVATION STRATEGY: "THE WOW"

Let's face it. As consumers most of us are obsessed with being cutting edge in what we purchase. Many products are "old hat" after six months. From a firm's perspective, however, old products do not necessarily mean bad products. The financial goal for any firm should be to depreciate the cost of developing a new product over as long a useful market life as possible before running the risk of obsolescence. The life cycle of different products and services differs radically. For some products, such as Heinz baked beans, that life cycle may be as long as 100 years. For others, such as PCs, it is a year and ever shortening. For firms it is a juggling act of profit maximization through product longevity and surfing the curve too long and falling off. It is a balance that

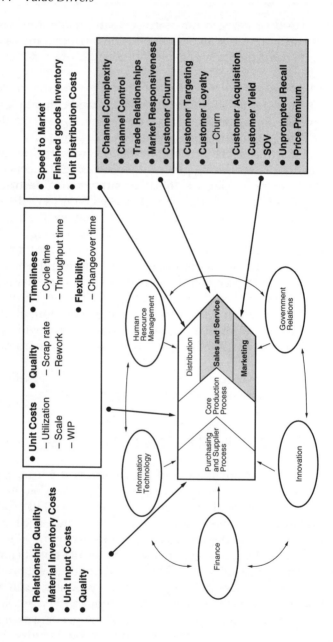

Figure 7.25   *Value drivers summary*

many great firms have got wrong. Those with a very high market share might have become complacent and assumed that nothing would ever change. Then suddenly consumer sentiments shifts, they appear anachronistic and a new competitor outpaces them with a new product formulation. This has been the story for many of the maturer segments of western industry faced with the appearance of more agile competitors from the East, from motorbikes through to textiles.

With the growth in international competition the pace of innovation has increased dramatically. The average life cycle of products and services has fallen and consumers have been habituated to an endless stream of annual upgrades. This has made the speed with which a firm can innovate into a primary basis of competition. The problem for many firms is the cost regime this imposes. The R&D cycle for many products is years or, in the case of pharmaceuticals, decades. This implies tremendous investment in a situation where there is no guarantee of market success at the end of the tunnel. In line with the growth in new product launches, there has been an equal growth in the rate of product failures. Around a staggering 80% of new products launched fail to make it! And once the new product is on the shelves its battle is not done. Since the average product life cycle has shortened, the time over which a new product can recoup the investment and generate a return for shareholders above its costs has also concertinered. All this has to be cast against the backdrop of an ongoing squeeze on costs in non-customer-facing functions. On the whole, R&D budgets as a percentage of revenue have only been going one way!

So what does this mean for how firms cope? The first obvious answer is that many do not. The rate of consolidation in many industries has been fuelled in part by the costs of keeping pace with innovation. Since R&D is scale sensitive and needs a deep pocket, big firms are on the whole in a better position to win. Although lots of great products have been invented in the garages of geniuses, they tend to get folded into the arms of big brothers in order to turn ideas into large scale commercial reality. This is particularly so if the product requires a large marketing push to gain consumer acceptance. And even the big boys are under cost pressure.

In response many firms have fundamentally changed their

innovation processes. Instead of innovation being invested solely in the arcane black box of the R&D department it is increasingly becoming a responsibility of a larger set of people within the organization. Innovation can, after all, occur anywhere along the length of the value chain, from improvements in the process technology of manufacturing to breakthrough methods in the way customers are handled by service departments. Each will impact the way the firm and its products are viewed by consumers. In the core product innovation process, firms are typically fast tracking the development cycle and reducing the risk of failure by ensuring close interaction of R&D with both market-facing groups and manufacturing. Amongst successful firms, innovation is hence becoming a goal which tends to pervade the entire organization rather than reside only in a piece of it. Whether a particular firm manages to deliver on the idea or not is a different story!

Down to Drivers

The key question to answer is whether the firm is leading the "innovation cycle" or lagging it. The innovation cycle curve may take many forms in different industries but roughly speaking can be divided into three stages: cosmetic upgrades, basic model modifications, and then major model redesigns or replacement (see Figure 7.26). Each stage has different risks and rewards depending on customer sentiment. For example, by introducing a new scent to an existing line of detergents a manufacturer may achieve a boost to product relevance without undertaking a major formula redesign. An auto manufacturer might smooth the shape of the exterior panelling but stick with the same chassis and engine. If both of them can give the consumer the impression that they are getting something fundamentally new, then they will have innovated at extremely low cost. Of course, if competitors are innovating in a more substantial fashion then cosmetic upgrades will not cut ice and the firm will be forced to follow. Different industries experience different speeds and types of competition in terms of evolving product specifications. Some may progress through tweakings of a fundamentally unchanging formula, others will experience regular fundamental redesign. Each will place different new product development demands on competitors.

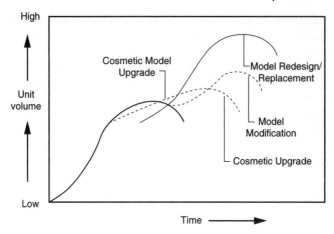

High

Unit
volume

Low

Cosmetic Model
Upgrade

Model Redesign/
Replacement

Model
Modification

Cosmetic Upgrade

Time

Figure 7.26 *Illustrative industry innovation cycle curves*

Different firms respond to the challenge of developing new products in quite different ways. Some firms may make the decision that everything they do should be driven by stated customer need. These type of firms will tend to conduct plenty of market research. Also their manufacturing group will probably have close contact with the marketing group since they will be waiting for market signals. Other firms, in contrast, will take the view that reference to existing customer tastes mitigates innovation. How can a customer know what they have never experienced? These firms will attempt to lead customer demand and it is likely that their manufacturing groups will be highly dominant over their marketing compatriots. This is the case with some Japanese auto manufacturers, for example.

Of course, there is no single best way to keep a product at the cutting edge. The only question is whether the firm is innovating in a way that is relevant to threshold and differentiating customer needs. For example, a manufacturer of chainsaws may be competing on regular upgrades to the power of its engines and be charging a 25% premium over a competitor who is aiming purely to minimize add-ons and perfect the reliability and handling of a long established model at lower price. Which better serves the dominant customer cluster, or do they compete in quite distinct customer segments? Is there enough of a specialist customer cluster available to support the non-dominant strategy?

The best way for a firm to ensure the success of a new product is to make sure that it serves a clear customer need which is not adequately met by an existing product or service. Typically this means focusing on a core customer cluster. If a firm succeeds in building a franchise with a core group of consumers the usual hope is that they will act as a driver of broader consumer acceptance. Word processing software packages, for example, were originally taken up by the secretarial departments of companies for whom they represented a distinct efficiency gain. Subsequently, however, all of us use them. Products which are not well positioned against the needs of a well understood core customer group will often flounder. Why would your average Tom, Dick or Harry need an Apple Newton in 1992? It was not until business users adopted targeted electronic organizers for the general market that we got used to the idea of electronic diaries with lower functionality than the Newton. If the firm you are analysing has not shown itself to be as good at targeting and understanding core customer groups, it is safe to assume that it will not successfully innovate.

Pulling it All Together

Where does this leave us when analysing a firm's innovation capabilities? The straightforward measure of the commitment of a firm to innovation is its level of spending on R&D as a percentage of sales versus the competition. Since innovation is also driven by a firm's manufacturing capabilities you should also check its relative levels of capital expenditure. If you are looking at a service company, the level of innovation will be driven by the quality of the people. Its level of investment in training as a percentage of revenues will give you a rough indication of its commitment. Commitment does not, of course, add up to results. How many patents per 100 employees has the firm registered each year for the past five years compared to the competition? How many new products has it brought to market over the past five years and what has been their market share performance? Where have they come in on the innovation curve? Depending where they sit on the curve, how sustainable do you think their innovation edge is? By taking a look at the company's past you should be able to make a judgment about how successfully it will innovate in the future. It is only the future that matters to shareholders.

Figure 7.27 summarizes the key value drivers for the innovation area of a typical firm's value chain.

FINANCIAL STRATEGY: "THE OIL"

Over the past decade, finance has risen to become easily the pre-eminent function of the senior management team. Any Board of Directors of a major western firm will probably be at least 50% dominated by finance people. One of the reasons for this has been the growth in the power of the financial markets in the mid-80s. The number of investment funds exploded and with them the intensity with which firms traded hands. A large number of holding companies and LBO funds came into being purely for the purpose of extracting incremental value from assets by managing the balance sheet. Firms such as KKR in the US and Hanson in the UK are the more infamous. Many firms which started off as financial holdings have subsequently developed into proper companies not reliant solely on management of the balance sheet to create a return. They have retained their financial orientation nevertheless. Normal operating companies have, in the process, had to become more sophisticated in their dealings with the capital markets. Hence the bias on their Boards.

The financial abilities of a firm will condition its capacity to raise and sustain financing in order to fund the activities necessary to compete. Financial strategy can be divided into three core areas:

- *Capital structure* or the type of funding used by a company;
- *Capital markets* or the source of that funding;
- *Financial management* which is all about putting the capital to efficient use.

Typically these will be overseen by the CFO but will also involve a wide number of players in the organization. As a manager the key issue to understand is whether the financial strategy pursued

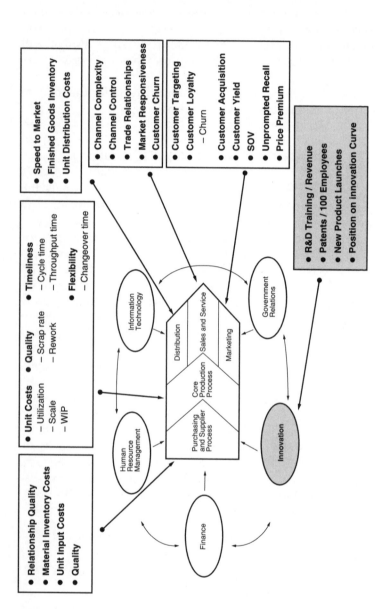

Figure 7.27   *Value drivers summary*

by the firm is appropriate to support its business goals given the competitive characteristics of the market. Whilst an understanding of accounting makes this stuff easier, it is not necessary and we will assume that the term accounting sends shivers through your spine.

Capital Structure: "The Type of Funding"

The capital structure of a firm is simply the collection of sources of cash used to fuel the business, from bank loans through to supplier credits. It appears as a block on the right-hand side of the balance sheet and is usually broken down into the pieces illustrated in Figure 7.28.[12] Jointly these items represent the capital necessary to keep the assets churning. They divide simply into liabilities and shareholder equity.

The liabilities of the company are debt owed to external parties. Usually these are divided into short-term liabilities, which the firm will have to meet over the next year or so, and long-term liabilities which do not have to be paid off for some time. Short-term liabilities will usually include items such as bills for goods received from suppliers which have not yet been paid, bank overdrafts, unpaid wages or bonus accruals of employees, taxes which fall due shortly and other items such as reserves created for write-offs which are anticipated to occur in the near future. Long-term liabilities will include items such as bank debt and long-term debt owed to bondholders, as well as preferred stock which carries a dividend coupon much like an interest charge on a loan. Most of these liabilities will carry interest which the firm will have to pay to service them. The balance on the right-hand side of the balance sheet is the equity invested in the firm. This equity is "book equity" and will not bear any relation to the actual value of the stock in the marketplace. The equity on a balance sheet is the accrued balance of all the reported profit the company has earned in its history, after payment of interest, taxes and dividends. This is notionally the money that will be owned by shareholders and has been reinvested in the company.

There is no need to go into the details of the balance sheet for

[12] The presentational format of balance sheets varies country by country and we have taken the US model as the most dominant internationally.

ASSETS		SOURCE OF FUNDING
● CURRENT ASSETS		● CURRENT LIABILITIES
– Cash		– Trade Creditors
– Inventory		– Bank Overdrafts
– Receivables		– Capital Leases
		– Taxes Due
● FIXED ASSETS	**=**	● LONG-TERM LIABILITIES
– Tangible Assets		– Bank Debt
● Plant and Machinery		– Debentures
● Buildings		– Preference Shares
● Fixtures and Fittings		● EQUITY
		– Called Up Share Capital
– Intangible Assets		– Additional Paid in Capital
● Trademarks		– Revaluation Reserve
● Goodwill		– Retained Earnings

Figure 7.28   Illustrative simplified generic balance sheet for an American firm

our purposes, which is to understand the contribution of financial strategy to company success. However, it should be pointed out that care has to be taken when using the liability and equity numbers from any balance sheet. For example, the company may have recently bought another firm and have accrued "goodwill" equivalent to the difference between the book value of the firm and the price paid for it. This goodwill will often be included among the assets with a corresponding inflation of equity. Were this goodwill to be written off, then it could potentially deeply reduce the size of the book equity. Similarly, there may be a number of other liabilities which the firm has not funded out of earnings on the balance sheet. These might include pension liabilities, uncapitalized lease financing, positions in derivatives markets or contingencies for outstanding legal suits which do not feature on the financial statements (although they will generally be disclosed in the notes). Creating a fund for these would involve moving money out of the equity pile and creating a liability. Clearly this would reduce the size of the equity on the balance sheet. Unless you have a good understanding of financial statements, it will be impossible for you to identify the quality of the balance sheet. It is simply worth bearing in mind that the numbers should not be taken at face value and your judgments should be tempered until you can get the numbers checked by an accounting buff.

Down to Drivers

The principal issue that should concern you about the capital structure is how much "leverage" the firm has on the balance sheet. Leverage is the ratio of interest-bearing debt (which includes preference shares carrying a coupon) to common equity on which no interest is paid. On its own this ratio will not mean much, but if you compare it to competitors it will. If a firm is much more leveraged than a competitor you will know it is taking a quite distinct approach to increasing returns to shareholders. As we have already explored, increasing the amount of debt will increase returns to shareholders because it enables more revenue to be financed for the same equity investment. Debt also has a tax advantage because interest can be written off against tax and therefore creates shareholder value equivalent to the interest multiplied by the tax rate.

The leverage ratio cannot be taken in isolation. Firstly, you need to check the level of "interest coverage", that is how comfortably the firm can afford to pay the interest on the debt. If the firm appears comfortable, with an interest coverage ratio in excess of the five times mark, then the leverage on the balance sheet is probably a safe method of boosting returns to shareholders. If, however, its coverage is low, say below three times, then it might be exposed to any potential downturn in the economy. Normally debt will come with bank covenants specifying certain financial ratios which have to be met, so it would be unusual for you to find an exceptionally low coverage rate in the firm you are examining.

The second issue to look at is the comparative cost of the debt. By taking the total sum of debt on the balance sheet (which may not be the same as its market value but we can ignore this for our purposes) and dividing it into the interest charge on the profit and loss statement you will get a sense of the cost of the debt. If the firm appears to be paying considerably more on its debt than its competitors then you know there may be a problem. Usually a firm will pay more interest on its debt because the banks or, in the case of traded debt, the markets, believe it is a riskier bet and therefore the coupon is set higher. This may be because the firm is highly leveraged. Typically there is a trade-off between leverage and the cost of debt. If a firm raises leverage very high it will have to pay more interest on its debt because of the increased risk to lenders.

As we mentioned, liabilities come in two basic flavours: short term and long term. Long-term and short-term debt carry different rates of interest. For instance, a loan which is payable in one year will carry a rate of interest which reflects market expectations for that year. Debt which is repayable in five years will carry an interest rate which reflects interest rate expectations five years out. Typically the further out the repayment, the greater will be the interest rate because of the inherent uncertainty about how the markets will move in the meantime. The resulting curve is called the "Yield Curve". This curve will shift all the time and in certain cases may invert. The only thing we need worry about is whether the firm has obeyed the rule that it is best to finance assets with matching debt. If an asset will only last for a year until its useful life is done, then it is best to fund that with debt that will mature in a year. Likewise if it will last for five years, it is best to finance that with five-year debt. The objective is to match the risk associated with the income from customers with the risk associated with the debt that has to be repaid from that income. Both are subject to similar shifts in the term rate of interest. If a five-year project is funded with one-year debt and interest rates soar in year two the project will have to entirely recalibrate its economics and may become not viable.

As a quick check you should calculate the ratio of short-term to long-term debt. If you compare this with competitor's numbers you may find some differences. If you then intelligently compare this to what you believe to be the maturity of the company's investment cycle you may be able to see whether there is a match or a mismatch. If, for example, the company is manufacturing swimming pools, are there major equipment changes on a yearly cycle or does the machinery last for ten years? If the firm is a travel agent with changes in its IT infrastructure every five years, then ten-year debt may be inappropriate.

So far we have discussed the total amount of debt versus equity on the balance sheet. There is also the issue of how that debt is secured against assets. Virtually all banks require the debtor to specify the value and identity of assets against which their loans are secured. This means that should the firm go under, the banks have clear recourse to things, or "liens", which can be sold to pay back that loan. In reality firms have a fair degree of discretion about where they choose to allocate debt and where they choose to do so can confer competitive advantage. Depending on how they distribute it against assets, they may be able to lower the apparent risk profile of the debt and therefore reduce interest charges. This may also increase their ability to augment their leverage. Both of these actions will increase the value of the company to shareholders. There is no way, without access to all the gruesome details, that you can perform this analysis. However, you should be aware of it.

Pulling it All Together

Capital is only of any use if it is put to use. Our only concern should be that the capital structure of the firm supports its business strategy optimally. Is the level of debt likely to hinder the level of capital investment necessary to maintain competitive unit costs? Is it undercapitalized to support its rate of growth? Is it disguising the risk of ongoing interest type charges by financing itself with convertible preference shares which holders may fail to convert to equity if the firm begins to slow? Conversely, is it so under-leveraged that it is likely to be the object of a hostile bid from an LBO fund? Is there any more juice that can be squeezed out for shareholders without damaging the fundamentals of the business? What price is it paying on the debt? Does this mean it is being punished for excessive leverage? You should also ask whether the balance of the liabilities appears to match the balance of the assets. Is it funding long-term assets with short-term debt in an act of ill-judged desperation?

Capital Markets: "The Source of Capital"

A business has a large number of places from which it can raise capital. Equity can be raised from personal sources or private investors and debt can be raised from local retail and commercial banks. However, a firm can also access both debt and equity through the traded financial markets. The advantages of doing so are that a firm can access sufficient capital to grow which may not be available at competitive rates from local sources. Firms which run into trouble under private ownership often do so because they are under capitalized; that is they do not have enough equity to support their growth and therefore keep on adding bank debt until the seams burst. This usually occurs because they are unable or unwilling to access the public markets. Once a firm makes recourse to a public market it opens itself to public scrutiny which is often unwelcome by CEOs or shareholders who have been accustomed to autonomy.

A firm need not access the public markets if it is able to fund its activities through private sources. It might be producing sufficient cash flow to fund its own expansion from retained earnings. It might also have the backing of a group of wealthy individuals who have taken a long-term view of their investment. However, if a private firm is to compete against international players, private sources of funding are unlikely to be adequate to fuel the capital investment and acquisitions necessary to make it competitive. Bank debt is also likely to be expensive compared to debt raised through the financial markets because of the high cost structure of local lending banks. It is, therefore, increasingly uncommon for major international players to still be in private hands. Most will be listed on a stock exchange and both their debt and equity will be traded. The exception may be firms which are controlled by investment, LBO or venture capital funds. Such funds, however, can only realize their investments by bringing these companies to market. Generally speaking, if the firm you are examining is still private, you should check to see whether its rate of capital investment, its rate of acquisition and the interest rate on its debt are comparable with quoted competitors. If not, it will probably be a sign of management weakness that it is unable or unwilling to access the financial markets.

Accessing the markets is one thing. Keeping them happy is another. A distinguishing feature of a successful company versus an unsuccessful one is its ability to deal successfully with the capital markets. The capital markets are ever vigilant. All the investment banks employ a large number of analysts to maintain a close watch on the more important firms listed on the major exchanges. Their opinions will have a decisive effect on the share price of the companies under their scrutiny. In order to interface with them successfully, a firm will need a good strategy for managing expectations and reporting events in a compelling and timely fashion.

Down to Drivers

It is possible, in a fairly superficial way, to evaluate the past performance of a company in dealing with the markets by judging its ability to manage valuation of its stock. If you plot out the movements of the firm's profits per share over a number of years versus the per share price movements you may be able to detect patterns of good management. For example, if profits fell during a quarter but the stock price held steady then you can bet the firm has managed the expectations of the market well. It may have done so through holding a convincing set of investor presentations or by managing its financial PR well. By contrast, firms which go on a roller-coaster in terms of price movements, even though earnings performance has been moderately predictable, will have managed expectations poorly. This means they may have serious problems when times get really tough. One example is The Body Shop in the UK which has suffered a volatile stock and whose CEO is known to have an adversarial view of market makers.

The other obvious thing you might cast a critical eye over is the annual report. These are usually quite revealing about the company's strategy and will give a flavour of its senior management style. The annual report is geared mainly at investors and analysts so it will give you a sense of the firm's handling of the markets. If, for example, a media firm simply talks about how tough the home market has been whereas a competitor spells out opportunities in new markets then you can make some subjective guesses about its market skills!

Firms do not access the financial markets directly. They will almost always do so through a number of intermediaries, most importantly the investment banks. If, for example, a firm wishes to raise a tranche of equity an investment bank will underwrite that issue or guarantee a certain price and then sell that issue on to its many clients through from institutional investors to private individuals, via its dealer network. The indicator to focus on is how many calls a company has made on the market and how well received they have been. One way to measure this is the reported level of subscription for those shares. If the issue has been heavily subscribed that will indicate clear investor sentiment in its favour. The other thing to look at is the pricing of the issue versus the subsequent market rate a week after issue. If the issue has been priced low and the stock leaps significantly, it may indicate that the bankers were sanguine about its attractiveness to investors.

Finally, you should take a look at the company's performance in terms of dividends per share. Dividends are a means for a company to return cash to shareholders annually without them having to sell stock to realize a gain. The markets are highly sensitive to movements in dividend rates. A rapid drop in dividends is almost always taken as a serious signal that the company is running into some type of trouble which is sucking up cash. The analysts therefore favour steady dividend policies. Firms sometimes use dividends to return large amounts of cash to shareholders above what they would normally grant on an ongoing basis. A firm will do this when it can find no better use for the cash. This in itself can be a worrying sign. If they can't do anything with it, it is probably time for a management change and some more imagination!

Financial Management: "The Use and Management of Capital"

Capital is neutral. What matters is what you do with it. This means it has to be allocated properly and the use of it once allocated has to be controlled. We will start our analysis the wrong way round, with the hot topic of the 90s, cost control.

Cost Control

Firms sink or swim on the basis of the rigour of their internal controls. This basically means budgeting for the amount of cost that can be incurred given reasonable revenue expectations. It also means managing down that cost to ensure a target margin is achieved even if revenues fall. This is all very familiar territory, of course, because of the funeral bells of the downsizing phenomenon.

Costs are costs, aren't they? Well, not quite. They can actually be divided into two categories, fixed and variable. Fixed costs, or overhead, are those costs that do not easily go away even if there is a downturn in revenue. They might include buildings, fixed assets and even employees, depending on the flexibility of local labour law. Of course, ultimately they can be removed but this tends to occur in chunks. For example, closing a factory represents a major loss of capacity, and it tends to cost a lot to do. These assets are therefore considered fixed because a firm would not choose to dispose of them just because there was a downward blip in sales. Variable costs, in contrast, are those costs which are driven by the levels of activity of the firm or, most directly, by revenue. For example, if a firm cuts production of cars it will consume a correspondingly smaller amount of electricity, metal and other raw materials.

The trouble with fixed costs is that they are there no matter what happens in the marketplace. The ratio that determines when they have got too much for a firm to bear is the "breakeven" point. Breakeven is reached when profits are sufficient to cover fixed costs. The simple calculation for breakeven is revenues minus variable costs divided by fixed costs. If this number is greater than one, then breakeven has been exceeded and the firm is in profit. Since variable costs can quickly be adjusted up or down, the size of the fixed cost pile will be the critical determinant of when a firm does and doesn't make money.

Calculating the proportion of fixed costs relative to variable costs for the firm in question and comparing this with the key competitor's ratios will probably throw up interesting clues about a firm's competitiveness. In the case of service companies, for example, a firm's ability to switch employees onto variable bonus-oriented pay deals, and away from fixed salaries, will affect its ability to achieve consistent margins enormously despite blips in the economy. In order to calculate fixed and variable costs you will need to establish a picture of the firm's "cost structure''. A cost structure is simply the pile of costs a firm incurs, grouped by discrete category. The basic cost structure can be taken from the firm's P&L statement. However, this will not usually provide the level of detail necessary to perform your analysis. Figure 7.29 demonstrates how, in the case of a service business such as an advertising firm, you might break down the cost categories into analysable chunks from the annual report.

Down to Drivers

Once you have the cost structure clear you should be able to ask some tough questions about the relative cost performance of the company. The best place to start is to recalculate the cost bar on a unit of output basis by dividing it by unit volume. In the case of the advertising agency, the output would be the number of adverts; in the case of a car manufacturer the number of cars produced. You should then convert the cost categories into percentages. Percentage unit cost bars can be compared across companies, although obtaining competitive data is a tough task (we will come on to how to do this presently). You will then be able to understand where the firm is out of line on costs. For example, it

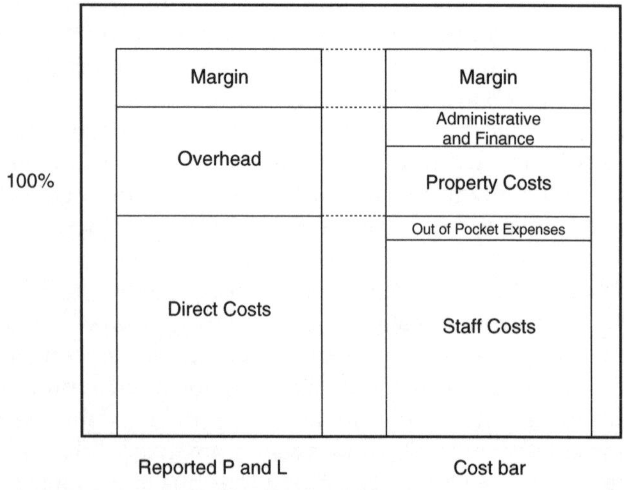

Figure 7.29   *Illustrative simplified generic cost structure of a fictional advertising agency*

may be that its ratio of employee costs to revenue is far too high compared to competitors. Or it may be that its fixed costs are excessive and that its breakeven hurdle is too high, leaving it exposed to economic downturns. The cost bar will form the basis for your evaluation of whether or not a firm is able to compete on the basis of price. If its cost bar is higher than that of its competitors it will have to rely on differentiating its product or service sufficiently to maintain a decent margin. If it cannot do this, it will have to address its cost position. Figure 7.30 compares the unit cost structure of a fictional fast-food restaurant with that of a Soho French brasserie. It should be pretty clear that the cost structure of the brasserie prohibits it from competing in the hamburger wars on price!

The cost bar will also be a useful litmus test for your analysis of a firm's success with its operations, marketing and human resources policies. If you have identified weaknesses or, indeed, strengths in these areas this should be reflected in the cost bar. If, for example, a market research firm is dependent on keeping costs low to win contracts but it is pursuing a strategy of hiring senior business advisors, its staff to revenue ratio will be adversely affected and hence its cost position. If, by contrast, an fmcg company is competing in branded goods but has a low advertising to revenue cost line and a large administrative overhead, it is probably putting resources in the wrong place. The

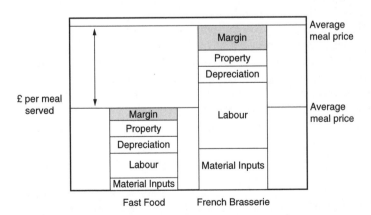

Figure 7.30 *Illustrative simplified unit cost bar of two generic restaurant businesses*

cost bar is the guide to a company's performance throughout its entire value chain.

Of course, costs do not simply happen. They are driven by revenue. The late 80s and 90s have been preoccupied with controlling the denominator, with downsizing, delayering, rightsizing and every other euphemism for cost reduction. The problem is that a firm needs costs to produce revenue. If an advertising firm does not have enough creatives it cannot pitch for work. If a steel mill does not have enough free capacity it cannot grow sales except through price increases. The other thing about the relationship between costs and revenue is that costs usually have to be added before revenues flow from them. The lag time between cause and effect will vary by industry but in some cases it can be quite long. It can, for instance, be ten years between the decision by a pharmaceutical firm to put cash behind a drug and the first pound hitting the cash register. A firm investing heavily in advertising may not reap the rewards of growing consumer equity immediately.

In recessionary periods, it is always a temptation not to wait and to cut costs right back. The boost to the bottom line is immediate. In the longer term, of course, the machine may seize up. You can save money by not eating but in the end you die. In many cases the decision to cut costs hard is now hampering firms' ability to grow revenues significantly. You should be wary of simply accepting low cost numbers as good in and of themselves. If they are combined with sales growth which is well below the industry average then it is possible that this has been achieved at the expense of growth (see Figure 7.31). And in many industries rapid erosion of market share can be calamitous and unrecoverable! Whilst competitive pressure will continue to force companies to chip away at the bottom line, most firms will have to concentrate equally on growing the top line if they are to deliver decent returns to shareholders.

Cash Flow Control

Assuming a firm has the volume of business to support its fixed cost base and that its cost bar is competitive, the other big issue is cash. Cash is not the same as profits but it is cash that keeps the wheels turning. We have already discussed how to calculate

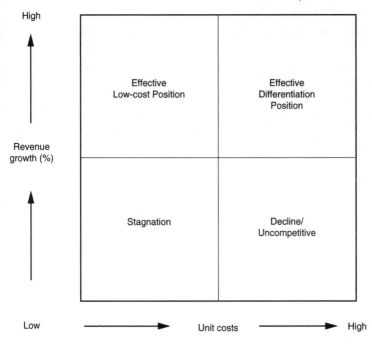

High

Revenue
growth (%)

| Effective Low-cost Position | Effective Differentiation Position |
| Stagnation | Decline/ Uncompetitive |

Low   ⟶   Unit costs   ⟶   High

Figure 7.31 *Illustrative relationship between revenue growth and unit costs in a generic business*

cash flow (Figure 5.2). But what makes the cash flow good or bad?

The most common reason a firm might be experiencing cash flow problems is because clients are not paying their bills on time. Meanwhile, the firm is still having to pay its suppliers on a reasonably timely basis or they cut off the shipment of vital inputs. A common way to compare the balance of what a firm owes and is owed is to compare a company's days receivable and its days payable. A firm's days receivable can be obtained by dividing its trade receivables by sales and multiplying by 360. Its debtor days can be obtained by dividing its trade payables by its cost of goods sold and multiplying by 360. This will give you the approximate number of days of payment a firm owes its suppliers and how slow its own customers are in their payments to the firm. In most firms you will find that these numbers are roughly in balance. If the balance is to tip in either direction it is better that a firm should be stretching payables because this will provide it with cash. If bills are due a month after receipt of goods this might mean holding out for two months typically. This can, however, carry costs since suppliers are likely to charge interest for late payment and may reduce the amount of credit they will grant if this is done repeatedly. If the firm is accumulating unpaid receipts from customers, it may be getting into deep trouble. This may be occurring because customers are having a tough time getting rid of the product.

The second key item which consumes cash is inventory. If too much unsold inventory gets accumulated then again the firm will have problems since inventory ties up cash. The best way to compare the efficiency with which inventory is being managed is to divide the value of inventory by sales and multiply this by 360 days. The resulting number represents the days of inventory the company has in stock. This will give you a sense of the speed with which inventory is being turned over. If one player is much slower than another you will probably know that it is carrying a lot of old inventory on its books. This may be an indication that the product line is superannuated and discredited with customers. It may also be because it has a poor manufacturing process, as we have already discussed.

In addition to receivables and inventory, most firms will also have a cash pile on the left-hand side of the balance sheet. All firms have to keep a certain amount of cash in the bank just to keep the wheels oiled. Of course, a firm may have an unusually large amount of cash because of exceptional circumstances such as the recent sale of a business, or the proceeds from a "rights issue"[13] which it has not yet invested. On the whole, however, a firm will not want to keep that pile sitting there long since it will not be earning any return; shareholders will soon enough realize this and wonder what's going on.

The balance of cash plus receivables plus inventory minus payables is called the "net working capital" of the business. If this number is very large relative to sales and growing, this will be a sure indication that the company is guzzling cash. You then have to make a judgment about how long this is sustainable. If cash flow is negative then it will have to have to access additional

---

[13] A rights issue is an issuance of the right to existing stockholders to acquire a certain number of additional shares for each share they currently hold, at a set price.

funding to stay alive without piling excessive debt onto the balance sheet. It will also need a clear route to turning the cash flow positive again. If debt is piling up and cash flow is a river of red ink, there will be real trouble in store.

Finally you should take a look at the depreciation line. Depreciation simply represents the notional annualized charge for a capital asset such as machinery. If, for instance, a chemical firm buys a machine valued at £10 million it can usually choose to write this off against profits over a number of years depending on the nature of the asset. If, in the case of this piece of equipment, it could be depreciated over five years that would mean an annual charge against profits of £2 million The rates at which different assets can be depreciated are set by the accounting standards boards in each country. The advantage to the company is that the depreciation charge will reduce the tax bill for the company by reducing its taxable profits and thereby boost its cash flow by the value of that tax break. For our purposes, the main thing to observe is that depreciation is a proxy for the amount of cash a company is investing in its productive assets. The easiest way to boost profits is to cut capital expenditure. This, however, will certainly weaken the future earnings capability of the firm and might ultimately lead to its substitution by a competitor who has invested in cutting edge machinery. As a test you should compare the depreciation charge against revenues. If this ratio in the firm you are looking at is curiously low compared to a basket of competitors then this will raise the question of the firm's long-term competitiveness. If, on the other hand, it is extremely high then you should try and find out why they have planned such comparatively high investment levels.

We will return to the issue of cash at the end of this book because cash is the driver of the value of a company's stock and shareholder value is all we need care about. But now you should be able to understand a little better what is driving that number. We should be as sanguine about cash flow as we are about profits. Just because a firm is pumping out cash now does not mean it will do so over the next few years. It might be cutting advertising spend or reducing its R&D budget which will damage its long-term earnings potential. The markets scrutinize the long-term cash potential of a firm, not one year's performance, and we should do the same.

SBU Control

All firms have an internal control mechanism for ensuring that SBUs are performing as anticipated by senior management. The quality of internal management data can have a tremendous impact on a firm's ability to manage itself effectively. The collapse of the venerable Barings Bank in the UK because of failure by management to understand its exposure to Asian markets is a salutary reminder. Most firms will have reasonable control systems. If they don't, erratic performance and surprise disclosures to the markets should expose this fairly quickly.

The first issue to clarify is the basis on which senior management measure the performance of their SBUs. All firms will gather the basic statutory information such as revenue, operating margin and cash flow. However, they will employ very different techniques for comparing the relative performance of units. In a capital intensive industry, such as machine tool production for example, it would be common to find senior management benchmarking performance based on return on capital employed or ROCE.[14] They would pick this measure because the major resource in the business is fixed cost and, unless this is effectively deployed to generate optimum sales, the firm will get into trouble. In the case of an advertising agency, by contrast, there is little capital deployed. The largest item in the cost structure is people. Therefore, it is likely that the CEO of the firm will keep a close eye on the staff cost to revenue ratio. If this rises beyond expectations, it will be a sign that people are being deployed less efficiently against revenue-generating activities.

Internal performance measures are a key driver of internal behaviour. If a managing director of an SBU is rewarded on the basis of ROCE he will most likely do everything in his power to ensure he meets that target. He might do this by ensuring he fully utilizes his machinery by aggressively winning new business, which would obviously be a positive outcome for the firm. Or he might freeze capital investment which would boost his numbers but would not be good for the firm in the long run. Similarly, the MD running the division of an advertising firm might simply cut his headcount to bring his ratios in line but in so doing will

---

[14] ROCE = after tax profit divided by the capital deployed in the business. In this context, "capital" refers to the value of physical assets such as machinery rather than purely cash.

undermine the opportunities for future growth. To be effective, the internal performance measures have to induce the appropriate behaviour. In the case of the ad man and the paper man, in addition to the measures discussed, it would probably be wise to incentivize them on the basis of revenue growth to ensure that shortcuts to good ratios are closed off.

The sophistication of internal control systems has increased dramatically over the past ten years and are a backbone of corporate strategy. Many firms for whom customer service is a vital driver of competitiveness have introduced non-financial measures by which to judge the performance of SBUs. The retail arms of banks, for example, might be evaluated on the basis of customer satisfaction. Commercial airlines might evaluate management on the basis of the percentage of flights arriving on time. Increasingly, customer-facing measures are being used to supplement inward-facing efficiency measures. The reason is simple: internal efficiency is a threshold performance standard, customer delivery is where firms differentiate themselves. The challenge of complex internal control systems is the burden they place on a firm's information systems. They also require more sophistication in terms of the structuring of compensation plans as we will come to in a later section.

It should be relatively easy to find out the exact basis on which SBU or divisional performance is measured. The question to ask is: How well geared is this to promoting the behaviours that will make the firm competitive? If, for example, a manufacturer of luxury shoes is measuring performance on the basis of ROCE, is this likely to be relevant to its need to sustain an outstanding customer franchise and superb quality? If a consulting firm is focused on the staff cost to revenue ratio, is this likely to foster the level of talent that it needs to maintain its competitive position?

Capital Allocation, Investment and Acquisitions

If you were given £10 million you could probably come up with a wish-list without much problem. Spending cash is not usually a tough affair. Within most firms it is not that simple. There are always many competing potential uses of capital, each with an advocate clamouring for investment. The allocation of capital within a firm should, theoretically at least, be based on the same analysis to which we have subjected SBUs. In allocating capital a firm needs to understand the value that any use of it will return to shareholders. To do this they would need to understand the value of the cash flows that it will produce into the future. The reality is, of course, that most decisions about where to allocate cash occur on a more "pragmatic" basis.

There is a hierarchy to the capital allocation decisions a typical firm faces. At the top end there is the issue of which SBUs to back, in the middle there is the issue of investment in major productive capacity and at the lower end is the issue of investment in discrete items such as single machines, minor IT systems or office refurbishment (see Figure 7.32). Ideally each decision should be subjected to cash flow analysis but, practically speaking, the importance of this rises as it moves up the investment hierarchy. The problem firms often encounter in terms of choosing where to put their money is the basis on which they judge the potential return on the investment. Assuming they understand what revenues it will produce, the tough part usually boils down to the "hurdle rate" they use. The hurdle rate is the minimum return on investment that management will accept for an investment. Sometimes, for simplicity's sake, they will apply a uniform rate to all investment areas across their companies. In many cases this will not be appropriate because the risk associated with different

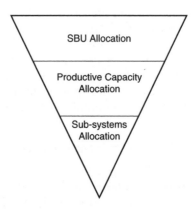

Figure 7.32　*Illustrative hierarchy of capital allocation in a generic manufacturing firm*

options will differ greatly and therefore the necessary return to make it viable will also differ. The other problem that often occurs is that the time period over which projects will pay out will not be the same. If, for example, a manufacturer of clothing is facing a choice between investing in a new machine for an existing line of clothes and production capacity for an entirely new garment range, both the risks and the critical time frame for getting a return will differ. The new line may be an uncertain market and consumer confidence will have to be built. Unless the firm builds these sensitivities into its evaluation of return on investment its decisions will be flawed. Whilst it may be difficult to examine a firm's overall budgeting processes, if it appears to be making consistently bad investment decisions then it may be using dodgy assumptions.

Down to Drivers

The most important investment decisions a firm has to make is which SBUs to fuel. This brings us back to our starting point. Has a firm made the correct decisions about the balance of SBUs in its corporate structure? Could the capital be used better elsewhere? Should the manufacturer of bicycles sell out its mountain bike division at the top of the market and reinvest the money in hi-tech material frames for racing bikes? This is the question we will return to at the end of this book. In terms of the lower tiers of the investment hierarchy the only thing you might scrutinize is the total capital investment charge as a percentage of revenue. If this number is significantly different from that of major competitors then it is worth probing further into where cash is being spent or not being spent.

One option open to firms is to not put their capital back into their existing businesses at all, but to buy new ones. This is very tempting – for one good reason. As long as the firm being acquired has positive earnings above the cost of any debt necessary to purchase it, then the acquisition of that firm will be "earnings positive"; that is it will contribute to the new parent company's reported profit and not detract from it. If the firm has paid more cash for the acquisition than its book value, as will be the case in almost all acquisitions, then it will have to put that difference on its balance sheet as goodwill. The firm may choose to write this off against profits over a number of years. To be earnings positive, the earnings of the new firm after payment of interest will need to exceed the write-off of goodwill. Assuming that it does so, a CEO can invest in acquisitions and immediately boost the bottom line, resulting in an instant appreciation in share price. Given that the alternative of investing in improvement to existing SBUs may not yield incremental profits for some time, the incentive for management is pretty clear. Buy your way to glory.

Faced with great pressure from shareholders to increase returns, many companies have continued to pursue a growth strategy through acquisition. If executed properly, there is nothing wrong with acquisition and it is an essential part of any company's pursuit of shareholder value. Good acquisitions will tend to be in areas in which the firm has some expertise and which it will be able to quickly exploit better than their previous owners. They will be "clustered" around existing segments and areas of competency. In situations where market share is consolidated, acquisitions may be the only viable route to entry. There are also likely to be only a limited number of targets at any one point in time.

The problem with basing a growth strategy on acquisitions is that the only way to grow tends to become to acquire. Sooner or later the good targets will be exhausted, prices will become inflated and, as with any narcotic, things go wrong. Long-term shareholder value will be eroded. Unless a firm is able to produce growth out of its core assets, acquisitions or no acquisitions, it will be in trouble.

Pulling it All Together

The only question you need pose is, do you believe the financial strategy supports the overall operating strategy of the firm? If a pharmaceutical firm has a high return on equity but appears more highly leveraged than its competitors, do you believe the high levels of interest payments will allow it to invest sufficiently in R&D to maintain its market edge? If a manufacturer of plastic toys has a low amount of debt and is returning a lot of cash to shareholders in the form of special dividends, is it putting enough effort into inventing an innovative range of toys for next Christmas? If a diversified light manufacturer is juggling a port-folio of small units do you believe that it is backing the right horses with its investment strategy? Figure 7.33 summarizes the key value drivers in the finance area of a typical firm's value chain.

There are a number of important issues relating to the financial management process which we have not dealt with here. For example, there is the whole deliciously tortuous issue of tax. Since tax represents up to around 35% of income (although business rates vary dramatically country by country) it is clearly an area to which firms pay a great deal of attention. By shifting tax liabilities between SBUs and across countries, companies can often minimize their tax obligations and directly boost returns to shareholders. As a result, different firms competing in the same segments may show quite different rates of tax as a percentage of pre-tax income. Similarly, there is the issue of currency manage-ment which is a major issue for firms with multi-country oper-ations. Failure to hedge against movements in currency values can have a major impact on the P&L number. These issues are beyond the scope of this book to examine in detail but may potentially have a decisive effect on the efficiency with which a firm creates shareholder value.

One final problem with finance, of course, is that the capital structure will usually exist for an entire firm and not for a specific SBU. Unless it is a single product company it is unusual for each SBU to have its own capital structure. You will, therefore, have to consider the SBUs jointly.

HUMAN RESOURCE STRATEGY: "THE OOMPH"

In the past it was capital that made companies tick. Now, in an age of developed capital markets, the finite resource is skills. In more basic terminology, that means people. In light of the issues we have discussed it should not be hard to understand why. Improved customer responsiveness, the increased pace of inno-vation and more flexible working practices have made skills the magic ingredient that distinguish one business from the next. The problem facing virtually all businesses is how to develop

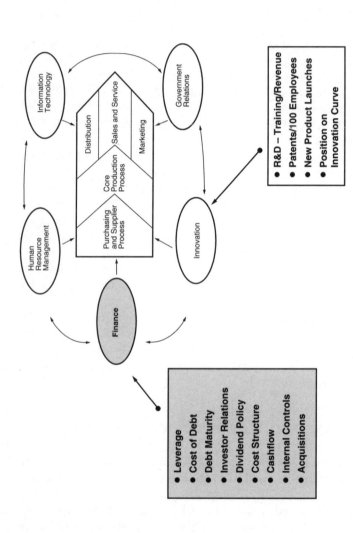

Figure 7.33 *Value drivers summary*

them and then – even tougher – how to hang onto them. A plethora of studies have shown that the level of employee loyalty has diminished over the past decade. In many industries career trading between companies is the surest way to achieve promotion and wage increases. This has reached epidemic proportions amongst service industries such as banking and advertising, for example. The challenge of skills retention has been exacerbated by the downsizing phenomenon that has gripped corporate America, Europe and even Japan over the past five years. The ironic by-product of an exercise that has been intended to reduce costs is that it just as often resulted in a need to pay more to retain the important people who have wisely ensured their own marketability.

The formal owner of these tough issues is the HR department. The HR function has had a mixed life over the past 20 years. In most firms it has been relegated to second or third tier status as an internal supplier. It is typically discussed in the same breath as the accounting function and is associated primarily with the routine tasks of payroll and recruitment presentations rather than as a participant in shaping the strategy of the firm. Consequently, the calibre of professionals in HR is often viewed as being inferior to those in other parts of the value chain. The result is often a downward spiral which will eventually impinge on the ability of a firm to recruit and retain. A typical undergraduate from Harvard, for example, will be interviewed at some stage by a partner if she applies to McKinsey, whereas in a manufacturing firm it will more typically be an HR specialist. The signal given is pretty clear.

This is, of course, a bad mistake on the part of companies who are dependent on the calibre of employees to sustain their competitiveness. Over the past five years most firms have been so preoccupied managing down their staff numbers without causing rebellion that they have taken their collective eye off this ball. Now that much of the easy fat has been cut in many firms, they are facing the challenge of growth as the only means to boost corporate profits. But how do you grow without good people? How do you get good people without investing in a good human resource strategy? Many firms are finding it much harder to formulate such a strategy than they did cutting out costs.

However, in successful firms, this imbalance is now beginning to be redressed. Along with it there is also a changing attitude towards the traditional role of HR. Firstly, its status within most companies is beginning to recover some lost ground. Areas such as employee communications, which historically were based on cheap broadsheets and photocopied letters from the CEO, are becoming more sophisticated. Firms are introducing corporate TV and company magazines. They are also taking more seriously the process of eliciting information from the grass roots level rather than solely pushing mandates down. The whole area of corporate values and the management of corporate culture are also being taken more seriously. In general, the level of spending on the vast plethora of activities which fall under the loose banner of employee motivation has shown sharp upward growth. Why? Because firms are beginning to realize that the only thing that can sustain corporate innovation, sustain high levels of customer satisfaction and generally differentiate one firm from the next is the quality of its workforce.

Down to Drivers

The key issue to address is whether the firm in question has the human capital to support its strategy effectively. This comes down simply to motivation and skills. If a firm cannot inspire good people to great deeds it will not excel competitively. Are the good people staying, are good new people joining, and are they exerting themselves creatively and energetically?

Let's start with retention. If a firm is suffering higher turnover of staff than its competitors this is a reliable indication that internal morale is low. Low morale quickly leads to loss of productivity and, if it extends to the wrong areas, a loss of revenue. Turnover is different from downsizing. Turnover is the percentage change in individuals in a normal operating year. When looking at these numbers you should ensure that exceptional redundancies are not included in this number. Statistics about average tenure can help qualify your interpretation of turnover numbers. But turnover numbers alone can lead you down a couple of blind alleys. Firstly, they are contingent on local labour laws which may limit a firm's ability to fire people without prohibitive cost. Secondly, if the wrong people stay and the good people walk, low turnover can be a drain on corporate resources rather than a boost. If, for example, one firm is German and the other American they will be constrained by quite different laws relating to layoffs. The same might be true also of two American firms, one of which is unionized and the other not. In this case, the longer average tenure of employees might indicate labour rigidity which would be a competitive disadvantage.

The complement to turnover numbers is application rates. Application rates are an excellent indicator of employee perceptions about a firm. A typical application rate for a first tier advertising firm such as J Walter Thompson, for example, will typically exceed that of a second tier firm by several orders of magnitude. Of course, quality is more important than quantity. There is always the issue of where the applications are coming from. High application rates from top schools is a good indicator of relative perceptions of the career offered by a firm. The fact that McKinsey, for example, regularly recruits over 15% of the graduating class of Harvard Business School is a reasonably good indication of how the company is perceived in the US marketplace.

The relationship between application and turnover rates is subtle. Situations where employee turnover is high but application rates are equally as high may indicate an environment which is highly internally competitive. This would often be the case for investment banks, for example, which typically sustain very high margins despite an apparently unstable employee base. Figure 7.34 illustrates the trade-off between application and turnover rates. Another interesting thing about staff turnover and application rates is that they have their marketing counterpart, loyalty and customer acquisition. Everyone knows that increased customer loyalty combined with a steady increase in new customers is a recipe for competitive advantage. Not everyone seems to know that high employee retention and successful hiring are also a recipe for competitive advantage. Indeed, one is often a precursor to the other. Unless a firm has a loyal employee base it will always be harder for it to retain loyal customers. Disgruntled employees will bad-mouth the firm, deliver poor customer service and, possibly, poor product quality and low productivity. Interestingly, therefore, successful firms will tend to pay as much attention to marketing to their internal constituencies as they do to their external constituencies.

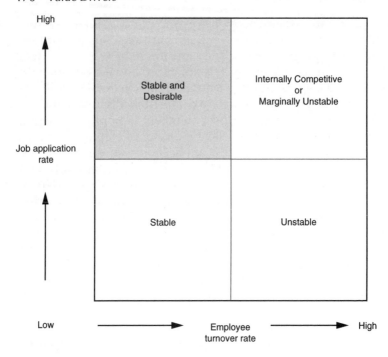

Figure 7.34   *Illustrative trade-offs between job application rates and employee turnover rates in a generic firm*

So, what drives turnover and application rates? The usual response is cash. Were this the case, HR strategy would be simple. Victory would go to whoever pays the most. The reality is not so simple. High remuneration does not correlate simply with competitive advantage. If a firm can achieve low comparative remuneration rates[15] combined with low staff turnover rates then it is likely to have the strongest position. Firms with excellent market reputations can often maintain people for below par salaries for the prestige value of the job. People will work for literally no money at premium auction houses because they know that the training and experience has a market value in itself. Conversely, firms with higher wage rates and high turnover are probably being forced to compensate for an intrinsic

---

[15] Dividing total employee costs by the number of employees will give you the approximate average pay per employee.

lack of prestige or quality through high pay. Ironically, this can occur after a firm has tried major downsizing exercises only to discover this has left them with a skills shortage.

What is the outcome of a good HR strategy? The first is productivity or the rate of output per employee.[16] The more motivated and skilled a workforce, the higher will be their rate of productivity. If the firm is achieving high productivity outcomes combined with good staff retention rates, then it is probable that its HR strategy is sound. If large productivity improvements are associated with a fall in employee numbers and high turnover, then this boost may be a result of a policy of headcount reduction which you will need to examine for sustainability (see Figure 7.35). Productivity gains achieved during periods of stability in the employee base will be a more enduring sign of competitiveness. Productivity improvements can only occur if customers are buying the output. It is no good a firm being excellent at producing something if it is not also excellent at selling. The second sign of a good HR strategy, therefore, is a satisfied customer base. If the rate of customer loyalty and new customer acquisition is high it is likely that the firm is also effective at attracting and retaining staff. Unless the two sides of the equation are in balance, it is unlikely that a firm will be able to maintain customer loyalty for long.

So far we have been talking about a firm's employees as a lumpen mass. In this we are guilty of the cardinal HR sin. Good HR policy, just like good marketing strategy, should be premised on segmentation and targeting. As a starting point, you should therefore also get a sense of all the basic variables by functional areas of the value chain, from finance, manufacturing, through to senior management. Do average turnover and application rates vary substantially by department in each SBU? Are average pay levels noticeably different? From your analysis so far, you will have determined which parts of the firm's value chain are most critical. This is where HR will be most critical also. If, for example, turnover rates and average remuneration are low in the manufacturing area of an fmcg player, this may not be as damaging as the same dynamics in the marketing group. Unless a firm's HR policies are well targeted and prioritized by critical areas of the value chain, it is unlikely to be highly competitive. As with a

---

[16] Productivity is simply the amount of revenue or, alternatively, pre-tax profit generated per employee.

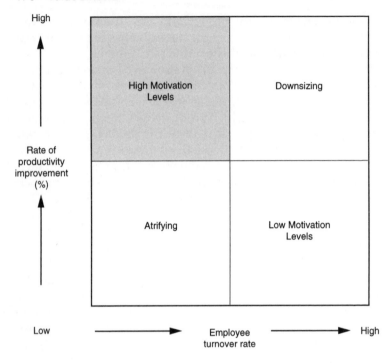

Figure 7.35   *Illustrative relationship between productivity gains and staff turn-over in a generic company*

firm's customer base, not all of its employees can be 100% satis-fied.

HR can too easily be confused with a firm being a "nice", "kind" employer. This, of course, means nothing. An employer can be very tender and politically correct but, if it does not achieve good returns for shareholders, it will go under and the workforce will be out of a job. In order to get good outcomes a firm has to ensure the alignment of personnel policies with desired business goals. The average firm has at its disposal a number of HR levers to achieve this alignment, the most import-ant of which are:

- structure and organization of human resources;
- remuneration and evaluation policies;

- career management policies;
- training and internal communications strategy;
- work environment management.

In an age where headcount reduction has become, and will remain, a managerial imperative, ensuring that the HR strategy delivers long-term competitive advantage is both a critical task and the single toughest task facing senior management today. The next few years are likely to see this issue assume increasing prominence. If you're considering careers, put your money on HR strategy!

Structure and Organization of Human Resources

Probably the most important, and certainly the highest profile, of the HR levers is the structure of resource – that is, how people are organized and deployed. This issue has been in the spotlight over the past ten years with the advent of "re-engineering". Classically, most businesses have and continue to organize their people into functional specialties corresponding to their value chain. This means that a product or service is handed from one specialist function to the next before being completed, much like the batch manufacturing process we discussed earlier. R&D invents it, manufacturing pumps it out, the marketers communicate its merits and the sales group ship it to market.

Re-engineering has prompted a revision of this organizational paradigm with the goal of streamlining the number of steps and internal transactions necessary to deliver output. This change typically imposes a "process view" rather than a functional view of the organization. It stipulates that the process should dictate the structure the firm adopts rather than the structure dictating the process. Most processes travel across the traditional basis of organizational structure, the functional departments. In the case of an insurance company processing claims, for example, this might mean that instead of a customer call that has been received by a telephonist being turned into a form by a clerk, in turn being handed to a claims agent, and then to a claims adjuster, ad infinitum, one person might handle the entire process for a target customer group. Usually the goal will be to reduce the number of steps necessary to deliver the output and the number of errors that occur between stages, thereby increasing the speed of delivery to the customer and reducing the total cost of the product or service.

Teams Versus Departments

To generalize somewhat, this thinking is propelling an increasing shift from traditional departments to multi-skilled teams as the basis of organization. This can have many benefits but also has its limitations. Departments are often referred to as silos, as if they contained manure. To the "re-engineers" they are associated with failure to communicate across the value chain and the defence of "dysfunctional" baronies by the people who run them. This is often not a fair accusation. Departments exist because firms need to develop different sets of specialist skills. Specialist skills are usually best nurtured in groups of likeminded people who can transfer learning between each other. In most firms, therefore, the reality is that there is a need for a careful balance between inter-departmental teams and departments themselves. However, the current swing of the pendulum is definitely in favour of teams.

In the case of service businesses, where the movement away from departmental structures has been most widespread, these teams typically will be organized around clients. The principal aim of teams is that by working together fewer people will be able to complete tasks faster and more accurately because there are less handovers between departments. The additional aspiration is that team members will feel more "ownership" of the outcome and can be more transparently rewarded for results. In a number of service industries the shift to client-facing teams has delivered results. Perhaps most significantly, it has allowed service firms to more closely match the needs of their clients. In the case of an advertising firm servicing a global client, with professionals dedicated to the account globally in each servicing office, it has meant better coordination, speedier transfer of ideas and more efficient sharing of resource across the world. The result is better, faster and cheaper work.

De-layering

A development in many companies associated with the re-engineering phenomenon has been that of "de-layering" or the eponymous "downsizing". The classical structure associated with departmentalism is the pyramidal hierarchy. The top issues orders which middle management fashions into tasks for the people actually creating the product or delivering the service at the bottom. The role of the wedge of people in the middle is to push information down, to feed it back up and hence exercise control. A basic tenet of re-engineering is that the percolation of information up and down the hierarchy of middle management has the drawback of being slow and expensive. The last five years have seen a substantial shortening of reporting lines. The information-transferring role of middle management has been partly removed by the growth in IT and the use of networks which permit the delivery of performance data direct to the desks of senior management at even the most desegregated level. As a result, there is a lesser need for order givers in the middle; organizations tend to look "flatter" and the span of control of remaining managers has widened dramatically. It has also fundamentally altered the cost structures of the firms that have done this (Figure 7.36).

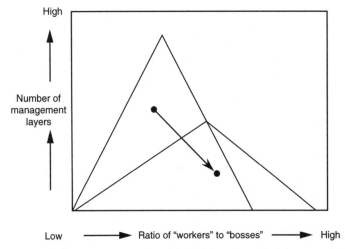

Figure 7.36 *Illustrative shift in organizational structure of a generic firm over the past 10 years*

Networking

Combined with de-layering has been the shift from rigid reporting lines to more flexible working practices which encourage networking. Normally, if a good idea is developed by a research group in an average company, this might be handed over to marketing to test its viability and then to a manufacturing group to test for manufacturability. At each stage it would be subjected to a laborious approval process by each department. The result would be a long time lag in getting the idea to market because of internal inertia. In good firms this process will increasingly be collapsed through use of a task force of people drawn from across departments to "fast track" the idea. Good firms are placing an increasing emphasis on cooperation between functional groups and the fostering of informal networks which can help speed the process of communicating ideas around the company. Often these networks will appear disorganized and uncontrolled which poses challenges for traditional firms and conservative managers. The advent of robust PC-based communications systems, from Notes to Intranet, has greatly facilitated this, as we will come onto shortly.

Empowerment

Also associated with the shortening of reporting lines in de-layered organizations has been the trend towards "empowerment". Although it may sound like a form of aromatherapy, this simply means the devolution of more decision-making responsibility to people nearer the coal face. Whereas a line worker welding car panels together might previously have relied on a quality inspector to find mistakes, in an "empowered" organization he might be encouraged to build in quality through personal commitment. There has been an evolving view that the more decision-making power employees are given, within reasonable limits, the more commitment they will feel to delivering outstanding results. The slimming of middle management has made this an imperative since the ability of many firms to impose control in the old command and control style has been gutted. The bad face of empowerment is when management simply expect fewer people to deliver the same level of customer satisfaction without any fundamental revision of working practices. The good face of empowerment is when increased responsibility is matched with increased autonomy of decision making, enhanced performance-based rewards and concerted investment in employee training.

Intrapreneurialism

At the same time everyone has been talking about empowerment, most firms have also begun to recognize that they are dependent on entrepreneurial activity at the local market level to secure growth. This has spawned the concept of "intrapreneurialism". Intrapreneurialism simply means the granting of greater degrees of freedom to local management to determine the course of the business under their control. Many highly innovative firms have actively spurred on their SBUs to experiment with new product and service formulations. An idea which cuts ice in one local market can rapidly be expanded across the organization. In many organizations there is an active investment strategy to back internal horses with capital in much the same way as venture capitalists back entrepreneurs in the external marketplace. The hope is that providing capital and incentives to seed projects internally will, in the long run, be a cheaper way of producing innovation than will the purchase of start-up firms which have brought a new concept to market. A startling number of successful new entrants, from Microsoft in the US through to Direct Line Insurance in the UK, have been incubated under the umbrella of a "sponsoring" corporation. Whether the corporation was wise enough to maintain its stake in the business before it took off or not is another matter! Of course, intrapreneurialism is no new invention. It is simply the name for a phenomenon which good firms have harnessed for a long time; the extraordinary competitive advantage conferred by highly motivated staff.

Most of what we have discussed may sound as if management have let go of the reins. Precisely the opposite is true. Senior management tend to scrutinize local performance to budget more closely then ever before. With active shareholders and bank analysts on their tails they have no choice. Developments in IT have enabled them to get the numbers faster and more accurately, without the bias of internal intermediaries. They can empower the management of an SBU because, if it begins to go off the rails, the numbers will show them what is happening fast. The leash has become longer but the tugs are all the harder and more timely if they stray too far.

Virtually all the structural changes we have discussed are instigated by senior management rather than by the HR department. Given that all the changes involve people, and not just abstract units or material assets, it should strike you as odd that the HR professionals are not usually the drivers of the action. The image of HR professionals as fusty guardians of the old order has had much to do with this. In fact, the structural changes taking place in many firms have simply raised the bar for the HR function. It is all very well chopping out middle management and giving the remaining people greater responsibility, but what if they are all left disillusioned or simply can't take the increased pace? This has been the almost universal problem facing firms who have been "re-engineered". The result is that, after an initial leap in productivity, competitiveness quickly erodes because of the discombobulation and anaemia of the workforce. And the HR group are left to clean up the blood. Firms that have put the people issues at the heart of their plans, and developed training, rewards and motivational tools, have fared much better out of restructuring. In these cases, a new breed of HR professionals have assumed board level positions alongside the financiers.

Down to Drivers

How do you evaluate a firm's HR structures and their impact on performance? The first thing to get a grip on is the dominant basis of organization. Does the firm comprise a series of departments or is it team based? How does this differ from competitors? If the dominant structure is still departmental, is there any evidence to suggest that it is slower to get product to market, slower to innovate and that its unit costs are higher? In the case of an advertising firm, for example, are there a large number of handovers between departments and does it take a long time for final copy to be produced? If a manufacturer of CD ROM games takes a long time to get new product concepts to market, this may be because of the transaction time between functional departments. Do you believe that the underlying structure of the firm you are examining will enable it to deliver against the key market characteristics you identified in your industry analysis? Will it lead to the retention and development of outstanding people?

One of the clearest guides to structure is the vertical hierarchy. How many layers are there in a typical SBU between the managing director and a line worker? What are the ratios between the number of managers and line workers or, in the case of service firms, customer-facing employees? Does this differ radically from the major competitors? What relation do you believe this might have to the level of turnover amongst line workers? Does this appear to be stifling the level of productivity achieved by the firm? If the depth of the hierarchy is significantly greater than that of immediate competitors it is likely not only to disadvantage their cost structure but also the level of motivation of staff lower down the business. Conversely, a company where the layers are excessively thin may have a difficult time coordinating its businesses successfully.

The second key to structure is where "accountability" is held in the organization. Accountability can obviously mean a wide number of things. The most important is some gauge of the bottom line such as the profit margin, ROI or ROCE or an equivalent financial measure. But the firm may also have in place a number of different measures such as customer retention or scrap rates depending on the piece of the value chain in question. A firm where bottom line accountability is held very high up will probably be a traditional vertical hierarchy. A firm where accountability is held at a desegregated level by people near the coal face will probably be a decentralized, empowered organization with a flatter hierarchy. A firm which has restructured itself around cross-functional teams will probably have shifted the basis of accountability away from geography alone to global business or service line units. Accountability drives the behaviours of individuals in an organization and unless a firm's basis of accountability alters any purported restructuring will quickly stall with it.

In general, it will be fairly well known which resource structures different firms are pursuing. It is probable that in the industry you are analysing there will be a limited number of experimental alternatives. If the firm in question is not taking an active hand in developing its structures at the vanguard of the industry, and has not placed the HR function firmly at the heart of these endeavours, then there is a good chance that it is in the process of being left behind.

Remuneration and Evaluation Policies

Cash is the great incentive of the late twentieth century. Whether we like it or not, we live in an intensely materialist age. The structure of compensation is a vital ingredient in making whatever resource structure a firm imposes, work. In most markets, skilled employees are able to switch employers with ease. Doing so is often the speediest route to promotion and pay rises. In industries such as advertising, at one extreme firms may accept a turnover rate of 30% as normal. In a manufacturing environment this may be much lower but nevertheless significant. One important way to keep good employees and to motivate them is to make them feel that they are fairly rewarded for their efforts.

The most powerful performance incentive is ownership. If you are in any doubt, just compare a set of rental apartments to a street of owner-occupied houses! Employee share ownership schemes or ESOPs have grown at a phenomenal pace over the past ten years. Amongst senior executives' bonuses, paid partly in shares or in options, have become the mainstay of compensation plans. Despite these developments, it is typically a small percentage of staff who have a meaningful equity stake in the businesses where they work. In the case of banks or consulting firms it is limited to the partners; in most industrial firms it is effectively limited to the Board.

In industries where ownership is only shared reluctantly, bonuses are often employed as a proxy to tie an individual's rewards to the economic outcome experienced by a firm. In investment banks, for example, bonuses usually exceed base salaries. Typically firms which pay out a higher percentage of total compensation in the form of variable bonuses will benefit from a greater level of commitment by the workforce to the effort of delivering outstanding customer results. Compare the hours a typical banker puts in compared to a those of a shoe salesman! In addition to providing a tangible reward for effort, bonus-related pay whether in the form of stock, options or cash also offers the firm a chance to control costs. The advantages for the employer are obvious; they only pay out when the performance of the company justifies it. If EPS and returns to shareholders begin to fall, they can limit the damage by controlling the wage bill without paying for redundancies. By turning what was a fixed cost item into a variable cost item the flexibility of the firm to respond to market conditions increases substantially. In the case of service businesses, where the largest item in the cost structure is wages, this can confer great competitive advantage. It should, therefore, be no surprise that most service companies and some manufacturing firms have seen a shift in their total wage bill away from fixed to variable costs.

In order to work, variable compensation systems require a robust evaluation methodology. In the past this was simple. Your manager evaluated you and submitted a recommendation to HR unseen by you. There may not even have been a meeting. This was the classic "command and control" type stuff. Clearly, if one of the reasons for variable compensation is to motivate people, this type of evaluation is counter productive. As a result, many firms are changing to a more collaborative approach to evaluation with an emphasis on building skills rather than criticizing mistakes. Its most extreme manifestation is the 360° evaluation procedure which involves you evaluating your boss as well as the other way around and you both discussing verdicts together before submitting them to the remuneration committee. This is a fairly common practice in environments where all employees make a direct client contribution, such as a management consulting firm for example. Whatever the system used, the basis for evaluation has to be felt to be objective by employees if it is to support a compensation scheme with a significant variable component.

For evaluation to work it also has to be based on meaningful criteria. It is tough to pin variable compensation plans to subjective criteria. Usually they have to be based on a measurable economic indicator. This is why historically it has only been managers with P&L (profit and loss) responsibility who have received significant bonuses as a percentage of base salary. Successful firms, however, are increasing the percentage of the employee base evaluated and rewarded on the basis of performance. Inevitably this means that they are experimenting with turning subjective concepts such as customer satisfaction and group cooperation into harder measures. In the case of customer satisfaction, for example, these measures might take the form of consumer ratings, number of returned items or customer complaints. Of course, as bottom-line accountability is pushed down the organization, the process of introducing wider bonus schemes is made all the more viable.

Down to Drivers

Usually the first indicator to look for is what percentage of employees have an equity interest in the company. If employees hold a significant position, it is likely to be in the form of an ESOP. What is the reserve per employee? Is this significant enough to be a motivating factor for most staff? It is most likely, however, that ownership will be confined to senior management. Do they hold a significant stake? Have they been accumulating shares or do they tend to sell them periodically? Unless they are prepared to hold major positions in the firm and invest their earnings in it, why should external investors do so? You should also estimate the proportion of variable compensation as opposed to fixed compensation in the cost structure. Whilst the absolute numbers may look respectable, you should check to see how variable pay as a percentage of base compensation for line workers compares to the same ratio for middle and senior management. If the firm you are examining loads variable rewards on the top end of the pyramid whereas a strong competitor distributes them more equitably, it is likely to lose many of the potential benefits of variable compensation.

The best indicator of distribution is the "remuneration ratio". A remuneration ratio will show the multiple different levels of seniority received in pay and benefits versus entry level employees. A ratio of ten between entry level employee and CEO might be normal for a Japanese firm. For an American firm this often stretches up to a factor of a hundred or more. If the company you are examining appears to have a set of ratios which are distorted versus the competition this is likely to influence its competitive position. Assuming that the base pay is reasonably in line with the industry, then the size and distribution of variable pay plans is likely to have a direct impact on staff turnover.

There has been a lot of flack about senior management compensation levels in the business press over the past few years. The reason is that, as employees have been "downsized", so corporate profits have enjoyed a sharp upturn and senior management have reaped the rewards in pay for performance. The transfer of wealth from the bottom to the top has therefore been unusually dramatic. As we have discussed, the windfall fruits of headcount reduction are not a lasting source of advantage. In order to achieve increases in returns to shareholders, most firms are having to embark on concerted growth efforts. The only way of delivering growth is if employees are pulling enthusiastically on their oars. This means, in turn, that the fruits of labour have to be equitably distributed. We should therefore anticipate a more balanced approach to variable compensation schemes among successful companies over the coming years.

The key issue with senior management is that their pay is highly geared to company performance. If the total percentage of remuneration paid in performance related bonuses to executive Board members is low, alarm bells should ring. How well does it appeared tied to genuine market performance or is it just another name for a guaranteed handout? How much of it is paid in stock or options as opposed to cash? If directors show a preparedness to accept stock and hold these stakes, this is a good sign that they are committed to enhancing shareholder value. A number of fund managers actually trade in and out of companies on the basis of the share dealings of their Boards of directors.

You should also make a judgment about the sophistication of the firm's performance measures. Has it introduced criteria by which to evaluate a significant percentage of employees? Are these criteria meaningful, both in the sense of reflecting the challenges facing the firm in the marketplace and in the sense of being objective? Do employees appear to be responding to them positively? How faithfully are rewards actually tied to these measures? One thing is for certain. Just as water will ultimately flow to the lowest point, so good employees will flow to the place where they are most appreciated. Unless evaluation processes and remuneration structures are effective, no organizational structure, however sophisticated, will deliver results.

Career Development

Closely related to the issue of compensation is the issue of career progression. This is simply a measure of the speed with which a good person will experience a titular promotion. Since titles tend to be similar for equivalent jobs across an industry, they enable an employee to become a tradable asset. Everyone familiar with the US banking industry, for example, knows roughly what a VP does. The result is that most employees can judge with reasonable accuracy whether they are moving as fast as their peers elsewhere.

Promotion is very much dependent on the structure of the hierarchy of a firm. For a consulting firm with a very flat pyramid, rapid promotion may be possible until you get below partner level when there is a bottleneck. This will foster a system of maximizing the leverage of partners and will create a shake-out at a senior level. Another firm may have a very steep pyramid which will mean slow movement up the ladder but room for a larger pool of senior executives who have shown long-term commitment to the firm. The tendency, as we have discussed, is to move to flatter structures. This means that there is room for quick reward of relatively new employees but a slim chance of making it to the very top. Such structures will tend to foster an up or out system, attract competitive individuals and place a premium on performance.

You will already have a sense of the depth of the hierarchy of the firm in question. You should also estimate the average length of time between layers for good employees. The depth of the hierarchy and the speed of promotion will be related. However, which model best fits a firm's competitive situation is a case by case issue. If, for example, one firm of software manufacturers has five layers and promotes typically every two years and its rival has three layers and promotes every four years, which is better suited to the competitive environment? The answer should be reflected in the employee churn and application rate numbers.

Training

Firms used to train, now they don't! This may be something of a generalization but it is not far from the truth. The average US firm spends under 1% of revenue on staff training. Why? Because the cost hits the bottom line immediately but the benefits don't for two or three years. That's too long for most senior managers. Since most firms are more service oriented than production oriented, investment in training is analogous to investment in capital equipment. This makes this low investment number all the more appalling.

Training has two benefits. Firstly, it improves skills at a time where employee skills are the key differentiating factor for most companies. Secondly, it is a personal benefit to employees and, at the early stages, potentially as motivating as cash. In the US, people still go to P&G for the best training in brand management, to JP Morgan for the blue chip entrée to investment banking and to J. Walter Thompson as the university of advertising. Firms have ditched training in part because of disillusionment with increasing employee churn and because they often feel they can buy the skills outside more efficiently than they can create them inside. This is a difficult argument to refute when in most industries the tenure for new graduate trainees is three years and firms that train tend to be seen as legitimate hunting grounds for talent by others.

Despite the incidence of employee churn, the impact of training on long-term competitive performance is clear. The five year moving-average spend on training as a percentage of sales by a firm will probably correlate to staff productivity and the rate of market innovation it achieves. Good firms will target their spend carefully. Typically it will be distributed through the hierarchy rather than concentrated excessively at entry levels where churn is likely to be highest. The massive growth in mid-career executive training programmes suggests that most firms have recognized this fact.

The importance of training is increasing dramatically with the change in organizational structures and work patterns. If a research scientist in a pharmaceutical firm has worked for 30 years in a secluded laboratory and is suddenly required to work as a team member with representatives from marketing and manufacturing, he will need new skills fast. In general, the process of de-layering and empowerment is forcing employees to master a broader set of skills and, most notably, to acquire the basics of financial management. Unless firms are prepared to reinvest the savings garnered from restructuring projects in developing these skills, the evidence is that the new cost advantage will be short lived.

Down to Drivers

The simple way to find out whether a firm is committed to training is to calculate its average spend per employee versus major competitors. If it is possible to find out the distribution of spend across the value chain, that will be a good indicator of whether it is targeting the spend where most competitive advantage is to be won.

Internal Communications

At the end of the day, when a CEO wants to deliver a strategy the asset she has to get moving in the right direction is employees. Employees are not like factories or warehouses; they have to be coaxed, wooed and won over. Internal communications is one of the critical tools in the CEO's armoury to make this happen. It is also one of those areas like public relations: a black hole into which executives dubiously pour money one year, then, disillusioned, strip it back the next. Historically, it has taken the form of low grade employee leaflets, brochures, videos, newsletters or "team briefing"[17] systems. The dominant direction of communications has been top down. The philosophy driving it has tended to be control and command. Although there has been a steady growth in the use of employee surveys to elicit the mood and opinions of the workforce, such tools have not until recently begun to fashion the nature of internal communications substantively.

However, over the past five years, the role of employee communications has been changing dramatically. As a result of the

[17] Team briefing is a cascade communications system involving groups of employees meeting to discuss pre-set issues.

erosion of the middle management function, senior managers have found themselves with no-one in the middle to communicate with employees. This is happening at a time when groups of employees within SBUs have been given increasing autonomy to determine their tactical response to local market conditions. The result has been a growing imperative for senior management to master internal communications or find themselves at the helm of a firm drifting away from the corporate strategy. This situation has become particularly acute in the wake of widespread re-engineering, restructuring and downsizing efforts. All of these changes require employee support to put them in place. Without legions of middle managers to communicate the messages clearly, employees have in most cases remained deeply suspicious of change. The result has been great difficulty getting new structures and processes implemented. It is widely acknowledged that about 80% of re-engineering efforts have failed and they have done so principally because of lack of employee commitment. Usually this means that the reasons for change have not been properly communicated. It also probably means that the communication has been one way.

Not surprisingly, there has been a surge in spending in the area of employee communications as senior executives have come to realize its importance to their success. The format has been upgraded to more sophisticated forms of delivery such as corporate TV and PC-based Notes systems As yet, however, it tends to lack the sophistication of external communications and there is no established mechanism for measuring its effectiveness. Employee satisfaction surveys are notoriously misleading for obvious reasons. It is also hard to control. Employees develop views on their employer based on a wide range of sources, including media intended for customers such as commercials. It spans a wide range of activities which fall into different budget areas, from training through to corporate PR. Unless there is a senior champion in the company, it usually proves tough to communicate a consistent message.

In general, management currently tend not to view employees as a set of customers and internal communications usually reflect this. How many boring memos have you received from the CEO about some abstract issue which is half buried in double-talk? Over the coming years this will change amongst successful firms as they recognize that engaging employees is equally as important as captivating customers and that many of the same communications skills are transferable between the two audiences.

The clarion call of this change is all the talk of corporate values, culture and identity. The wiser firms have realized that simply telling employees about the intentions of the company, even if phrased nicely, does not condition behaviour. Instead, they have focused on communicating a set of values which embody the ideas behind the corporate strategy in a more motivating form. The usual expression of this is in the corporate logo, the design of its literature and presentational material as well as the nature of the work environment itself. It might even take the form of certain types of language and norms governing the structure of memos. The idea behind values and culture is that they can act as a binding force, uniting the firm behind shared goals, even if those goals are not explicitly stated. The British Airways identity, for example, is a symbol which reflects the values of the corporation to its employees of solidity and reliability. The Virgin identity, by contrast, embodies a set of values relating to accessibility, youthfulness and service. These indirect metaphors are usually a more powerful form of communication than words on a page. Interestingly, they are usually equally as relevant to consumers as they are to employees and therefore bind the two audiences together.

Down to Drivers

As a starting point you should try to find out how much the firm in question spends on internal communications as a percentage of sales. Since the budgets for different pieces of the pie are often under separate control, this can be a tough number to pin down. It also gives no sense of its impact. The most informative way to sense its effectiveness is to interview a small number of line workers and test how well informed they are about the strategy of the company and how committed they feel to delivering it. You should also try to get a sense of whether they can articulate the values of the firm and describe its culture. The better their understanding of the firm and the greater the interest in it, the better will be the internal communications process. The way a firm's internal communications will improve over time is if there is a robust system for management to get feedback from the front line. Communications is about two way, not one way. Is that how it works in the firm you are examining?

Work Environment

No one likes working in a hell-hole. The quality of the work setting can be a major emotional benefit to employees. Indeed, if wages are at competitive levels, then the quality of office space can be a crucial differentiating factor which will allow firms to attract and retain the best. This is known as "corner-office syndrome". In addition, the way space is used can have a significant impact on the efficiency of work flows and the transfer of information and ideas around the company. The sophistication with which a firm configures its work space is therefore a serious driver of competitiveness.

For most service businesses lease and upkeep costs are number two in the cost structure after salaries. This has focused minds on one key number, square metres per employee. Firms have pursued various strategies to lower this ratio, particularly in situations where they have been unable to relocate to cheaper locations because of lease restrictions or because it would represent a loss of competitive advantage. The most common strategy has been breaking down individual office walls to create open plan areas. Typically shifting from individual offices to open plan will reduce the space ratio by around 40% if there are no structural limitations such as fixed walls or pillars. The second common tactic is moving away from dedicated desks. In most service or non-manufacturing operations only about 25% of space is occupied by employees at any one moment. As a result the shift to "hot-desking" or "hotelling", as it is euphemistically called, offers the opportunity – in theory – to reduce space usage by a further chunk. Finally, firms are increasingly encouraging home working in some industries, facilitated by the growth in computer networks and video conferencing.

The usual objection put forward is that cost and productivity of staff in a space are, to some extent, a trade off. As square footage per person falls so does the quality of the environment. As it happens, the movement to open plan offices has facilitated team working and therefore supported a structural shift in the organization of resource which increases productivity. Similarly, hot-desking supports a strategy which aims to get as many people as possible on the road and client facing. Ideally it should be possible, therefore, to lower total real estate costs per employee and to witness a sustainable rise in underlying productivity.

Cost is driven by location as well as metres per person. Most industries have a preferred location. For example, the US investment banking business is clustered around Wall Street. For an investment bank to be located in suburban Connecticut would constitute a major loss of advantage when it came to hiring and retaining employees. The location trade-off could appear to be a simple one; cost per square metre. You can't get a great location unless you pay for it. However, the trade-off is usually not so straightforward. Location does not necessarily correlate with the quality of the work environment. A reduction in unit rental costs can permit both enlarged space per employee and higher spends on upgrading the internal environment. This is the sugared pill offered by many firms who relocate out of town. The question is, does this outweigh the location advantage?

Down to Drivers

The most important thing about the design and location of a space is that it should support the resource and organizational structure best suited to achieving competitive advantage in the business. If, for example, an advertising firm moves to cross-functional teams to reduce the cycle time necessary to provide an ad, this is unlikely to work properly if the interior is made up of individual offices. People will still tend to work alone and to locate themselves on floors of functional departments. Similarly, if the most important informal network that exists in a sports shoe manufacturer is between marketing and R&D, it probably is not the best configuration of real estate if they operate out of buildings at the opposite ends of town.

In analysing the firm in question you should exercise some subjective judgment. Interiors are organic and it is relatively easy to judge a motivating design from a poor design. Chiat Day in Venice, California, looks very different from a Midwest accounting firm. But which suits the internal needs of employees? In comparing the interior of the firm you are analysing and that of a competitor, ask yourself which would most appeal to you as a client and as an employee? Then find out how much it is costing. Most firms are under increasing pressure to cut real estate costs. Unless they can optimize the performance of the space whilst reducing unit costs it is likely that at some point they will be tempted to go for the cheap option. The cheap option can erode competitiveness with amazing speed, particularly in the case of a service organization.

Caveats (Just in case it sounds like we're saying everyone should just love each other. . . .)

We have advocated the benefits of commitment by employees with unqualified enthusiasm. There are, of course, two sides to any contract. What about when a firm wants to get rid of employees that are redundant or non-performing? In many markets and in many industries this can be a major issue. Labour rigidity has the same effect as high exit barriers; it leads to a downward spiral of competitive standards just as surely as a bad HR strategy.

Labour Rigidity

In terms of comparing two firms competing in a single country, the source of any labour rigidity is likely to be the level of unionization of one workforce versus another. If one firm has to engage frequently in collective bargaining and its nearest rival doesn't then the former will be at a competitive disadvantage. This will prevent it from adjusting its cost structure during market changes. More importantly, it will prevent it from imposing a competitive internal market that will encourage the best and dispense with the weak. If, for example, a firm wishes to introduce a wage system with a large percentage of pay contingent on company performance, the unionized firm is likely to have this blocked whereas the un-unionized firm will not encounter organized resistance. Unions were created in the mid-nineteenth century for a reason: to prevent abuse of power by management. Unscrupulous managers can cut swathes out of costs by reducing headcount or freezing salaries. In the immediate term this may hike share values but it will quickly lead to an erosion of value if employee motivation is dampened. A confrontational approach to staff management is, in many cases, tantamount to bad management. Consequently, firms suffering regular union problems often are firms which have been mismanaged and require fundamental restructuring due to years of inefficiency. Unionization is a symptom as much as a cause.

Assuming you have no desire to bury yourself in tomes of local employment law, the best way to compare two firms in terms of labour flexibility is simply to compare the level of unionization between the two firms. Then check for the number of recorded instances of collective bargaining over the past five years. As long as there is no major difference between the two firms, structural labour rigidity will not be an issue.

Comparative Labour Rates

More significant in a globalizing economy is the differential advantage enjoyed by firms competing in a market but from different home manufacturing bases. One may have easy access to raw materials in its home market, the other may have to import them; one may be subjected to a heavy tax regime whilst the other isn't; one may be located near a university supplying outstanding talent whilst the other has to compete for foreign graduates. Each factor will confer a competitive advantage on the more fortunate firms. However, assuming that both firms have managed to get around these obstacles, the most critical difference between economies is the cost of labour. Whilst most material inputs are internationally traded and price differentials between markets compress, labour tends not to be so mobile and therefore cost differences can be dramatic. An average automobile assembly-line worker in Korea, for example, will be paid one-fifth the amount of his counterpart in a US plant and one-eighth the amount of his counterpart in Germany.

The opening up of trade zones such as the EU, ASEAN, AN-DEAN and NAFTA will liberalize the flow of labour and slowly erode wage differentials. But major cost variations will persist for the foreseeable future. In part, they will be driven by differences in national labour laws. For example, a Korean steel manufacturer with no unionization can respond to a fall in market prices by cutting the workforce. A German steel manufacturer does not have the same liberty because of local labour law which imposes a heavy cost on lay-offs. Similarly, the Korean manufacturer will not have a minimum wage imposed by the government and its rates will reflect the low national average. The German manufacturer, by contrast, will have to maintain a minimum wage in line with EU law which will far exceed that of its foreign rival. This will dramatically alter its cost base and the strategy it can pursue.

Because of large differences in national wage rates, low value-added manufacturing continues to migrate to low wage countries. This will tend, over time, to limit the cost advantage one firm will enjoy over another by virtue of unit labour costs since everyone can site manufacturing in low wage countries. The important point, however, is that low cost labour tends to be a fleeting source of competitiveness. Efficient firms will redress a labour cost imbalance by automating all aspects of their activity to ever-increasing degrees and substituting capital for manpower. Alternatively, they will build advantage on the basis of employee quality rather than cost and move into higher value added or more differentiated categories. Cost advantages built on strong productivity increases or on specialized business focus will be more enduring than bleeding the labour pool till it drops. That means worrying about improving skills rather than driving down average wage levels. This lesson is lost on many firms and governments in the pursuit of short-term profit. Does the firm you are examining appear to be shirking the long-term issues by pushing down wage rates?

Pulling it All Together

HR suffers the misfortune of being associated with crumpled grey suits and dingy back offices. It is also seen as an area which does not deliver quantifiable returns. Of course, it is always the intangible areas which deliver most competitive value because they cannot be easily replicated. The impact of HR strategy on the performance of the firm is undeniable, which makes it all the more odd that HR should have been relegated to a non-strategic role in most organizations. This is in the early stages of changing as firms become dependent on smaller groups of ever more highly skilled individuals to maintain their competitive position. The level of loyalty of good staff to their employers has diminished and employers are having to be as sophisticated in their dealings with employees as they have become in their dealings with customers.

The most effective HR strategies will ensure close alignment between all the HR levers and between the HR levers and the business objectives of the firm. It is no use a firm investing in training, for example, if staff turnover is high because of a poorly conceived career development strategy. Equally, it is no use restructuring resources around cross-departmental teams if the people running the teams have no idea how to manage a complex process. Engaging in training may, on a grander scale, be inappropriate if the firm in question is facing a margin crisis which will require it to shift to a lower wage environment. It is when HR does not specifically deliver against the corporate strategy of the firm that it loses any credibility and gets bundled with back office functions.

Figure 7.37 summarizes the key value drivers for the HR function of a typical firm's value chain.

INFORMATION TECHNOLOGY STRATEGY: "THE BACKBONE"

If cash is the blood, data is the grey matter of the corporate brain. Without it no company can function. Over the past 20 years data has made the leap from being a building block of basic company functions to being one of the primary sources of competitive advantage. What has carried it to the top is the rapid development in information technology. IT is the backbone that has facilitated most of the changes taking place in corporations we have discussed.

Even up to ten years ago, IT was still viewed by many firms as a back office concern focusing primarily on automating basic, low value-added accounting systems such as payroll, accounts receivables and general ledger. In this capacity IT has substituted human labour and made the process of assembling financial reporting information more speedy, more accurate and cheaper. Simultaneously, it began to make a ubiquitous appearance in the

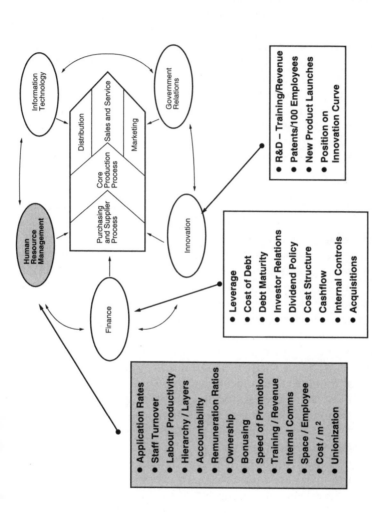

Figure 7.37   Value drivers summary

front office; most people have had a PC on their desks for some time and the role of secretarial and other overhead functions has already been substituted by computing power. More recently, IT has been transformed into a far more potent tool. It has been the fundamental driver of changes in the underlying business processes on which companies are built. This is the realm of re-engineering. We have already explored how an insurance firm which previously required five people to process a claims form, with a throughput time of a week, might now conduct the same transaction in six hours with a single operator using networked PCs and customized software. That constitutes a steep change in performance levels. It also constitutes a major boost to the market value of a company's stock. It is the thing which makes it happen.

IT has gone through a number of stages of metamorphosis over the past 30 years. It all started off with the use of mainframes which acted as central processing hubs. These were bulky and expensive and tended to be restricted to the processing of large computational tasks such as sorting customer information. Then processing power was bundled into smaller boxes and dropped on the desk in the familiar form of the PC. These tended to operate in stand-alone environments, with a connection to printers via local area networks or LANs. More recently, IT has begun the process of evolving into a fully networked configuration with servers acting as network processing hubs (see Figure 7.38). Shared data resides in a central location on large databases but can be accessed and processed through individual PCs. These PCs can also actively communicate with each other. There are a number of communicational databases such as Lotus Notes which are capable of supporting these proprietary networked environments. There is also the growing use of Internet technology in the form of Intranets to support closed company networks. In most large firms one form or other of these networks is being deployed through their operations worldwide. It is the networking of data around companies which is driving many of the structural changes taking place in firms.

Communicational Role of IT

The role of IT in reshaping underlying business processes can be divided into a communicational role and an operational role,

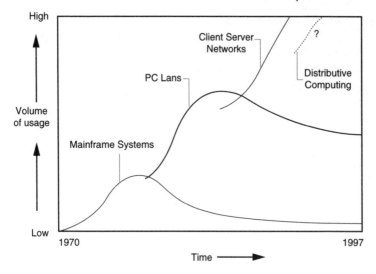

Figure 7.38 *Illustrative simplified evolution of IT in the workplace (1970–1997)*

although the two are intimately interrelated. The communications applications of IT are the most familiar to everyone since they are becoming a part of everyday work life. The most basic application is, of course, e-mail (if you haven't got an e-mail address on your business card, get one or risk extinction!). However, the same networked PCs can be used increasingly for data share, image share and even teleconferencing with real time, high quality video direct to the desktop. Most systems are capable of supporting databases which are either of limited or general company access. The result is that information can flow around the organization much more freely and at higher speeds. For the average employee it means quick access to shared knowledge and intellectual resources from every corner of the firm. In the case of a management consultancy, for example, it means that all presentations and research about a particular industry can be centrally stored and made available to consultants working on cases in that industry from their PCs. For an advertising agency it means that all work from a particular multinational client can be accessed by local servicing offices anywhere in the world, avoiding the need to reinvent advertising concepts. For the marketing firm it means that experiences of consumer reactions to NPD work in one country are immediately available to executives in another. This opens the doors to a new dimension of competitive advantage: "knowledge share".

In many firms the greatest asset at their disposal is their collective knowledge of the marketplace in which they compete; in terms of the evolving nature of customer demand, the shifting basis of competition and the competencies "owned" by the firm which can be deployed against these moving targets. The motor of innovation for many firms often will be limited to a dozen brains on a dozen shoulders wandering somewhere around their global operations. The progress of the firm will probably be nothing more than the collective learning of a limited group of highly dispersed people. Unless their knowledge is shared and institutionalized through a material medium it can either walk through the door or fail to convert into commercial advantage. Assuming that most competitors can achieve similar scale, have mastered similar process technologies, possess equally strong brands and offer not dissimilar incentives to employees, often the most significant source of differentiation will be the speed and efficiency with which a firm can gather and deploy its collective knowledge. The birth of the concept of the "knowledge worker" is an acknowledgment that the people who are likely to succeed in organizations are those who can sift and make use of the collective learning available through the firm's IT networks.

The interesting thing about knowledge and learning is that it possesses economies of scale. The larger the organization that uses a set of ideas or learnings, the greater will be the benefit. A single concept generated in some far flung reach of a corporate empire can, in theory, be leveraged across an infinite number of applications as long as it is communicated. If broadly adopted, this would virtually eliminate the cost of research by depreciating the investment across a wide set of outputs. In the case of an advertising firm servicing a global client, for example, a creative idea generated, tried and tested successfully in one market might be accessible to every local market manager across an Intranet. This would mean a significant lowering of risk in the new copy development process for the agency and potentially lower costs for the client. Through such knowledge networks, companies have the opportunity to ensure that all parts of the organization attain the level of best internal practice across the entire value chain. This can happen quite independently of any central mandate as long as information is flowing rapidly and freely around the organization.

Knowledge share is a horizontal process which cuts across the fixed boundaries of a corporation. Traditionally, knowledge has tended to be "hoarded" either departmentally or, in the worst cases, by individuals. The traditional role of middle management was justified as long as those people could lay claim to information not privy to others either above them or below them in the hierarchy. Slowly, IT networks are beginning to do away with all that. A spirited fmcg brand manager in the UK, for example, might now draw upon the expertise of an NPD team in Australia who report to an entirely different management group. Similarly, two research teams in different parts of a pharmaceutical firm might decide to collaborate on a joint project by exchanging research details electronically. Perhaps more importantly, an ordinary employee in one corner of a company can connect directly with another in an entirely different division. They might trade information about good job openings in their respective divisions or exchange gossip about the likely outcome of merger talks they have overheard in corridors. Management can either make a commitment to harnessing these knowledge networks productively or they can put up sea-walls. Few walls can keep back a sea for long!

As well as facilitating knowledge flows across a company, IT networks also fundamentally change the nature of the flow of information to senior management. The IT backbones in most companies enable the rapid gathering of information from the periphery for use by the centre. Whereas in a paper-based environment, the collection of monthly performance data by SBU might have taken months in itself, this can now be done in real time. This means that, even in a large corporation, top management can react swiftly to address any developments at a very local level. In the case of a consumer goods company, for example, salesmen might input stock and orders data into a hand-held computer every time they visit a retail outlet. In a networked company this data could, in theory, be aggregated daily on an international basis to give management a breakdown of movement in orders and WIP across all SBUs and markets.

The important advantage this brings to a firm is performance clarity. In a networked company senior management should be able to see the red cells pumping around the corporate system. This will tend to make them more comfortable with delegating full business authority to SBUs. The paradox of the control implied by IT is that it is those same systems which allow empowerment to happen! It is also the dynamite which has blasted out the middle-management blockage.

Just as data can flow up it can also flow down. Networked PC environments provide the CEO with an invaluable internal communications tool through which to build employee commitment to the corporate strategy. The trouble with the historical system of memos was that it only allowed for one-way communication, it tended to be sporadic rather than regular and relied on middle management as a filtration and distribution force. A joke changes with each telling and the same was true of senior management communications. With PC-based communications there is no intermediary other than a wire and server. It also allows for real time feedback. The result is that in a networked company, senior management can literally plug straight into the front line and understand how their corporate strategy is translating into reality and, if not, why not. The analogy is very much the boss walking the factory floor. But now they can – in theory – do this every few days, globally, and provoke a more honest dialogue.

Finally, networks also allow firms to extend their community to include the external constituencies of clients and suppliers. As we will come to, this offers tremendous opportunities to reinvent the value chain. In pure communication terms, it means that clients and suppliers can be closely consulted. Instead of a firm navel-gazing, it now has every opportunity to ensure that it is intimately plugged into its marketplace. This might mean that consumers are solicited for on-line feedback or it might mean that they are kept regularly updated about product developments. A ski fanatic, for example, might visit Rossignol's web site to investigate equipment planned for the following season. In general, the closer a firm can keep its finger on the pulse of the market the better it will be able to pre-empt the process of change. Networked PCs are the nerve system that will support that effort.

Operational Role of IT

However, the most significant value to the new IT networks is operational rather than purely communicational. The first key impact is that they are facilitating greater integration of the firm's internal value chain. IT networks mean that teams can practicably be composed of people who are not physically situated near each other and who may reside in distinct functional areas of the company. If, for example, an fmcg firm is proposing to launch a new toothpaste, it is viable for a team to be assembled comprising a product designer in Switzerland, a manufacturing designer in Thailand and a marketer in the UK. Most of the re-engineering efforts that have taken place have involved the breaking down of old departmental structures and the re-grouping of people into cross-functional teams. IT enables such teams to form even if the department framework is still the fundamental basis of physical organization. Work can be done in "virtual" space rather than physical space. The result of electronic proximity is that decisions can be made faster and better. The cost of internal transactions is also lowered. If ten meetings are necessary instead of 50, if the project is completed in five months instead of ten, if the product is fully designed for manufacturability before it gets to the production line; if all these things happen then costs will fall away and client expectations will be exceeded.

The second key advantage of networked IT systems is that they facilitate integration of the external value chain by linking the firm with both suppliers and customers. In the case of the toothpaste launch, for example, it would be viable to have a group of freelance designers working off site but communicating regularly with the internal team about concept development. This would reduce fixed costs. Similarly, an automotive manufacturer would be able to reduce its inventory of dashboard lights from a major supplier by providing real time, detailed information about work in progress and stock levels on a daily basis. Networked IT links are increasingly central to Just-In-Time manufacturing systems by linking the manufacturing cycles of the buyer and the supplier. The result is lowered inventory costs and probably better utilization of machinery. In the case of a supermarket, electronic point of sale (EPOS) data collected at the cash register can be used to generate electronic orders to distributors who can then restock shelves. This cuts out the need for laborious stocktaking and order placement. Again, resource is freed up for more value-adding activity such as customer service.

The most extreme form of the networking of external value chains is the "virtual company". The virtual company is an assembly of firms, joined together for the express purpose of delivering a product of service which neither would be able to produce on their own. Each participating firm would tend to contribute an area of competence that the rest do not possess. One might have an outstanding marketing capability whilst another has invested heavily in the R&D, and a third may have spare manufacturing capacity. The relationship would tend to resemble a partnership of collaborators rather than a supplier-buyer arrangement. The vital glue binding them together would be a free flow of complementary ideas and knowledge. The number of virtual companies springing into being has grown significantly over the past five years. Usually they are structured as alliances to crack a particular product or service opportunity. As soon as the product expires or is superseded, the arrangement is often disbanded. The "firm" is virtual in the sense that all the activities take place in the participating companies; the "firm" itself might have a name and executives with business cards, but may exist only as a conceptual space where ideas are shared and where a consumer impression is forged. This might sound futuristic, but the future is never far away!

A lot of re-engineering has an excessively internal focus. IT can also suffer from an inward orientation. Much of the benefit IT offers is in linking the firm more closely with the outside world of its customers. Since the spends on networks are so large, unless they can deliver customer value they would not be justified on productivity grounds alone. The cost gains associated with increased productivity will lower prices for customers. However, the most concrete form of potential customer benefit from IT networks is the degree of responsiveness or customization in a product or service. The efficiency with which usage patterns and evolving tastes can be captured greatly improves the ability of firms to condition and target their offer. The speed of collection of client orders and the transmission of this information to production greatly enhances the ability of a firm to respond to needs on a timely basis. An increasingly common example of this is the process of ordering food in a restaurant. The techno-savvy waiter can use a hand-held computer to take your order which, at the same time, sends this direct to the kitchen whilst preparing the bill. This means that firms have more time to be attentive to customer needs whilst potentially lowering overall staff costs.

It also allows firms to ensure that they are producing what consumers actually want; in the case of the restaurant, swift service, freshly cooked food and an accurate bill. In the case of a supermarket, the use of EPOS data will allow the store to judge much more accurately what exactly customers want to find on the shelves from week to week and season to season. In the case of an fmcg company, information about consumption patterns will drive their communications and promotions strategies. The closer the electronic tie between the point of purchase and the company, the more consistently it will be able to exceed customer expectations and achieve "mass customization".

Networking still has a long road to run in most companies before it realizes its full potential. Once wide-area networks such as Intranets are able to support real time image transfer at proper speeds, at acceptable cost and securely, the value chains of many businesses will alter fundamentally. In general, the number of layers between the "manufacturer" of a product or service and the end customer will tend to diminish in exactly the same way the layers inside companies between management and line workers have thinned. The mail order business, for example, which has mushroomed over the past 20 years will probably in time be dwarfed by the growth of the on-line order business. Many retailers are gearing up their web sites to permit customer transactions over the PC. Firms such as Peapod in San Francisco, for example, have already captured a significant share of the local retail market through the internet. A number of manufacturers have also seen the possibility to bypass the retailers and sell direct to consumers, capturing a larger margin and mitigating the corrosive power of own label. In the future, we might expect a wide array of firms, from the auto manufacturers to music publishers, to switch to on-line selling without intermediaries other than a digital satellite.

Down to Drivers

So, assuming you haven't got an electronics degree and that you are not a computer buff, how do you evaluate a firm's IT strategy? Looking at absolute spending levels on IT as a percentage of revenue will only give you a sense of the firm's commitment to it. What you are more interested in is how effectively IT is being deployed to increase productivity and the level of market responsiveness.

Firstly, you should ask what advantage the company has taken of the communicational aspects of IT. Does the firm have a Notes-based or Intranet communications network in place? What percentage of employees are linked to a network from desktop PCs? What type of shared database resources does it have available to these people? Does the firm still appear to conduct most of its internal transactions using paper and fax? Is there still a comparatively high ratio of secretarial staff compared to professional staff? If the firm in question has an efficient internal network and encourages knowledge share, then it will probably be the case that best internal practice is spread rapidly and operating standards are uniformly high. It will probably also mean that it is getting innovative products or services to market faster. In the case of an advertising agency, for example, is there evidence of rapid spread of advertising copy concepts across international markets? In the case of an fmcg player, is there evidence of rapid deployment of great new brand concepts across markets?

The second question you should ask yourself is: Has the firm taken hold of opportunities to tie together its internal value chain? Has there been a progressive increase in the speed of product innovation? Has there been a steady increase in productivity which is not attributable to a simple headcount reduction? What stories has the press carried about the working practices of the firm and what are you hearing from employees? If there has been a change of organizational structure which appears to have delivered results it is likely that the IT side has been competently implemented.

The third question you should ask is: Has the firm seized opportunities to tie together its external value chain? On the supply side, what are the levels of inventory in both inputs and finished goods? Are there any indications that it has successfully implemented a JIT system in its manufacturing group in alliance with key suppliers? On the customer side, does the firm you are examining appear to have a good understanding of its customers by virtue of its data collection capability? Is there any evidence that it has used IT to increase its speed of responsiveness to order taking? Does it appear to be running an effective database driven marketing programme? Is it spoken about in the press as being "customer focused"? Figure 7.39 summarizes the key value drivers for the IT function of a typical firm's value chain.

Pulling it All Together

If a firm is taking IT seriously it will usually have a chief information officer or CIO. Ideally this person would report directly to the Board. If it is not viewing it as a core competence, a firm will tend to have outsourced many of its IT functions to an independent supplier. Usually the rationale behind outsourcing will be that costs can be lowered by subcontracting out this activity. For many companies this is a mistake. The operational and communicational implications of IT networks are far too important for firms not to treat them as core competencies and central to their corporate strategies. Knowledge alone may be one of the most valuable assets of the successful firm of the twenty-first century. Without an intimate understanding of how to gather it, process it and deploy it, that advantage will be surrendered. Increasingly the good firms will put a stake in the ground by not only having a world class CIO but also by having knowledge managers to keep the knowledge ball rolling.

LOBBYING POSITION WITH GOVERNMENT: "THE PULL"

In an international marketplace it will not always be the case that a firm's principal competition will be based in the same country. This means that the issue of the role of the state can be vital in conditioning the competitive advantage of one firm versus another. With the tremendous growth in international trade, there

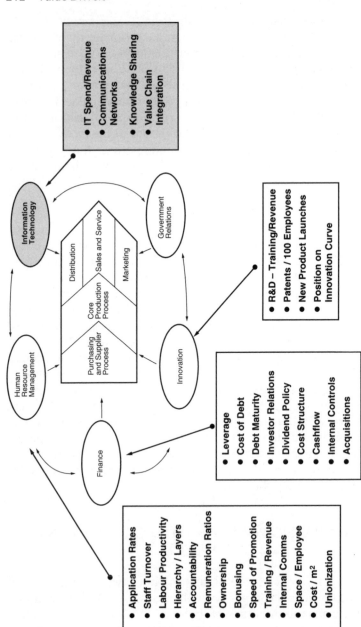

Figure 7.39   Value drivers summary

is a lot of energy being put into levelling the international playing field and removing government-induced distortions. Nevertheless, government policy can still play its part in shaping the advantages enjoyed by favoured firms.

Your previous analysis of market conditions may have brought to light some competitive distortions that affect the company you are analysing. For example, a steel exporter from Spain may have been the recipient of a loan guarantee from the European Bank for Reconstruction and Development (EBRD). This will substantially lower its cost of borrowing and place it at a financing advantage relative to a US exporter to Europe. Similarly, an exporter of electronics from Japan may have a quasi-public bank as a majority shareholder and its cost of capital will have been lowered. Equally common are restrictive market policies. If a firm is protected in its home market it will be able to achieve healthy cash flows to subsidize its entry into foreign markets. This may not be sustainable but, temporarily at least, this asymmetry will place it at a competitive advantage.

In the advanced economies of the West and some of the developed economies such as Japan, there has been a major thrust towards market liberalization over the past decade. This has meant that governments have opened their markets to foreign competition. The idea behind it is simple; firms are more likely to reach world class standards in a competitive environment than in a regulated one and consumers benefit at the same time. If you are examining a company that competes primarily in a western market the issue is, therefore, less likely to be about the impact of relative government distortions and more about the impact of deregulation. If, for example, the firm currently enjoys a monopoly of supply of a basic utility what are the odds on the government passing legislation to open it up to new competition? If currently it enjoys an unusual tax holiday, is there a likelihood that this loophole will be closed? How able do you believe the firm will be to cope in a deregulated competitive environment?

The other main focus of government legislation is to protect consumer interest. If, for example, you are looking at a supplier of paper to the tobbacco industry, how likely is it that legislation against its major customers will stiffen? Does this mean that the firm should make provisions in its financial reports for the effect of potential lawsuits against its customers which will dampen their consumption of paper and which, in turn, will drive down the firm's own share price? If you are looking at a pharmaceutical firm that has invested heavily in a new drug formulation which is proving controversial, what is the probability that it will get government approval? Whatever industry you are examining there may be some glaring risks on the horizon concerning changes in regulation and the value of the stock should be discounted to reflect this risk.

Because public policy is continually changing (governments tend to have far less consistent economic strategies than firms!) it is a competitive advantage for a firm to be a competent lobbier of government. If it can lobby successfully it is more likely to be able to ride any changes in legislation that may come along. It will also be able to fight for a level playing field against foreign competitors who may be enjoying favourable government policies in their home markets. Because of its strategic importance, many firms invest substantial sums in maintaining lobbyists on their payroll under the guise of the PR budget. They may also have non-executive directors who have been either politicians or who are plugged into the political world. They may even donate to a political party, although this carries risks.

Down to Drivers

There are two simple questions you should ask. Firstly, is the firm potentially exposed to adverse government regulation in its core markets? This might be because it is a monopolist or because prices have been unusually high for an extended period of time. Or it might be because a lot of its business comes from areas which are subject to changing government policy. An obvious example might be a supplier of warships to the defence industry. The second question you should ask is, what evidence exists of the company's level of competence in lobbying with government? Does it appear to have close ties with the dominant political interest groups? Has it successfully fended off adverse legislation in the past? Has it successfully deflected consumer actions in the courts? Unless there is the possibility of a major sea change of political party, a good track record will probably be an indicator of future success (see Figure 7.40).

Pulling it All Together

As economies and firms continue to globalize, the impact of public policy on companies will shift with it. For the growing number of truly multinational companies the impact of government policy is receding as a driver of competitive advantage. The major multinationals will typically divide their operations into four regions: Asia; Latin America; North America; and Europe, the Middle East and Africa. Within each region they might operate in a dozen or more countries on a significant scale. The impact of the regulatory environment of any one country will therefore have a diluted effect on their overall business. Often their more senior employees will feel as much loyalty to the identity of the firm as to their own home market. Senior management will perpetually be balancing the risk profile of their portfolio by moving manufacturing into low wage environments and shifting resources from low growth to higher growth markets. The CEOs of such firms will probably be the only people in the world to take an entirely global view of economic opportunity, in a way that not even the President of the USA can. As these type of firms continue to grow and gain market share, their annual revenues are already beginning to outstrip the GDP of the smaller countries. Governments are always keen for such firms to establish manufacturing capacity in their country, and offer opulent subsidies to induce them to do so. Since these firms can easily play one market off against another, their bargaining position is often stronger than that of the governments with whom they negotiate. If you are analysing a multinational firm or a company which is moving in that direction, you can be sure that the issue of government policy will diminish as their revenue base grows more geographically diverse. The future dominant political unit will not be the country but the multinational company!

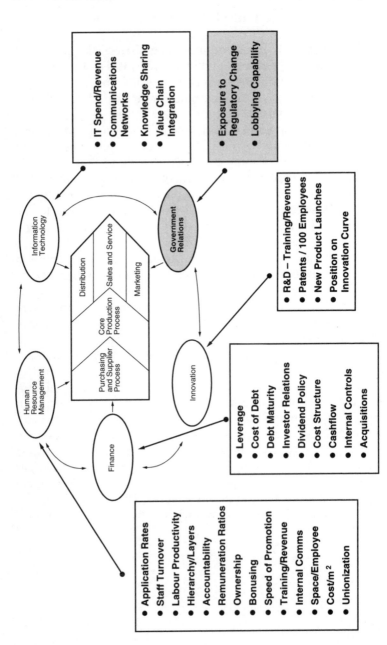

Figure 7.40   Value drivers summary

8
Core Competencies Revisited

"Do we have it where it matters?"

By now you should have a more thorough understanding of the relative strengths and weaknesses of each piece of the value chain of the firm you are examining and how they contribute to value creation. Of course, no firm governs itself on the basis of a set of independent strategies for each part of the value chain. Each piece has to be unified towards delivering the overall business strategy of the company. If the marketing director of an eye wear manufacturer, for example, is hell bent on competing against Emporio Armani in terms of premium positioning in the retail environment, whilst the head of manufacturing is focusing single mindedly on reducing unit costs, there is likely to be a problem. The quality won't hit the mark and the positioning will be an absurd illusion given the manufacturing capabilities of the firm. Similarly, if the key purchase criteria for the major customer of an industrial furniture supplier is speed, then it may be inappropriate for a firm to be focusing on perfecting its customer service capabilities and intensive quality control procedures.

In evaluating the overall competencies of a firm, there are three key questions to ask:

- Does the firm have strength in those parts of the value chain that matter?
- Are these activities well aligned with market requirements?
- Are they well coordinated to drive value creation?

Most firms will need to hit basic operating standards in each area of the value chain as a threshold to compete. However, not each piece will be as important to delivering the company's strategy. In the case of the branded eye-wear firm, for example, it is likely that the manufacture of rims can be subcontracted out to a number of suppliers. What cannot be subcontracted out is the marketing function which is where most value will be created. In the case of a paper manufacturer, in contrast, the scale of the manufacturing operation and the level of capacity utilization is likely to be far more important than the sophistication of its marketing activities. This brings us back to the concept of ''core competencies'' which is where we started. Most firms have finite resources. In order to excel they need to focus these resources on those activities which will add most customer value. Just as we drew up a hierarchy of customer values earlier, this has its counterpart in terms of the competencies of the value chain (see Figure 8.1). Do you believe that the firm you are examining has achieved world class standards in the key areas of the value chain which represent core competencies for the sector?

The problem with core competencies is that we tend to form an impression that they are based on accepted industry norms. In the insurance industry, for example, claims processing efficiency might be one standard performance benchmark. In the computer

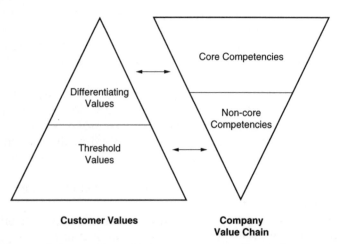

Figure 8.1   *Illustrative relationship between customer values and core competencies in a generic firm*

chip market unit price might be the traditional indicator of customer value. The problem with established norms, however, is that the best performers tend to be continually breaking these norms. An innovator such as the Virgin Group in the UK, for example, might reinvent the insurance game and introduce hip branding as a primary consumer benefit. Similarly, a firm such as Intel might shift the nature of competition in the market for chips from price to customer loyalty by deploying a powerful branding idea. Such innovators lead markets and do not follow them. In so doing, they tend to shift the areas of the value chain in which competitors have to forge their competencies.

What does this mean for us as we evaluate a company? It means that we should keep a weather eye on the firm's ability to innovate and stay ahead of the game. We discussed earlier how innovation does not occur simply in the R&D department but at all points in the value chain. You have made a judgment about whether the firm has strength in those areas which the market values at the present time. Does it also appear to be actively exploring methods of shifting the game? Innovation across the value chain is most likely to happen when the pieces are working closely together. A member of the marketing team, for example, might spot a customer need which she knows R&D looked at some time ago but stuck on the top shelf. A plant manager might identify a simple change to design that could be easily accommodated and communicate this to sales to see if customers would value it. The result might be a shift in emphasis about where customer value is built. This brings us to coordination.

Coordination of the value chain is as important as excelling in each part of it. It is no good putting out a powerful marketing message to consumers if manufacturing cannot deliver the promised quality. It is no point promising end users lower prices if supplier costs are going up. As we have already discussed, the traditional organization of firms into functional silos has hampered the coordination of the value chain. Manufacturing tends to be going one way and marketing another. There is often a high degree of disregard or even animosity between professionals in different groups. We have already mentioned that one way firms are trying to change this is by moving to cross functional teams and enhancing the networking capabilities of the firm. In essence, these are attempts to tie together the value chain behind shared goals.

Measuring the degree of coordination across the functional silos of the value chain is difficult to do. "Coordination" is usually based on informal working contacts between people rather than reflected in organization charts, although some firms may have instituted formal team structures. It is also a function of the intangibles of the cohesiveness of corporate culture and whether the firm has inculcated a shared set of values. However, on the basis of your analysis, it should be possible to ascertain the degree to which the pieces of the value chain are focused on a shared set of business goals. This brings you back to the starting point: the tightness of the fit between customer needs and the firm's capabilities.

Down to Drivers

During the course of your analysis you have:

- Made a thumbnail sketch of the corporate strategy of the firm;
- segmented the business into discrete operating units or SBUs;
- analysed the market context within which each SBU operates;
- evaluated the underlying value chain of the firm and its ability to support the competitive requirements for success in each SBU.

Figure 8.2 visually summarizes our journey through the value creation process. Your segmentation of the business will have clarified the nature of customer demand and the core skills necessary to meet that demand in each SBU. Your analysis of the market will have provided a gauge of the key drivers of industry profitability and the competitive standards a firm needs to meet to achieve advantage. Your analysis of the value chain should have identified how each function potentially drives value, and have established whether the company has the necessary capabilities to meet the competitive demands placed on it by the market. On the basis of this information you should be able to judge how well each of a firm's SBUs are positioned to drive shareholder value.

Whilst the model implies a balance between a firm's capabilities and the demands of the market, it is a firm's capabilities that will allow it to succeed, either by meeting existing customer needs more effectively than competitors or by creating a new set of customer needs. Some firms will evaluate a market, declare that it looks like a nightmare and sell the business. This is appropriate if the firm can do something more productive with the money it releases or if that business activity was not one in which it could realistically gain competitive advantage given its skill base. Another firm surveying the same nightmarish market environment might decide that this constitutes a great opportunity. By focusing its activities well it might introduce a new twist to the customer proposition and outmanoeuvre the incumbent players. The point is that the competitive nature of a market does not mean anything alone. It only means something in the context of what a firm can bring to the party.

It may be the case, of course, that an individual SBU, or even an entire company, is being managed well enough but the market itself is poor. For example, there could be a temporary period of excessive price pressure because a losing firm is unable to exit, because of an aggressive new entrant or due to structural over-capacity in the industry. In this case the firm will simply have to ride out the storm with potentially depressed profitability. However, it is usually the case that a world class firm can make money in any market, however competitive. If margins are being pushed down they might try to shift the basis of competition by introducing a product innovation or by merging with a competitor to reap manufacturing scale economies. Whilst earnings might go through a temporary dip, you would expect such a firm to recover its profitability within a discrete period of time.

As a manager this means that you should first make sure you understand a firm's capabilities before deciding whether the markets in which it is competing are attractive or not. If a market is easy but a firm has an imperfect set of competencies to serve it, you can bet that new entrants will soon raise the bar. Conversely, if a market is tough but the firm has strong competencies, that is more likely to drive sustainable returns for shareholders.

Pulling it All Together

Now you have worked out how well a firm's SBUs are positioned to create value. Is that the holy grail? Can you lie back and sigh with satisfaction? The answer is, of course, no! As we discussed earlier, it is unusual for a firm to be so focused that it is effectively one big SBU. What our analysis does not answer is whether the corporation is managing the correct mix of SBUs and whether it is managing them optimally as a portfolio. This boils down to whether it is extracting incremental value from them, above and beyond what they would achieve if they were free standing businesses in their own right. This brings us back to the "glue" of corporate strategy. Corporate strategy should lay out a clear mechanism for the firm to extract incremental value from its SBUs, or else the corporate structure serves no use for shareholders.

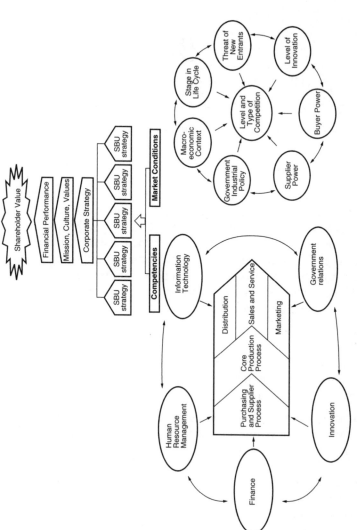

Figure 8.2 *Value drivers roadmap*

9
Back to Corporate Strategy

"Does it hang together?"

As we discussed at the beginning of our odyssey, corporate strategy is a logic governing the combination of SBUs under the umbrella of a single firm. Having got this far, you should be in a good position to ask whether such a logic exists in the firm in question. Is the union of the SBUs under a single roof driving shareholder value? Could the cash be better invested elsewhere?

The question of whether a firm has a good corporate strategy can be broken into two sections:

1 Does there appear to be a logic uniting the various SBUs in the portfolio?
2 Does the firm in question have a structure and set of management processes which are likely to enable it to maximize value from those holdings?

We have explored the first question in terms of portfolio strategy as well as vertical and horizontal integration. As we concluded, the more substantive the points of commonality across the value chains of the SBUs, the more likely it is that the firm should be able to add value through its holdings. The firm will develop expertise in those common areas, focus its resources and outclass the competition. It is more likely that SBUs will share common value chain characteristics if their market positioning is similar. If most of their products or services are geared to the mass market, low costs will be critical. If most are targeted at premium niches their ability to differentiate their products will be vital. These two generic strategies will place quite different stresses and strains on the value chains of SBUs. If most of the SBUs are either having to sustain premium pricing or keep costs to the bone (rather than a mixture of both) it is likely that a corporation will be able to leverage ownership of multiple SBUs by building unique areas of competence.

However, just because a set of SBUs appears to be clustered does not mean that a firm has a compelling corporate strategy. It only means that there is clear potential for it to have one. In order to extract value from clustered holdings, a firm needs to have a structure and a set of management processes which allow it to do so.

CORPORATE STRUCTURES

Different firms take very different approaches to organizing their SBUs. At one extreme the management system can be highly centralized. This would mean that the head of an SBU might report through a regional or sector head into the Board. They would probably be monitored on a monthly basis and their discretion over capital expenditure and diversification would be limited. The centre might also maintain personal contact with the largest customers to limit autonomy. No investment decision would be allowed without it passing over the CEO's desk. Firms which are centralized will tend to have homogeneous cultures; managers of SBUs will gravitate to a norm, HR policies across the group will be highly synchronized and many operating systems will be shared. Basic functions such as back office, purchasing and treasury might be centralized. Systems, structures and business processes will be uniform and the centre will be highly interventionist. Value will be added to the component parts by ensuring operational integration. For example, in the case of a professional service firm such as Arthur Andersen, a client might be handed seamlessly from the auditing group in the UK to the consulting group in Venezuela without any particular change in operating style. In the case of an fmcg firm, such as Procter & Gamble, core brands may be run on a global basis, reaping scale economies across the entire value chain.

At the opposite extreme, some firms employ a federalist structure. Here SBUs would be allowed to operate with relative autonomy. The management processes and systems might differ quite widely. The HR policy in one SBU may emphasize quite different qualities in recruits. Divisional management, if it exists, will tend not to intervene directly in local operational decisions, unless budgets are shot. The centre will be left with the task of ensuring that the portfolio of SBUs is balanced. It will probably focus its energies on financial control and on managing the overall corporate balance sheet. It would almost certainly appoint the CEOs to staff those units. Value will be created through stern financial target setting and the efficiency of the overall capital structure. This type of structure would typify a decentralized organization such as Unilever or Nestlé, for example.

The decentralized and centralized models tend to be associated with different operating realities. Centralized management structures will suit situations where products or services are being delivered on a multinational basis in a reasonably uniform fashion. An example would be an international brand of shampoo such as Elida Gibbs' "Organics" which employs similar advertising copy globally. Product formulation might be done centrally by a single R&D team and manufacturing might be centralized into a single location for each region. For the service firms (such as advertising agencies) supporting the product, services would probably be delivered seamlessly on a global basis by a dedicated team of professionals. Many large firms are choosing to impose their corporate brands over those of the sub-brands of their SBUs and advertising under a single brand to reap economies of scale and enhance impact. This is driving centralization into even the historically local areas of the value chain such as marketing communications.

Federalist structures, by contrast, tend to be associated with firms whose products and services are fundamentally local. They tend to be firms which have grown through acquisition of large numbers of smaller local companies. If a corporation has a portfolio of SBUs marketing food brands which are highly culturally distinct, the benefits of coordination may be low. Fruit salad in Uruguay will pose quite distinct, different challenges from spaghetti in Milan. Back-room functions such as tax and treasury, which do not affect the consumer directly, may be the only areas that the company can effectively centralize.

Both centralized and federalist firms will tend to organize

themselves along both product and geographical lines. Typically, groups of similar products will be clustered into divisions and each division will have a director in charge. Unilever, for example, has classically broken itself into foods, detergents and personal products such as shampoo. At the same time, most firms will also organize themselves by geographical region. All the operating activities that occur within the UK, France, Germany and Italy, for example, might be clustered beneath a European management structure. The difference between federalist and centralized structures will be the degree of power that these divisional heads will exert over the business and the number of functions they manage on a coordinated basis.

Product-based organizational forms and geographically-based organizational forms obviously overlap. A manager selling toothpaste in Italy will have a boss dealing with a personal care division globally and a regional boss dealing with Europe as a geography. Where these reporting lines cross, firms have coined the concept of the "matrix" structure (see Figure 9.1). The logic of the matrix is to allow firms to capture both the benefits of local market attention and the benefits of specialization in product areas of scale. A pharmaceutical firm, for example, with a new antidepressant might centralize manufacturing in one site per region to depreciate R&D costs and reap economies of scale in production. Local brand managers, however, might adopt highly localized marketing opportunities that would be irrelevant globally; the Indian advertising copy would be fundamentally different from that for the Australian market. Whilst firms such as ABB have made a real go of matrix management, the reality is that it is tough to do. Wanting to be global and local sounds good in theory but it puts tremendous strains on an organization in practice. You may have had personal experience of reporting into two bosses, one running a region and one a product line. The schizophrenia this induces can lead to poor outcomes.

Down to Drivers

You will now have a good sense of the effectiveness the pieces of the value chain in the firm you are examining in meeting the demands of the market. What has been the impact of organizational structure on ensuring that SBUs are positioned to build on

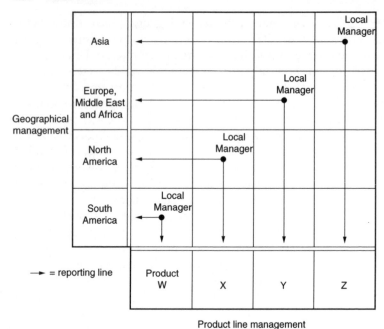

Figure 9.1   *Illustrative generic matrix structured organization*

this? Have inappropriate levels of centralization robbed SBUs of local market responsiveness? The use of a common salesforce in a diversified insurance firm, for example, may be leading to consumer confusion when the salesman tries not only to sell life insurance to a housewife but also house insurance, when these are fundamentally different products. Or has the firm failed to fully exploit the scale economies available through the centralization of shared functions? A set of SBUs selling soap powder, for example, may not be able to achieve the share of voice (SOV) necessary to compete without the strength of an umbrella brand. The ability of the company to centralize effectively will clearly depend on the nature of the SBUs under its charge.

ROLE OF MANAGEMENT

At the end of the day, whatever the theoretical benefits of a structure, any organization will be as weak as the management whose job it is to make it work. The only people who can formulate the corporate strategy of a firm are its executive Board directors since they are the only people with a purview of the entire business. The impact of senior management on the performance of a firm is decisive. This is why shareholders are prepared to pay them such extraordinarily large sums of money. It is also why, if performance flags, they are amongst the first to go (although often they will take lots of heads out first). Although it is something of a black art, you cannot therefore afford to ignore the leadership issue.

The conundrum of how to judge senior management has been flogged to death by the academics. They have tried to determine what makes a good CEO by measuring their average height, their average IQ, their family history, their sexual appetites. You name it, they've tried it and yet have failed to come up with any workable generalization. There is a lot of talk about visions, missions and other types of quasi-religious rites that CEOs are supposed to perform. But, at the end of the day, what they have to do is deliver a corporate strategy which drives shareholder value.

As with all employees, a major driver of the performance of senior management is the vested interest they have in the firm. You only have to look at the difference in performance of most MBOs, prior to purchase by management and after, to corroborate the relationship between ownership and results. You can easily identify the size of the management team shareholding by looking at the annual report. You might also be able to determine how closely bonuses have been tied to company performance through stock and option grants. If management's holding is high and bonuses are paid out in stock, clearly there will be a much stronger commitment to upholding performance. The opposite situation might be one where there has been a regular reshuffle of senior management and the management stake in the firm is low. Typically this might occur in a situation where a highly active shareholder has pressed for tactical measures to boost stock price in the short term, such as downsizing.

Down to Drivers

It is always illuminating to rootle out as much as you can about the history of key managers in the business. Searches in the press about previous roles and results may give you a flavour of what to expect. Some CEOs may be known as ruthless cost cutters, others as long-term value drivers. The acid test of prior performance is how well the companies under their charge have performed in periods of slow or negative growth. High growth situations are often panaceas for poor practices lurking beneath the surface which do not get exposed until the tide recedes. The history of a manager's behaviour is likely to be a reasonable guide to their future performance. If the company you are examining is stuck with a dud, then it is unlikely that its future performance will be stunning.

Of course, most of the world class firms in existence today have outlived a dozen CEOs. The IBMs, the DuPonts, the Mitsubishis of the world have survived and thrived under many different guiding hands. This observation leads to the idea that there is something about such firms which is more enduring than a corporate strategy concocted by an individual CEO at a given point in time. The name given to this phenomenon is "corporate culture". Corporate culture is a set of values which conditions the employees who work in a firm and which guides the decision making of senior management. It is sometimes called "the smell of the place" or "the way things are done". Its tangible manifestation is the visual identity of the firm but its power is its ability to influence behaviour. It is often the case in such firms that senior managers are promoted through the ranks rather than recruited from outside. As a result they don't get their hands on the wheel until they live and breath those corporate values.

That said, in most firms the corporate culture is not static but changing. It tends to evolve with the changing corporate strategy of the firm. It can also be altered by a powerful, charismatic CEO. Since markets are continually shifting, successful firms have to continually adapt. Smart CEOs harness the power of culture and corporate values to drive continual change through the organization. If employees can be made to believe in a course of action and adopt it as their own, the likelihood of them supporting it becomes far higher. Firms such as IBM and General Electric both had strong corporate cultures in the mid 80s, but they were inappropriate for the changing market conditions in which those firms found themselves. New CEOs such as Jack Welsh and Lou Gerstner have since redirected those corporate values behind more appropriate goals and the cultures of these organizations have subsequently shifted. Whilst a firm may have a culture which is larger than one person, the onus of ensuring it is conducive to building competitive advantage falls squarely on the shoulders of the CEO. All ships, however large, can be turned (see Figure 9.2).

PULLING IT ALL TOGETHER

Nothing good in life is free and CEOs cannot implement their strategies free of charge. Any corporation incurs costs to control the assets in its portfolio. This goes by the name of "corporate overhead". Overhead can often be estimated approximately if it is possible to identify how many people are employed by a corporation. Assuming that the corporate cost structure is just people, property and expenses, you can build the total overhead charge by adding the reported pay of the Board, top salary for the rest, the firm's average property cost per employee and about 100% of salary as expenses. If this number as a percentage of revenue appears large compared with competitors then the corporate strategy will have to deliver a commensurately higher level of profit to maintain shareholder value. If the accumulation of corporate overhead has occurred faster than the growth in corporate profits and share price, then you know there will probably be a problem.

So how do you determine whether the corporate strategy, the organizational structures put in place to deliver it and the overhead costs associated with managing it are creating value for shareholders? The answer is straightforward. If the value of the pieces or SBUs exceeds the market capitalization of the company then there is something wrong. Most corporate raids occur in situations where corporate functions only represent a cost and not a benefit and can be eliminated. The assets can then be spun off and value created by giving them their independence as stand-alone firms. The calculation of whether the whole is worth more than the sum of the parts is not straightforward. We will discuss this in the next chapter.

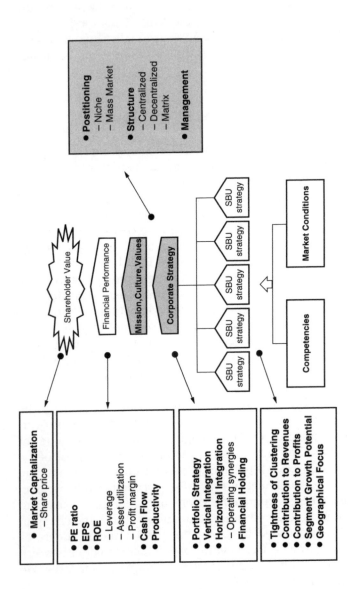

Figure 9.2   Value drivers road map

10
Back to the Bottom Line

"Let's talk cash"

At the end of the day, when all is said and done, all anyone is interested in is money. Or to be more precise, cash (as distinct from that accounting based term, profits). It is on the basis of a firm's ability to deliver cash that it is valued. The quoted value of the shares of a company on Wall Street, LSX or the Paris Bourse is a function of the anticipated cash flows that will be thrown out by a business. Or to be more exact it is a function of the sum of cash that the firm is anticipated to throw out from now to eternity, discounted by the cost of the capital employed in the business.

What you want to know is, could the firm generate more cash? If so, what has to happen to make this a reality and push up the stock price? This is the calculation that bank analysts will be making about the companies they follow all the time. It is also the calculation that corporate raiders will be making when they peruse the companies they might take over. Management should, of course, be preempting them all by making decisions to optimize long-term cash flow based on their superior understanding of the value drivers of the business. All of these people should ostensibly go through the same analysis of drivers as we have in the course of this book. The trick is then to state this analysis in terms of cash flow. In reality, management often don't do this or they do so incompletely. That is why they are forced to take surgical action from time to time (such as downsizing) to get back on track!

CALCULATING FUTURE CASH FLOWS

How do we look at the firm as a stream of cash? We have already gone through the process of calculating the cash flow for a SBU in a single year (Figure 5.2). Ideally you should also project this cash flow out for five to ten years. Estimating future cash flows, of course, assumes a good understanding of how market conditions and business performance are likely to alter. On the basis of your evaluation of the market you should be able to make an informed judgment about how revenues and profits are likely to behave over the coming years if the firm remains on its current course. If, for example, you expect a new firm to enter the market with discounted prices, you should adjust the revenue line to reflect anticipated lower unit prices. If, by contrast, you anticipate that a loss-making company will exit the sector then you might raise unit prices and therefore revenues as well as margins. If you anticipate a consolidation amongst suppliers, then prices of inbound goods are likely to rise. If distributors are suffering the adverse effects of increases in fuel prices, the difference will probably come out of the manufacturer's margin. If a major innovation is about to come off patent it is likely that prices will fall sharply and market share will be eroded by generic competitors. Jointly such anticipated changes in market conditions will have a decisive impact on driving a firm's future cash flows.

Profits and revenues are not the only numbers that will be affected by changing market conditions. The company's rate of capital investment may have to alter to meet new competitive demands. If a competitor is fundamentally more productive because of greater production line automation, the firm may have to invest aggressively to redress the balance. This will increase the size of its depreciation number and its capital investment charge. Alternatively, it may be forced to alter its consumption of working capital by changing conditions in the buyer and supplier chain. Pressurized by suppliers to shorten payables and by buyers to stretch receivables, a firm may find itself with an increased working capital requirement above what might otherwise be projected. In addition to these items, a firm will have discretion over altering its capital structure to meet competitive demands. This might, for example, involve a reduction in debt and an increase in equity through a call on the equity markets. This will influence the amount of interest it has to pay and the size of debt on its balance sheet.

In translating your observations about the drivers of value creation into their impact on the firm's financial statements, you will be able to account for the impact of these drivers on its future cash flows. You should be able to do this for each SBU independently (see Figure 10.1).

Future Key Financial Variables*	Impact of Changes in Level of Market Competition	Impact of Possible Actions in Key Areas of the Value Chain										Overall Net Impact
		Purchase and supply process	Core production process	Distribution	Sales and service	Marketing	IT	Government relations	Innovation	Finance	HR management	
Revenue	↓					↑		↑				→
Direct costs	↑	↓		↓								→
Overhead	↑											↑
Interest	→											→
Profit after tax	↓	↑		↑		↑		↑				↓
Depreciation	→						↑					↑
Net working capital	↑	↓		↓								→
Capital expenditure	→						↑					↑
Cashflow	↓	↑		↑		↑	↓	↑				→
Debt	→											→
NPV	↓	↑		↑		↑	↓	↑				→

↑ Increase ↓ Decrease → No Impact

* As a base starting point all projections assume straight line revenue growth and stable financial ratios.

Figure 10.1 *Summary impact of market and value chain changes on future financial variables of an SBU or firm*

VALUING CASH FLOWS

All these cash flows have to be funded by capital, both debt and equity. Capital has a cost. The cost is a blend of the interest cost of the debt and the expected return associated with the equity for shareholders given the riskiness of the investment. There are a number of ways to calculate this number, but these are somewhat complex and beyond the scope of this book.[1] For our purposes, assuming that the company is based in one of the major western economies, you might take an average cost of capital of 15% as a standard benchmark. (In reality this number will differ firm by firm depending on the underlying riskiness of the sector in which they are competing and the capital structure of the firm itself.) Whilst most corporations will have a single balance sheet rather than a capital structure for each SBU, the cost of capital for each SBU will in fact vary because of the differing risk profiles of the business. The likelihood of a start-up venture in fashion clothing folding will be much higher than the likelihood of an established menswear operation going belly-up. Ideally, therefore, each SBU should be attributed with a different cost of capital. For our purposes, however, we will assume a uniform rate across all SBUs. This number can then be used to discount the cash flows back to their present value as illustrated in Table 10.1. (The last year has to be treated as a "perpetuity" by dividing it by the discount rate before discounting it back to its present value.) The number that pops out of this calculation will be the Present Value of the SBU. Subtracting from this number the long-term debt attributable to the SBU, you will have the Net Present Value of these cash flows or what they are worth to shareholders.[2]

---

[1] The most common method of calculating the cost of capital is called the Weighted Average Cost of Capital or WACC. However, there are a number of alternative methods which avoid complications concerning the capital structure of the firm which are raised by use of the WACC. For a detailed explanation of various alternatives you should refer to "Valuation: Measuring and Managing the Value of Companies" by Tom Copeland and Tim Koller (see Bibliography).

[2] Many SBUs won't have debt directly secured against them. The best way to attribute them with notional debt is to apportion them a share of the corporation's overall debt based on their contribution to corporate revenues.

Table 10.1 *Illustrative calculation of NPV for a fictional SBU or firm (£m)*

Year	0	1	2	3	4	5
Cash flow	100	110	120	130	140	150
Discount rate	1	1.15^1	1.15^2	1.15^3	1.15^4	1.15^5
Discount factor	0	1.15	1.32	1.52	1.75	2.01
Perpetuity*					$((150 \times 1.05)/0.15)/1.15^5$	
Present value	100	95.7	90.9	85.5	80	597
Debt	200					
NPV	849					

* Assuming 5% growth rate into the future.

Down to Drivers

Once you have done this for all the SBUs in the firm, and added them together, you will have the value of the entire enterprise to shareholders. You should try to compare this to a similar valuation for the entire company, including the cost of corporate overhead. This calculation simply involves repeating the same exercise, but for the entire firm based on its reported P&L and balance sheet statement.[3] If this number differs substantially from the collective valuation of its SBUs, the red flags should go up. If, for example, the aggregate value of the SBUs appears to exceed that of the overall corporation by a substantial amount then it is likely that the corporate strategy is not adding value to the enterprise in excess of the costs of corporate overhead (see Figure 10.2).

The acid test is to compare your NPV calculation of the company's SBUs to the valuation of that firm's stock on the open market or its market capitalization. This can be obtained by multiplying the total outstanding shares by their current stock price. If there is a major difference then you will know roughly speaking whether the corporation is perceived by the markets to be adding or detracting value from its holdings. If it is taking value away then something is badly wrong. This can be corroborated by comparing the earnings multiple (market value divided by after tax earnings) and the revenue multiple (market value divided by sales) of the firm against its closest quoted rivals. If

[3] This is not an easy process since it requires making assumptions about the firm's aggregate changes in revenue, profit and other elements of cash flow.

Value Drivers

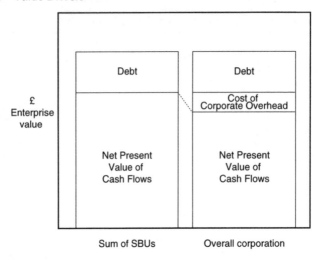

Figure 10.2 *Illustrative comparison of the valuation of an underperforming fictional corporation versus the sum of its SBUs*

the company you are examining is underperforming, these ratios will typically be depressed, reflecting the pessimism of the markets about prospects for future performance (see Figure 10.3).

Of course, it is easy to criticize and much harder to remedy. On the basis of your analysis of the value chain you should have identified areas where you consider the company could improve. This may involve cutting costs or investing to build sales volume. It could also extend to the softer areas of employee morale. If motivation was increased, would productivity also be boosted? You should cast your mind back along the value chain and decide whether the firm has hit world class standards where it matters. Where do you believe it could make some quick kills? If you build these adjustments to value drivers into your cash flow projections (Figure 10.1) then you will be able to calculate a new value for the equity which will reflect these improvements. You might, for example, estimate that were it to alter its basic organizational structure by forming teams, the firm could probably halve the cycle time for producing a product. This would mean it could either increase its revenues substantially or reduce its costs which would immediately boost cash flow. Similarly, if you believe an SBU could be sold and the cash deployed more pro-

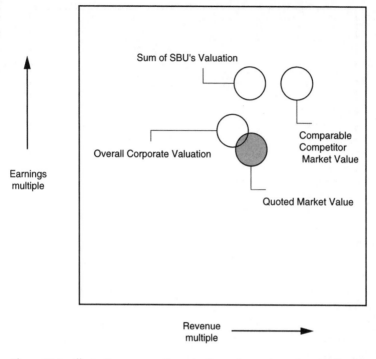

Earnings
multiple

Revenue
multiple

Figure 10.3 *Illustrative comparative valuations of an underperforming firm based on market indicators*

ductively elsewhere in the company, you should build this into your projections. Alternatively, you might surmise that the firm could halve corporate overhead because it is adding little to the efficiency of the SBUs. If collectively these improvements to SBUs produce a total corporate valuation far in excess of its current market valuation then there may be grounds to antici-pate a management change (see Figure 10.4). It is unusual for the markets to fail to identify or to tolerate such a "value gap" for long and not do something about it.

PULLING IT ALL TOGETHER

Do not get depressed if this all sounds daunting. Cash flow valuation analysis is a highly complex art. That is why the

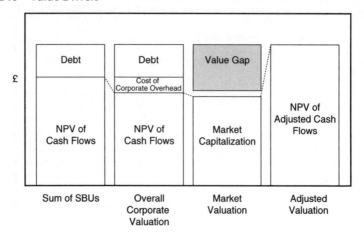

Figure 10.4   *Illustrative effect of revaluation based on adjusted cash flows for an underperforming firm*

investment bankers are able to charge their exorbitant fees for advice during acquisitions. It is also one reason why analysts' opinions can have such a dramatic effect on share price. In this book we have glossed over valuation in a superficial manner and you should not hope to master it on the basis of a little light reading. What it has aimed to do, however, is to give you an understanding of how a company's strategy and the competitive position of its SBUs drive that cash flow value number. And make no mistake, long-term cash flow is the only number that matters! (see Figure 10.5)

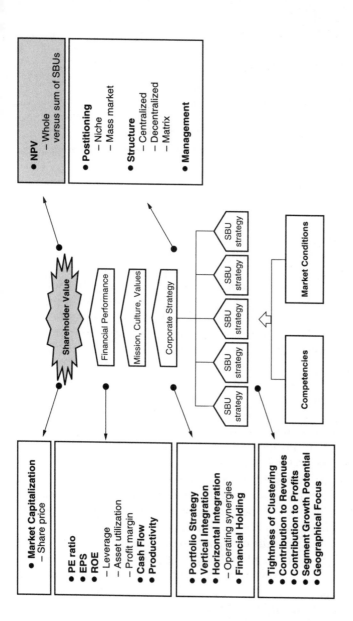

Figure 10.5 Value drivers roadmap

11
Conclusion

"What's in it for me?"

Most large modern corporations are highly complex entities, operating across a wide range of business areas and a wide range of geographies. The competitive and market influences they are subject to tend to be subtle and hard to unravel. The internal structures they adopt are typically complex to match, usually involving a matrix of product lines and quasi-independent business units. The majority of managers in a large company will probably not be aware of the precise logic binding the pieces together.

It should not be surprising, therefore, that many firms unwittingly succumb to the Leverhulme conundrum, by failing to clarify which activities drive value and which drive cost. As long as the equation nets out sufficiently in favour of value, lots of skeletons may go ignored. Whilst the growth in international competition and the increasing power of the capital markets have conspired to put the spotlight on this issue, many major companies still have a lot of potential value left on the table. As a manager this presents both a challenge and an opportunity. The issue as a manager is how to turn it into an opportunity.

Most managers still occupy functionally specific roles. This might be as specialized as designing point of sales promotion campaigns, orchestrating the accounting department, running an inbound logistics system or managing a business unit. What distinguishes Board level directors from the average manager is that they have to discern where overall value is being added and where it is being detracted and take action accordingly. Making the leap from the functionally specific to the general business perspective is a big one. That is why so few people manage to do it. It is in the interests of most firms that their managers and employees assume this responsibility in their daily activities but in reality it rarely happens. Despite an increasing need for strategic thinkers at all levels of the organization, the obstacles for managers have – ironically – increased faster in many cases.

The impact of most of the trends we have discussed has been to facilitate the dismantling of the traditional hierarchy. This has meant that many of the middle management roles which would have served as the traditional training ground for people coming up from functional roles have disappeared. What many firms are left with are two groups: a large group of doers and a disproportionately small group of thinkers/controllers. Since top management are often drafted in rather than home grown, this further reduces the potential for people to grow into senior roles as a matter of natural progression.

Meanwhile, management consultancies continue to fill the void left by middle management, acting as props to senior management decision making in much the same way as middle management would have done historically. The consulting industry continues to achieve consistent growth rates over 20% per annum. Of course, this comes at a high cost to clients. It is probable that as the business cycle moves back from the cost cutting of the mid-90s to an imperative for growth, firms will re-hire middle management to put growth strategies in place. However, these will probably not be the same people as before. They will look much more like the consultants in terms of their structured approach to understanding the drivers of value creation.

Over the next decade, the cruel reality of the employment market is that it will increasingly divide into those employees who understand how shareholder value is driven and those who can't tell whether they are contributing to creating it or not. This will correspond to an ever-widening disparity of career opportunities and wages. Making sure you land the right side of the line is up to you. The best lever you can use is to demonstrate a strategic understanding of the firm's drivers of value creation, how they can be strengthened and what you can do to help that happen. Hopefully, working through the simple framework laid out in this book is a useful step in that direction.

Appendix 1: Benchmarking

"Only looking in the mirror makes a firm vain"

Firms do not exist in isolation. In order to understand a firm it is necessary to understand the competition with equal clarity. If the firm in question is achieving a 15% return on equity, it does not mean a thing if the other ten competitors are achieving a 25% return. All the way through we have been assuming a comparative perspective. In consulting lingo this is called "benchmarking". Benchmarking has become a huge area of consulting activity, fanned by the birth of the concept of "best practice". Subjected to continual scrutiny by the markets, most firms are becoming more alive to the need to emulate best practice players rather than viewing themselves in a vacuum. Benchmarking has also grown as a consulting area because it is difficult for an insider to gain an accurate sense of how competitors are performing and, more interestingly, why they are doing so.

The key for benchmarking firms is to ensure that you are comparing apples with apples, both in terms of the companies you have chosen and the numbers you use. Ideally, the competitors should have a similar range of businesses competing in similar segments and be of a reasonably comparable size and geographical spread. This is, of course, rarely the case. The precise mix of SBUs will tend to differ along with the strategic focus of the overall business. By conducting your analysis at the SBU level you will be able to get more accurate benchmark information. Once you aggregate these SBUs and compare one whole company to another, the basis of comparison will almost certainly be blurred. If you were benchmarking Rolls Royce against Ford, for example, it would make more sense to benchmark it against Ford's luxury car units such as Jaguar than against the entire company. No consumer in their right mind will be weighing up a Ford against a Rolls Royce! Comparing GM and Ford might be more legitimate but, again, the two companies do not necessarily compete for the mind of the consumer. The consumer will be thinking about utility trucks or luxury sedans. Although the company's overall brands will play their role, most consumers will not be not be weighing one entire corporation against another.

In addition to the mix of SBUs being compared there is the issue of the numbers being used. Different firms will treat many items in their reported financials quite differently which will affect most of the ratios we have considered over the course of this book. One firm may choose to use an accelerated depreciation schedule, to write off goodwill or have a number of other exceptional charges against profits. Another may have recently absorbed a number of acquisitions which will distort its profit statement. Similarly, items such as inventory and provisions for liabilities may be accounted for differently, depending on the approach the company adopts. The largest distortions are likely to result when comparing firms that report their results in different markets where the generally accepted accounting practice will differ. The acceptable treatment of many items, from depreciation rates to leases, may vary dramatically. All these factors will compromise the validity of any comparison between two firm's profit statements and balance sheets without adjustments being made to ensure that the reported numbers are constructed on a comparable basis.

Comparing apples and oranges is an acceptable approach if you are looking simply at the operating features of the business rather than their financial performance. It is often the case, for example, that one company can learn good tricks from another even though they are competing in different markets. The idea of single person operators for claims processing in the insurance industry, for example, came straight from manufacturing cells in the machine tools industry.

If you have two "apples" which have the same rate of return on equity, it will almost certainly be the case that the two firms have found different ways to reach the same result. For example, one firm may be outstanding at managing its utilization of fixed assets to reduce costs whilst the other firm achieves a better price point because of heavy advertising. Both routes may lead to the same outcome in terms of return on investment. Whilst a pattern often emerges among those firms that succeed and those that fail in an industry, in reality there is not usually a single right way to gain competitive advantage.

You should also be aware that the relative performance of firms may have exogenous explanations which are quite independent of the underlying competitiveness of the company. The previous CEO might have been involved in an insider dealing scandal which will have left the markets scathing about any claims made by the firm. The firm may also have been subject to an antitrust suit or be involved in other legal disputes which are not reflected in the annual report. When you are looking at a firm it is worth doing a quick review of all the previous press articles for any indication that such events may have influenced the stock market valuation of the firm.

Most companies now engage in ongoing benchmarking. In its most extreme form it takes the form of competitor analysis, which can involve everything from on-line searches about competitor news, interviews with clients of competitors, to false job interviews and rifling through a competitor's waste paper bins on the street. Major firms now often have a professional dedicated to competitor research and almost all of them will have employed consultants to help them with benchmarking. Obtaining the data is tough and ensuring its comparability is an accounting art. Therefore, don't be dismayed if you can't do this with great precision. As long as it is, in that seminal consulting phrase, "directionally correct", you will be on course.

Appendix 2: Where Do You Get the Data?

"Data is power. Well processed, it's gold!"

We have assumed that you are familiar with the firm that is the subject of your analysis, that you have access to information about SBU performance as well as the internal structures and processes. In short, it assumes you are an insider analysing the firm for which you are working. To complete a robust analysis, however, you will also need information about the industry, about competitors and about how your firm is seen to be positioned in the market. How on earth do you lay your hands on this?

For any industry it is always extraordinary how much data is commonly available either through public or university business libraries and industry associations. Between them they will always hold research reports, industry surveys, technical books and on-line databases. Many of the consulting firms get their basic information from these sources where it is easily available to their clients without paying gargantuan fees.

The second key source is industry experts. These might range from the heads of industry associations, to academics in the relevant university departments with an industrial background, to journalists who have covered the sector in trade magazines or newspapers. It is surprising how happy people are to share their experiences and give basic numbers. The *quid pro quo* is that you can offer them some insights or data checks which are more up to date on the basis of your ongoing research. They in turn will usually have networks of contacts which they can refer you to.

The third source of data about a firm is its customers. Customers are not usually proprietary about information pertaining to suppliers unless the relationship is a strategic one, such as that between a car manufacturer and a components supplier. You will almost always be able to get them to offer some insights about the performance of suppliers against benchmark standards. Often the trade or distributors will have a good story to tell and usually have low loyalty to one firm. Clearly the larger the sample you use the more accurate your information will be.

The fourth key source is ex-employees of the firm. These people may be listed as retired in the annual report or be quoted in an article concerning the company. Usually they will have invested a lot of their lives in the company in question and may feel somewhat rejected by it after leaving. They are often more than happy to give an incisive insight into how it works and how effectively it is managed, although the information can be outdated.

Fifthly, the brave new world of the Worldwide Web holds an inexhaustible source of information on markets, products and competitors. Whilst the proprietary on-line services such as Compuserve or AOL host conventional data sources such as Dun & Bradstreet, as much if not more insights can be gleaned by surfing sites related to the business you are analysing.

Finally, you can always try to get an objective view from analysts at the investment banks. Most major companies, and all industrial and service sectors, are covered by analysts who will produce regular reports on them. If they won't give you the reports without charging an exorbitant amount, they may offer a personal insight based on their thinking.

You may despair that there is no way you can get to understand the industry as incisively as a CEO with a panorama of the firm and its competitors. This is not the case. Whilst most consulting firms will have people who have sector experience, they have to be deployed carefully to avoid client conflicts and potential law suits for disclosure of confidential information. As a result, external consulting teams will tend to be green and go along a steep learning curve. This will mean that it usually takes them about 75% of the length of a project to catch up with the client's level of understanding, leaving the last fraction for them to race ahead and add value. There is no reason why, armed with the right frameworks, you shouldn't go a long way to doing the same thing.

A data gathering model is illustrated in Figure A2.1.

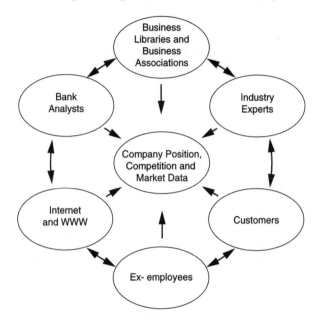

Figure A2.1 *Illustrative data gathering model*

Select Bibliography

The following is a selection of books which will provide more depth on the major areas we have covered.

Barabba, V.P. and Zaltman, G. (1990). *Hearing the Voice of the Market: Competitive Advantage Through Creative Use of Market Information*. Harvard Business School Press.

Bleeke, J. and Ernst, D. (1994). Is Your Strategic Alliance Really a Sale? *Harvard Business Review*, July/August.

Bower, J.L. and Christensen, C.M. (1995). Disruptive Technologies: Catching the Waves, *Harvard Business Review*, Jan/Feb.

Boxwell, R. J. (1994). *Benchmarking for Competitive Advantage*. McGraw-Hill.

Buzell, R.D. and Gale, B.T. (1987). *The PIMS Principles: Linking Strategy to Performance*. The Free Press.

Camp, R.C. (1989). *Benchmarking: The Search for Industry Best Practices that Lead to Superior Performance*. Quality Press.

Campbell, A., Goold, M. and Alexander, M. (1994). *Corporate Level Strategy: Creating Value in the Multi-Business Company*. John Wiley & Sons.

Champy, J. (1995). *Reengineering Management: The Mandate for New Leadership*. Harper Business Publishing.

Christensen, H.K. (1994). *Portable MBA in Strategy*. John Wiley & Sons.

Cooper, R.G. (1993). *Winning at New Products: Accelerating the Process for Idea to Launch*. Addison Wesley.

Copeland, T. and Koller, T. (1994). *Valuation: Measuring and Managing the Value of Companies*, 2nd edition. John Wiley & Sons.

Creech, B. (1994). *The Five Pillars of TQM: How to Make TQM Work for You*. Dutton

Davidson, B. and Davis, S. (1991). *2020 Vision: Transforming Your Business Today To Succeed Tomorrow*. Simon and Schuster.

Davis, S. (1987). *Future Perfect*. Addison-Wesley.

Deming, W.E. (1982). *Quality, Productivity and Competitive Position*. MIT Press.

Fuld, L.M. (1998). *Monitoring the Competition: Find Out What's Really going On Over There*. John Wiley & Sons.

Gilad, B. (1994). *Business Blind spots: Replacing Your Company's Entrenched and Outdated Myths, Beliefs and Assumptions with Today's Reality*. Probus.

Halberg, G. (1995). *All Consumers are not Created Equal*. John Wiley & Sons.

Hamel, G. and Prahalad, C.K. (1994). Competing for the Future. *Harvard Business Review*, August.

Hamel, G. and Prahalad, C.K. (1994). *Competing for the Future: Breakthrough Strategies for Seizing Control*. Harvard Business School Press.

Hammer, M. *Beyond Reengineering*. Harper Business Publishing.

Hammer, M. and Champy, J. (1993). *Reengineering the Corporation*. The Free Press.

Hammer, M. and Champy, J. (1994). *Reengineering the Corporation: A Manifesto for Business Revolution*. Harper Business Publishing.

Hampden-Turner, C. (1992). *Creating Corporate Culture: From Discord to Harmony*. Addison Wesley.

Hart, C.W.L. (1988). The Power of Unconditional Service Guarantees. *Harvard Business Review*.

Hart, C.W.L, Heskett, J.L. and Sasser Jr, E.W. (1990). The Profitable Art of Service Recovery. *Harvard Business Review*, July/August.

Henderson, B.D. (1982). *Henderson on Corporate Strategy*. New American Library.

Heskett, J.L., Sasser, E. and Hart, C.W.L. (1990). *Service Breakthroughs: Changing the Rules of the Game*. The Free Press.

Heskett, J.L. *et al.* (1994). Putting the Service Profit Chain to Work. *Harvard Business Review*, March/April.

Imai, M. (1986). *Kaizen*. Random House.

Kanter, R.M. (1994). Collaborative Advantage: the Art of Alliances. *Harvard Business Review*, July/August.

Kaplan, R.S. and Norton, D.P. (1993). Putting the Balanced Scorecard to Work, *Harvard Business Review*, September/October.

Katzenbach, J. and Smith, D. (1993). *The Wisdom of Teams*. Harvard Business School Press.

Kohn, A. (1993). Why Incentive Plans Cannot Work. *Harvard Business Review*, September/October.

Kotler, P. (1989). From Mass Marketing to Mass Customization. *Planning Review*, September-October.

Kotter, J.P. (1995). Leading Change: Why Transformation Efforts Fail. *Harvard Business Review*, March–April.

Kotter, J. and Heskett, J. (1992). *Corporate Culture and Performance*. The Free Press.

Larkin, T.J. (1994). *Communicating Change*. McGraw-Hill.

Maister, D. (1997). *Managing the Professional Service Firm*. The Free Press.

Meyer, C. (1993). *Fast Cycle Time: How to Align Purpose, Strategy and Structure for Speed*. The Free Press.

Meyer, C. (1994). How the Right Measures Help Teams Excel. *Harvard Business Review*, May/June.

Mohrman, S.A., Cohen, S.G. and Mohrman, A.M. (1995). *Designing Team-Based Organizations: New Forms of Knowledge Work*. Jossey-Bass.

Ostroff, F. and Smith, D. (1992). The Horizontal Organization: Redesigning the Corporation. *The McKinsey Quarterly*, No. 1.

Peppers, D. and Rogers, M. (1993). *The One to One Future: Building Relationships One at a Time*. Currency Doubleday.

Peppers, D. and Rogers, M. (1995). A New Marketing Paradigm: Share of Customer not Market Share. *Planning Review*, March/April.

Pine. B.J. II (1992). *Mass Customization*. Harvard Business School Press.

Pine, B.J. II., Peppers, D. and Rogers, M. (1995). Do You Want to Keep Your Customers for Ever? *Harvard Business Review*, March/April.

Porass, J.J. and Collins, J.C. (1994). *Built to Last: Successful Habits of Visionary Companies*. Harper Business Publishing.

Porter, M.E. (1980) *Competitive Strategy. Techniques for Analyzing Industries and Competitors*. The Free Press.

Porter, M.E. (1985). *Competitive Advantage: Creating and Sustaining Superior Performance*. The Free Press.

Porter, M.E. (1987). From Competitive Advantage to Corporate Strategy. *Harvard Business Review*, March.

Poynter, T.A. and White, R.E. (1990). Making the Horizontal Organization Work. *Business Quarterly*, Winter.

Prahalad, C.K. and Hamel, G. (1990). The Core Competencies of the Corporation. *Harvard Business Review*, May/June.

Rappaport, A. (1986). *Creating Shareholder Value: A New Standard for Business*. The Free Press.

Ray, D.W. and Bronstein, H. (1995). *Teaming Up: Making the Transition to a Self Directed, Team-based Organization*. McGraw-Hill.

Reichheld, F.F. (1993). Loyalty Based Management. *Harvard Business Review*, March/April.

Richman, T. and Koontz, C. (1993). How Benchmarking Can Improve Business Reengineering. *Planning Review*, December.

Risher, H. and Fay, C. (1995). *The Performance Imperative: Strategies for Enhancing Workforce Effectiveness*. Jossey-Bass.

Sammon, W.L., Kurland, M.A. and Spitalnic, R. (1984). *Business Com-*

petitor Intelligence: Methods for Collecting, Organizing, and Using Information*. John Wiley & Sons.

Schlesinger, L.A. and Heskett, J.L. (1991). The Service-Driven Service
Company. *Harvard Business Review*, September/October.

Spector, R.A. (1995). *Taking Charge and Letting Go: Breakthrough Strategies
for Creating and Managing the Horizontal Company*. The Free Press.

Stalk, G., Evans, P. and Schulman, L.E. (1992). Competing on Capabilities: The new Rules of Corporate Strategy. *Harvard Business Review*,
March/April.

Taguchi, G. and Clausing, D. (1990). Robust Quality. *Harvard Business
Review*, Jan/Feb.

Wellins, R.S., Byham, W.C. and Dixon, G.R. (1994). *Inside Teams: How 20
World Class Organizations are Winning Through Teamwork*. Jossey-Bass.

Wheelwright, S.C. and Clark, K. (1995). *The Product Development Challenge: Competing Through Speed, Quality and Creativity*. Harvard Business School Press.

Index